Echoes in the Mist

PICTORIAL RESEARCH BY
NANCY KNECHTEL

"PARTNERS IN PROGRESS" BY
MITCH FLYNN

PRODUCED IN COOPERATION
WITH THE NIAGARA FALLS AREA
CHAMBER OF COMMERCE

WINDSOR PUBLICATIONS, INC.
CHATSWORTH, CALIFORNIA

ECHOES IN THE MIST

An Illustrated History of the

Niagara Falls Area

by Michael N. Vogel

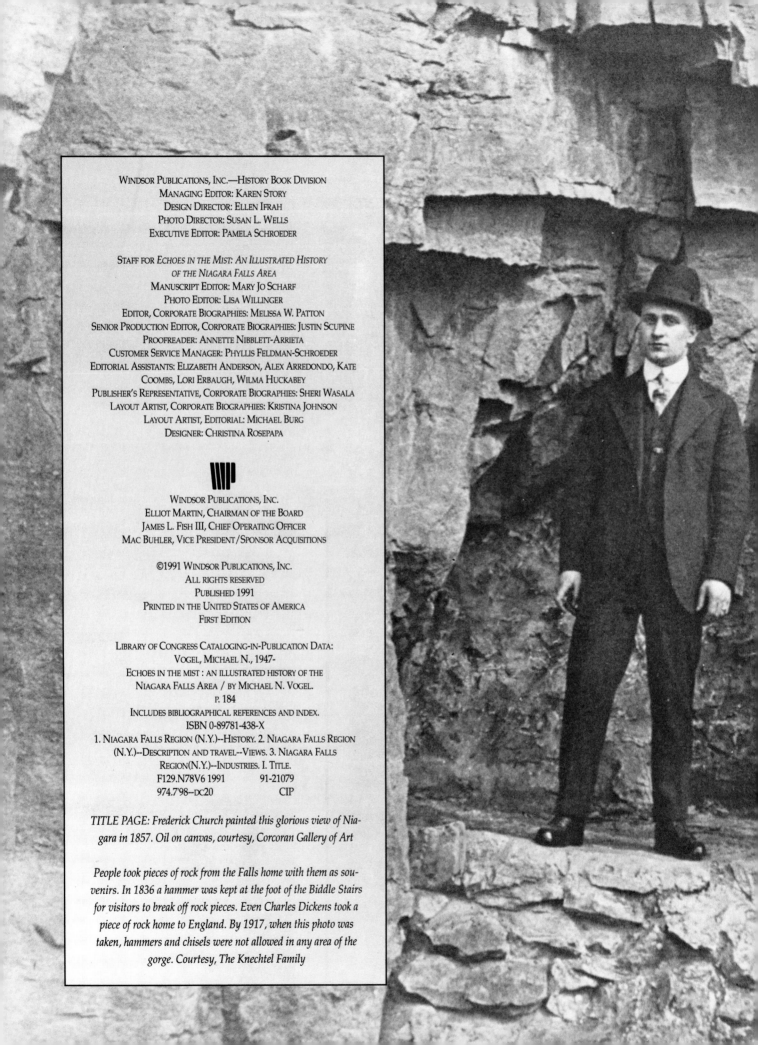

WINDSOR PUBLICATIONS, INC.—HISTORY BOOK DIVISION
MANAGING EDITOR: KAREN STORY
DESIGN DIRECTOR: ELLEN IFRAH
PHOTO DIRECTOR: SUSAN L. WELLS
EXECUTIVE EDITOR: PAMELA SCHROEDER

STAFF FOR *ECHOES IN THE MIST: AN ILLUSTRATED HISTORY
OF THE NIAGARA FALLS AREA*
MANUSCRIPT EDITOR: MARY JO SCHARF
PHOTO EDITOR: LISA WILLINGER
EDITOR, CORPORATE BIOGRAPHIES: MELISSA W. PATTON
SENIOR PRODUCTION EDITOR, CORPORATE BIOGRAPHIES: JUSTIN SCUPINE
PROOFREADER: ANNETTE NIBBLETT-ARRIETA
CUSTOMER SERVICE MANAGER: PHYLLIS FELDMAN-SCHROEDER
EDITORIAL ASSISTANTS: ELIZABETH ANDERSON, ALEX ARREDONDO, KATE
COOMBS, LORI ERBAUGH, WILMA HUCKABEY
PUBLISHER'S REPRESENTATIVE, CORPORATE BIOGRAPHIES: SHERI WASALA
LAYOUT ARTIST, CORPORATE BIOGRAPHIES: KRISTINA JOHNSON
LAYOUT ARTIST, EDITORIAL: MICHAEL BURG
DESIGNER: CHRISTINA ROSEPAPA

WINDSOR PUBLICATIONS, INC.
ELLIOT MARTIN, CHAIRMAN OF THE BOARD
JAMES L. FISH III, CHIEF OPERATING OFFICER
MAC BUHLER, VICE PRESIDENT/SPONSOR ACQUISITIONS

©1991 WINDSOR PUBLICATIONS, INC.
ALL RIGHTS RESERVED
PUBLISHED 1991
PRINTED IN THE UNITED STATES OF AMERICA
FIRST EDITION

LIBRARY OF CONGRESS CATALOGING-IN-PUBLICATION DATA:
VOGEL, MICHAEL N., 1947-
ECHOES IN THE MIST : AN ILLUSTRATED HISTORY OF THE
NIAGARA FALLS AREA / BY MICHAEL N. VOGEL.
P. 184
INCLUDES BIBLIOGRAPHICAL REFERENCES AND INDEX.
ISBN 0-89781-438-X
1. NIAGARA FALLS REGION (N.Y.)--HISTORY. 2. NIAGARA FALLS REGION
(N.Y.)--DESCRIPTION AND TRAVEL--VIEWS. 3. NIAGARA FALLS
REGION(N.Y.)--INDUSTRIES. I. TITLE.
F129.N78V6 1991   91-21079
974.7'98--DC20   CIP

TITLE PAGE: Frederick Church painted this glorious view of Niagara in 1857. Oil on canvas, courtesy, Corcoran Gallery of Art

People took pieces of rock from the Falls home with them as souvenirs. In 1836 a hammer was kept at the foot of the Biddle Stairs for visitors to break off rock pieces. Even Charles Dickens took a piece of rock home to England. By 1917, when this photo was taken, hammers and chisels were not allowed in any area of the gorge. Courtesy, The Knechtel Family

CONTENTS

Aside from a nearly lifelong consumption of Niagara hydropower and the occasional visit to Niagara Falls as a tourist or journalist, the author of this volume has only two significant links to Cataract City history: As a young Scout, I toured the Schoellkopf Power Station the week before it slid into the gorge, and as an adult who should have known better I joined the ranks of the daredevils (lower class) by riding the upper wing of a Stearman biplane a thousand feet or so over the Falls.

Neither event is chronicled herein. But I do treasure a clipping from the Niagara Falls, Ontario, newspaper about a mystery wingwalker seen high over the Falls, and I keep a picture of the stunt on my office wall as a reminder, in future, to always book seats on the inside of the plane.

I would be remiss indeed if I didn't add some special thanks to those with truer links to Niagara Falls history—those who have treasured it and kept it alive, and in so doing have earned a measure of thanks from all the residents of the Niagara region.

Special and invaluable guidance has been provided by Donald E. Loker of the Niagara

Falls Public Library, who both guards and shares a treasure trove of local history, and by Hamilton Mizer, a former *Niagara Gazette* publisher and columnist whose memory is equaled only by his writing skill. Both of them, indeed, are themselves cultural treasures, and their assistance is deeply appreciated.

They provided only true guidance; any errors, and any arbitrary judgments, such as the use of the spelling Stedman instead of the equally common Steadman for one of the early pioneers, are mine.

Fred Caso of the Niagara Falls Area Chamber of Commerce provided the impetus for this book and encouragement and assistance for its writer. Nancy Knechtel deserves special thanks for her efforts in compiling the photos and other illustrations, as does Mary Jo Scharf for her shepherding of this manuscript.

And certainly not least, my deepest gratitude as well as my love go to my wife Stacey and our children, Charity, Becky, and Alex, for their support and patience, which made the project possible.

I'm also grateful to the historians, chroniclers, and writers listed in the bibliography at the end of this text. You will be too, if you take the time to explore their work and reap your own rewards from their labors.

George Catlin's Portage Around the Falls of Niagara at Table Rock *was painted in 1847 or 1848. Catlin became famous for his images of Native Americans in the wilderness. Courtesy, National Gallery of Art, Washington, Paul Mellon Collection*

Acknowledgments

*C*easelessly, endlessly, the wide green river hurls itself into the abyss. Churned by the drops and eddies of rock-studded rapids, its waters come at last to a final, awesome plunge, arcing gracefully into a broad wall of white before cascading nearly 170 feet to the deep pools of the Niagara Gorge below.

Three hundred years and more have passed since Europeans first heard the distant thunder of the falling stream, untold generations since the first Native Americans peered with wonder from the bordering forests to see the plunge of the bright waters. But time means little to the river.

A million and a half gallons of water reach the brink of the Falls each second, as a huge heartland drainage basin feeds one fifth of all the world's fresh surface water through the Great Lakes and toward the river and its cataracts. Each second, more than 2,800 tons of water hit the surface of the river at the base of the Horseshoe Falls, and more than 300 tons cascade down the rocks below the American and Bridal Veil falls, before joining turbulent pools as deep as the Falls are high.

Parkland now lines the boiling rapids, and cities stand atop the high rock walls of the gorge that straddles a peaceful border between two nations. To the river, it is all one with the alarms of war and the bustlings of industry that have marked humanity's few centuries along its banks.

Timeless and hypnotic, the river thunders over the Falls of Niagara. In thousands of years, it has carved a seven and a half mile path through the rock of the Niagara Escarpment; left to itself, it would take thousands of years more to

This engraving, by an unknown artist, is from Father Louis Hennepin's book, A New Discovery of a Vast Country in America, *first printed in Utrecht in 1697 and then in England in 1699. This view exaggerates Hennepin's description of Niagara Falls. Courtesy, Royal Ontario Museum, Toronto, Canada*

DISTANT THUNDER

CHAPTER ONE

• • •

9

crumble into a long series of rapids from Lake Erie to the lower river and Lake Ontario.

Humanity has slowed its progress, diverting water for hydropower and cutting the rate of erosion to a mere foot or so each year. Change was once more rapid; the Falls of 12,000 years ago—when the first nomadic hunters reached the Niagara Frontier, as the last of the Ice Age glaciers retreated northward—was only one of at least five major spillways draining a now-vanished ancient lake.

Only the Niagara River survived, and where it met the 300-foot Niagara Escarpment, at what is now Lewiston, New York, a massive waterfall was formed. By the time of Abraham, it had formed a whirlpool at a bend where an even older river once had flowed; through the days of

Aristotle and Jesus Christ, it was cutting the rock walls that now mark the edge of the city of Niagara Falls.

Some 900 years ago, the single Niagara Falls neared yet another turn in the channel. The cataract bowed, and broke; the American Falls thundered its separate way down the side of the gorge, as the Horseshoe Falls continued its slow recession. Soon, in geological time, the larger cataract eroded its way past Luna Island, and the American Falls' smaller sister, the Luna (or Bridal Veil) Falls, was born.

Four hundred years ago the cataracts looked much as they do today. The large land mass of Goat Island separated the 800-foot-wide American Falls and the 100-foot-wide Bridal Veil Falls from the Horseshoe, which was straighter than

its current 2,500-foot crescent but still carried 90 percent of the river's flow.

To that wonder, at the beginning of the seventeenth century, came the first of the white men.

Samuel de Champlain, exploring "New France" as his kin sought an ice-free northern route to the Orient, was the first to report hearing tales of Niagara's wonders—but there is no evidence he ever saw the cataracts. In his *Des Sauvages*, published in Paris in 1604 and based on accounts he received from Indians in the New World the year before, Champlain provides only sketchy descriptions of the Great Lakes and large waterfalls.

Étienne Brûlé, woodsman and interpreter for Champlain, may have been the first European actually to set foot in the Niagara region, on his

way to the Andaste Indian territory in the Susquehanna Valley in 1615. He also may have been the first non-Indian to see the Falls—legend says the young *coureur-de-bois*, or woodsrunner, made his way to the cataract despite the desertion of Indian guides who featured to enrage the Spirit of the Thundering Waters, but there is no proof.

Next came the seekers of souls, the French missionaries to the Hurons, who reached at least the region of the Falls and heard of its wonders.

The Recollet priest Joseph de la Roche Dallion and two companions journeyed to the Niagara Frontier in 1626, spending three months in the region west of the Niagara River in an attempt to convert Indians of the Neuter, or Neutral, Nation. The Jesuit missionaries Jean de Brébeuf and Pierre Chaumonot journeyed to the area in the winter of 1640-41, and in 1641 the Reverend Jerome Lalemant wrote to his Jesuit superior of a river called "Onguuiaahra" that carried the waters of Lake Erie to Lake Ontario.

A doctor, Le Sieur Gendron, wrote in 1644 of Erie's flow "from a terrible height" into Lake Ontario, over falls whose spray deposited a yellowish salt of medicinal value. The falls also carried enough animals to their deaths, he noted, to provide plentiful food for the natives living nearby.

But it was a Sulpician missionary, the scholarly Father René de Bréphant de Galinée, who left the most tantalizing early account in 1669, during a journey with the 6 1/2-foot-tall Father François Dollier de Casson, who was an ex-cavalry captain famed for his ability to hold a seated man in each of his outstretched hands, and the yet-unsung 27-year-old explorer René-Robert Cavelier, Sieur de La Salle. Galinée reached the mouth of the Niagara River and heard the distant thunder of the Falls—yet, apparently, wasn't curious enough to travel inland for a look at what the Indians' descriptions convinced him must be "one of the finest cataracts or water-falls in the world."

"All the Indians to whom I have spoken about it said the river fell in that place from a rock higher than the tallest pine trees—that is, about two hundred feet," he wrote in a remarkably accurate estimate. "In fact, we heard it from

The American Falls are split into the large falls and the smaller Bridal Veil (or Luna) Falls, separated by tiny Luna Island. Water travels about 15 miles an hour over the Falls and drops 160 feet. This view of the American Falls was drawn by August Köllner in 1848, the year Niagara Falls was incorporated as a village. Courtesy, Buffalo and Erie County Historical Society

Niagara Falls With Trappers, *an 1837 oil painting by J.W. Carmichael, shows both Falls from beneath Prospect Point, with a rugged foreground full of rocks and gnarled trees. In the distance, Terrapin Tower and a covered staircase are visible. Courtesy, Royal Ontario Museum, Toronto, Canada*

where we were. But this fall gives such an impulse to the water that, although we were ten or twelve leagues away, the water is so rapid that one can with great difficulty row up against it . . . our desire to go on to our little village called Ganastaogue Sonotoua Outinaouatoua prevented our going to see that wonder."

La Salle went on to explore the Ohio River, and Galinée and Casson eventually camped on the shores of Lake Erie and formally claimed the entire region for Louis XIV, the Sun King of France—all without bothering to see the Falls.

In the annals of Niagara, the incurious Galinée becomes a footnote—leaving center stage to a colorful and controversial Recollet missionary known as Father Louis Hennepin, the first European known to actually have seen the Falls.

Hennepin, who perhaps loved to excite men's imaginations as well as he liked saving their souls, reached the Niagara nine years after Galinée, on St. Nicholas Day—December 6—in 1678, as a member of La Salle's second North American exploration. With Indian guides, he set out on foot for the Falls.

"Four leagues from Lake Frontenac [Ontario]

there is an incredible Cataract or Waterfall, which has no equal," he wrote in 1683 in what became the most widely read work on America in that century.

"The Niagara river near this place is only an eighth of a league wide, but it is very deep in places, and so rapid above the great fall that it hurries down all the animals which try to cross it, without a single one being able to withstand its current. They plunge down a height of more than five hundred feet, and its falls is composed of two sheets of water and a cascade, with an island sloping down. In the middle these waters foam and boil in a fearful manner.

"They thunder continually, and when the wind blows in a southerly direction, the noise which they make is heard for more than fifteen leagues."

Hennepin, whose later accounts became less trustworthy and who was not averse to claiming exploratory credit perhaps more rightly due La Salle, was a little off on his estimate of the Falls' height—unless you count the depth of the cliffs underwater. But his is the first eyewitness account and the most detailed description of the Falls region up to that time, even if later editions

Goat Island divides the Niagara River into the American Falls and the Canadian Horseshoe Falls. On the right of Goat Island, the Three Sisters Islands and Little Brother Island can be seen. They are named after the Whitney family, who walked to the islands over ice floes in 1816. The sisters' islands are individually named Asenath, Angeline, and Celinda Eliza, and the brother's island is named Solon. Courtesy, Buffalo and Erie County Historical Society

This nineteenth-century engraving shows the Falls before the shanties and souvenir stands were erected. Visitors who described the Falls in the 1840s and 1850s mentioned that the village was in the wilderness, with paths running through thick underbrush. Since the turn of the century, when commercialism took the area by storm, images of the naturalism of the Falls have been very popular with tourists. Courtesy, Buffalo and Erie County Historical Society

of his books did increase the height of the awesome cataracts to "six hundred Foot and more."

The missionary, who said the first Catholic Mass in the Niagara region on December 11, 1678, described the portage around two leagues of river rapids at the Falls as "a very fine road, very little wood, and almost all prairies mingled with some oaks and firs, on both banks of the river, which are of a height that inspire fear when you look down."

Henri de Tonty, La Salle's lieutenant, visited the Falls about two months later and agreed with Hennepin's height estimates.

"I can only say that it is the most beautiful fall in the world," he wrote some five years later. "By our estimate it falls perpendicularly 500 feet and is some 200 toises wide. It throws off vapors which may be seen at a distance of sixteen leagues, and it may be heard at the same distance when it is calm. When once the swans and bustards are caught in its current it is impossible for them to take flight again, and they are dead before they get to the bottom of the fall."

Hennepin and Tonty were at Niagara Falls

because La Salle was burning with the desire to forge a major fur trading route into the continental heartland he had probed. Part of that scheme involved a fleet of ships to ply the waters of this land of broad lakes and rivers—and a ship would indeed be built just above Niagara Falls to open those routes.

Hennepin, a priest with a decidedly secular bent, and Tonty, known to fearful Indians as "The Man with the Iron Hand" for the metal replacement for an appendage lost in battle in Sicily, were part of that expedition, and Hennepin and a few companions from the expedition's advance party made the first journey by canoe and foot to see the Falls.

The wilderness wasn't the only problem for the French explorers. There was unrest, too, among the Indians of the region.

The Niagara region, when Europeans arrived, was controlled by the Seneca Nation of the great Iroquois Confederation. It had been gained by the Senecas through warfare and assimilation of conquered tribes—among them the Neutral, Erie, Tobacco, and Huron nations.

In 1679 the leaders of the Seneca Nation gave La Salle permission to build a ship on their land, providing the vessel was used solely for exploration. This print is from Father Hennepin's book, New Discovery. *Courtesy, Buffalo and Erie County Historical Society*

The Senecas are the "Keepers of the Western Door" for the six-nation Iroquois Confederation, and they had helped push the earlier tribes of Algonquin stock northward into Canada. The Hurons, part of the even larger but more loosely organized Wyandot Confederacy, held sway beyond the Niagara to the northwest when the Europeans arrived, and there was enmity between the two nations.

When La Salle arrived to open his trade routes, the Senecas already were engaged in moving furs to Albany for trade with the British. To both the Indians and the Europeans, it was obvious that control of the Niagara meant control of the fur trade—and the French sought to convince the doubtful Senecas that their arrival in the region meant trade opportunities.

The Senecas were unschooled, but not unwise. They were part of a confederation that was to provide a model for the Albany draft document that became a precursor of the United States Constitution, and eventually to the Constitution itself; they were wary of all Europeans, but well aware of the power inherent in the prospects of trade.

After visits from the French to Seneca settlements near Rochester, first by Hennepin and Dominique de La Motte-Lussière and shortly after by La Salle and Tonty, the Indian leaders gave the explorers grudging permission to build a ship—strictly for exploration—near the Falls. Of even more lasting importance, they also agreed to let the French erect a warehouse at the mouth of the river on Lake Ontario.

The ship was the *Griffon,* the first large vessel to sail the Upper Lakes. La Salle led the French, in January of 1679, up the Niagara Escarpment and past the Falls to the banks of Cayuga Creek. Oaks were felled, and shipwrights—their temporary huts the first European settlement in Niagara Falls—spent February and half of March building the 45-ton sailing vessel.

Travelling back to the mouth of the river, La Salle began work on his "warehouse"—actually two stone blockhouses, to be called Fort Conti. The Senecas, however, were perhaps even more uneasy about the strange vessel taking shape near what is now Griffon Park in Niagara Falls. They stopped bringing corn to trade to the

Frenchmen, and only the hunting done by friendly Mohicans kept the Frenchmen's larders stocked. Soon Seneca warriors were plotting to burn the new vessel—but the French, warned by an Indian woman, foiled the plot.

Father Hennepin blessed the ship in mid-March, and it set off down the lakes on its maiden voyage. Strapped for cash and unable to buy supplies on credit, La Salle violated the terms of the agreement once more by loading a cargo of furs at Green Bay. While he stayed to push inland, eventually following the Missis-sippi to the Gulf of Mexico before dying in Texas, the *Griffon* set sail for Niagara—never to be seen again.

Fort Conti fared little better, burning to the ground after less than a year. It would be replaced, in 1687, by the buildings of tiny Fort Denonville—but that, too, would last less than a year.

It was built by an expedition led by Jacques René de Brisay, Marquis de Denonville, and among the members of that troop was the first non-priest to write of Niagara Falls. Louis Armand de Lom d'Arce, Baron La Hontan, in fact, was very much a non-priest—satirical, loose with the facts, adventurous, and military.

"As for the Waterfall of Niagara," he wrote in a book translated into English in 1703, "'tis seven or eight hundred foot high, and half a League broad. Towards the middle of it we descry an Island that leans towards the Precipice, as if it were ready to fall. All the Beasts that cross the Water within half a quarter of a League above this unfortunate Island, are suck'd in by force of the Stream. And the Beasts and Fish that are thus kill'd by the prodigious fall, serve for food to fifty Iroquese, who are settled about two Leagues off, and take'em out of the water with their Canows."

More than exploration was afoot in the New World in these years. France and England were at each other's throats in a series of wars that would span the next century. While armies battled in Europe and navies clashed on the seas, the vortex of war drew in the soldiers of the New World frontiers and the Indian nations who dealt with them.

In general, the Senecas supported the British and the Hurons the French. Early in "King William's War," the earliest of the conflicts, Senecas from the Niagara region captured a 17-year-old soldier named Louis Thomas de Joncaire.

Joncaire, later Sieur de Chabert, was a native of Provence, France, but had been in Canada since his boyhood. By his own account, his life was spared in admiration for the way he resisted attempts to prepare him for burning at the stake; while his companions who begged for mercy were tortured to death, Joncaire knocked down an old chief who tried to burn his finger in the bowl of a smoking pipe. For his spunk, the young soldier was adopted into the tribe and given an Iroquois wife.

Joncaire was to live among the Senecas for years, and to have a decided impact upon the region's history. Through him, many Senecas would be won to the French side. His knowledge of the Seneca language would prove of immeasureable value to French trade hopes, and his sons Philippe and Daniel would also win the trust of the Native Americans. The Joncaires

La Salle's ship, the Griffon, set sail on the Great Lakes on its maiden voyage in 1679. La Salle left the ship at Green Bay to follow the Mississippi River to the Gulf of Mexico. The Griffon then set sail to return to Niagara, but mysteriously, it was never seen again. Courtesy, Buffalo and Erie County Historical Society

would be major factors in the region's century of French domination.

In 1720 Joncaire won permission from the Senecas to build a trading post near Niagara Falls. His bark cabin, built at the foot of the Niagara Escarpment in what is now Artpark at Lewiston, was the first house in the area; Joncaire's mill, built later by his son Daniel along the shoreline just above the American Falls, would be the first such device to harness the power of the river.

Joncaire's trading post was built at the northern end of the portage route, where Hennepin, the other early explorers, and the Indians before them had landed to continue the journey upriver on foot. The portage led from the low and relatively level fields near the landing up the steep, three-tiered face of the escarpment itself, and then paralleled the gorge to an upper river landing above the Falls.

A year or two before the post was built, an unknown French officer passed through the region and recorded the scene at what would become Lewiston and Niagara Falls:

The Niagara portage is two leagues and a half to three leagues long, but the road, over which carts roll two or three times a year, is very fine, with very beautiful and open woods through which a person is visible for a distance of 60 paces.

The trees are all oaks, and very large. The soil along the entire length of that road is not very good. From the landing, which is three leagues up the river, four hills are to be ascended. Above the first hill there is a Seneca village of about ten cabins, where Indian corn, beans, peas, watermelons and pumpkins are raised, all of which are very fine.

These Senecas are employed by the French, from whom they earn money by carrying the goods of those who are going to the upper country; some for mitasses [leggings], others for shirts, some for powder and ball, whilst some others pilfer; and on the return of the French, they carry their sacks of furs for some peltry.

This portage is made for the purpose of avoiding the Cataract of Niagara, the grandest sheet of water in the world, having a perpendicular fall of two or three hundred feet.

The importance of the portage, which traversed what is now the downtown area of the city of Niagara Falls, has been dimmed by the passage of centuries. In early America it was the absolute key to control of the interior and of the lucrative trade in beaver pelts; whoever held the route along the 36-mile Niagara River held the upper hand, militarily and economically, in the development of vast stretches of the continent.

Niagara—the survivor of a multitude of spellings of an Indian word that most probably meant "the neck"—was a poor region to settle, otherwise. The portage trail led through land partly forested with oak, pine, and other trees, with the greatest profusion of plant life in the unique environment of the gorge and the spray from the Falls, but the soil was generally considered indifferent for farming. The Falls' reputation as a natural wonder was growing—but commerce kept Niagara on the map.

Joncaire's palisaded trading post stood on the site of what once had been a Neutral Indian village, and near the place where a hut and storehouse built by La Salle once stood. It was the start of the Indian portage route followed by Father Hennepin half a century before and followed since by other Europeans shifting cargo and military force between Lakes Erie and Ontario.

The location gave Joncaire virtual control over the trade route until his death in 1739, and he used trade goods as currency to hire Indians to carry loads of material up the steep escarpment between the landings. But the importance of his post pales in comparison to the other concession he gained from the Senecas—permission to build a stone "House of Peace" for trade purposes, at the mouth of the river.

The stone house occupied the ground at the Lake Ontario shoreline once occupied by Fort Conti and Fort Denonville, but it was to last much longer. Despite bombardment, age, neglect, occupation by troops of three nations, and finally the attention of tourists, the "French Castle" still stands today as the centerpiece of Fort Niagara and as the oldest building in the Great Lakes Basin—perhaps the oldest between the Appalachians and the Mississippi.

Construction was started in 1726 and finished in 1727, giving the French a firm foot-hold on the strategic strait. The British, who had been hundreds of miles to the east and had only pushed inland as far as Albany in the time of La Salle, had to content themselves with Lake Ontario trade through a port at Oswego or the costly, lengthy journey across the Appalachian Mountains farther south. English protests against the French fort went unheeded, as the tensions unresolved by King William's War and Queen Anne's War early in the century built toward the mid-century conflict known as King George's War.

The flow of trade goods and furs through Fort Niagara, more of a guard post than a trading center, kept building, and the portage became ever more valuable. In 1751, three years after King George's War, the French built "Little Fort Niagara" at the head of the portage, in what is now Niagara Falls, to protect that end of the route and keep Indians from the upper lakes from bypassing the main fort to reach the British trade center at Oswego.

Arriving in New France that year was one J.C. Bonnefons, a gunner who in the spring of 1753 found himself en route over the portage with an expedition taking provisions, ammunition, and trade goods to Lake Erie. He used the occasion to descend into the gorge at the Falls, despite the objections of his companions.

"Presently I began to descend with the intention of making sure of the branches which I encountered on my way, descending backwards so that I would not let go one after another until I had seized others of the same firmness," he wrote. "I was about an hour in getting down, not with commending myself to Providence, for I perceived the rashness of my undertaking, but I had to finish as much from pride as from curiosity."

Bonnefons reached the foot of the Falls and made his way across the rocks to a cavern behind the falling wall of water. Blocked by crevices, he retreated.

"All shivering with cold, and drenched, I hastened to take again the road by which I had descended," he reported. "I climbed up the bushes quicker than I had descended them. Arrived on top, I found the two people with whom I had come. They wished to interrogate me. This was futile. I was deaf and not about to

The "French Castle" of Old Fort Niagara, built in 1726 at the junction of Lake Ontario and the Niagara River, is shown here in 1890. In this image, it is apparent that the stone surface has been covered and that a porch has been added. Today the building has been restored to its original appearance. Courtesy, J. Carl Burke Studio

The South Bastion and "Gate of Five Nations" at Fort Niagara are seen here after reconstruction in the 1930s. Photos prior to this do not show the gate at this position, as the brick bastions and the stone construction were from different periods of the fort's history. Courtesy, J. Carl Burke Studio

hear them . . . it was not until two hours afterwards that the deafness left me and I was able to give an account of what I had seen."

The Swedish naturalist Peter Kalm also visited the Falls in these years, dining at the fort en route and pausing to watch the work of the Indians, who would soon be complaining to the French government that horses were being used on the portage, depriving them of their livelihood. While Bonnefons thought he may have made the first gorge descent, Kalm offers proof a year or two earlier that Indians and even Europeans had been there before him; in the earliest account of the region written in English, he tells of Indians descending to the foot of the Falls after having been stranded on the island that divides the cataracts, and he himself sent two young Frenchmen to the bottom of the abyss to gather herbs, shells, and stones for him.

The main fort, already used as a starting point for Indian raids on British settlements, also became a staging area for French military expeditions into the interior. Starting along the portage, the French troops began a string of outposts along the Lake Erie shore and as far south as Fort Duquesne, at what is now Pittsburgh.

The move sparked yet another conflict, known in Europe as the Seven Years' War and here as the French and Indian War. While the British forces, including a young Virginia colonial militia officer named George Washington,

campaigned to the south and suffered early setbacks in their attempts to strike north toward the Falls, efforts were being made to strengthen Niagara against the British threat from Oswego.

Captain Pierre Pouchot expanded the fortifications at Fort Niagara, but the labor was in vain. French domination of the Niagara Frontier, which had started even before the English colonized Jamestown or landed at Plymouth Rock, was about to end.

The French had not moved to settle the Niagara's banks, merely to hold the portage. For them it was a strategic point on a thoroughfare—a place that, if lost, could desolate Canada and force France to abandon its New World colonies, as one report to the Royal ministers noted.

Aside from Joncaire, some traders, and soldiers, those who came to Niagara—including Madame Cadillac and her companions, the first European women to reach the region as they travelled to join the founder of Detroit in 1701—were merely passing through. But the threat of a military loss at Niagara imperiled all the French holdings in the Great Lakes, not just in the unsettled region at the Falls.

Fort Niagara was enlarged and redesigned along the classical lines of a Vauban-style fortress, the work progressing despite the comings and goings of throngs of Indians of myriad nations. French-inspired war parties headed out against the English, but the English efforts led in New York by Sir William Johnson were turning more of the nations and warriors against the French.

As conflict along the Niagara neared, and Fort Frontenac at the other end of Lake Ontario fell to a British army, the commander of Little Fort Niagara—Lieutenant Daniel de Joncaire, son of the former chief Indian agent and often referred to simply as Chabert—was ordered to abandon his post and reinforce the main fort with his Indian allies. In so doing, he burned the water-powered sawmill he had built just above the American Falls in 1757 to cut planks for a chapel at the fort, and for two ships that were never finished.

Finally, in 1759, the British reached Fort Niagara. Supported now by 1,500 Iroquois warriors, Brigadier General John Prideaux's 2,000-man force from Oswego landed unnoticed and unopposed, and surrounded Pouchot's 600-man garrison.

What followed, historian Brian Leigh Dunnigan of restored Old Fort Niagara notes, was a classic European-style siege operation. While the cannons of the opposing forces hammered away at each other, English soldiers and sappers painstakingly advanced trenches toward the walls of the fort. After 19 days they were within a hundred yards of the battered fort.

The only hope for the fort was a hastily-organized relief force of French troops and Indians from the interior, which arrived at the Lake Erie entrance to the Niagara in a massive flotilla. The 1,600-man force moved quickly to the upper end of the portage and made their way toward the fort.

At a place near modern-day Youngstown called La Belle Famille, probably a riverside shrine, the French relief force was routed by British regulars on July 24, 1759. The next day, all hope lost, Pouchot surrendered the fort.

The Battle of La Belle Famille ended French hopes in America. Communication with forts deeper in the continent was severed, and Detroit and other posts also would soon surrender. The era of British dominance at Niagara and through much of Canada had begun.

John Stedman rebuilt Chabert's mill, mark-

ing the return of commerce. Captain John Joseph Schlosser took command of the upper portage, where at least part of Chabert de Joncaire's Little Fort Niagara still stood, and built what became Fort Schlosser. The simple French fortifications at the lower end of the portage also were replaced by a British post.

Disease and hardship reigned, though, until the French surrender at Montreal in 1760 allowed the British to turn their efforts westward.

Fort Niagara became a staging area for those efforts, and in 1761 Sir William Johnson held peace conferences at the fort to win allegiance from the Indians formerly allied with the French. But the Indians' distrust of all the invasions of their lands would continue to cause trouble for the region's new masters, and at Niagara more blood would be shed.

This stone chimney was built by the French in 1750 for the barracks of Little Fort Niagara, the upper terminal of the Portage Road. When the British marched against them in 1759, the French burned and abandoned the fort. Only the chimney remained. Without delay the English rebuilt the fort and called it Fort Schlosser. The "Master of the Portage" lived here in the Stedman House, which was built around the chimney. In 1808 the building became the Broughton Tavern, which burned in 1813. Industrial expansion caused relocation of the chimney in 1902 and again in 1942. The last move was to Porter Park, where it can be seen from the exit of the Robert Moses Parkway. Photo by Gail Salter

*J*ohn Stedman could taste the fear, as he spurred his horse away from the screams and the war cries behind him. Death had flashed from the woods in a blaze of gunfire, and the Seneca warriors who sprang from ambush after that first deadly volley were finishing their victory with the tomahawk.

Most of the British troops, caught between the brink of the Niagara Gorge and the trap laid by hundreds of enraged Senecas, had fallen in the musket volley. As balls cut the air near the fleeing wagonmaster, Indians already were driving fear-crazed oxen and wagons over the cliff and scalping their fallen foes.

Stedman spurred madly back toward Fort Schlosser at the Falls, while at the other end of the Portage Road the soldiers of the 80th Regiment of Foot were standing to arms at the sound of gunfire. As teams and wagons plunged to the river far below, Indians dropped the bodies of some of the British soldiers and wagoneers after them. Stedman, the portage master who had taken over the profitable post established by the unlucky Chabert de Joncaire, reached the fort safely; only three others of his wagon convoy also escaped, leaping from the cliff to flee the Indians but saved by trees and bushes that broke their fall.

As one of the survivors, a young drummer boy, watched his drum disappear down the turbulent river in the direction of Fort Niagara, the rescuing force of British soldiers rushed up the escarpment—and straight into a second bloody ambush.

This aerial photo was taken from the Moose Tower on Riverway in 1895. The canal basin is surrounded by industries, including the Kelley and Morgan Advertising Novelties Company, seen to the right. Note the ad on top of the roof at lower left for a 15 cent carriage ride at Prospect Park. Courtesy, Buffalo and Erie County Historical Society

CITY BY THE FALLS

CHAPTER TWO

• • •

In 1763 enraged Seneca Indians attacked a wagon convoy of the postmaster of Fort Schlosser. It is estimated that some 85 soldiers and wagoneers were either scalped or thrown into the river from the Devil's Hole, seen here. Courtesy, Local History Department, Niagara Falls, New York Public Library

FAR RIGHT: In an adaptation of the Indian myth, the maid of the mist was said to be a trial sacrifice sent to please the serpent god, Hinu. The Indian maiden's spirit returned to save her village, and Hinu twisted into a curved shape when he died, creating the shape of the Horseshoe Falls. Legend has it that visitors who look closely at the foot of the Falls can see the Indian maiden rising through the mist to the sky. This 1891 painting by James Francis Brown is called The Red Man's Fact; The Maid of the Mist. *Courtesy, Buffalo and Erie County Historical Society*

Within moments, it was over. Death had come to 5 English officers, 60 soldiers, perhaps a score of wagoneers. Teams and wagons—estimates of their numbers range from 25 to 40—littered the face of the cliff and the gorge floor, and the creek running through the ravine had become "Bloody Run."

The date was September 14, 1763, and as the Senecas melted back into the forest, the name of the place they had chosen for their ambush—the place near the Niagara Gorge Whirlpool where the shape of the land forced the portage trail to the very edge of the cliff—had taken on new menace. Forever after, the battle would be known as the Devil's Hole Massacre.

Three legends about Niagara stand out in Indian lore. One is mythic and tells how the Horseshoe Falls was formed by the death throes of a great, pestilence-spreading serpent slain by the lightning bolts of the great good god Hi'non and rolled into the river; a second is romantic and perhaps pure fiction, telling how Indian maidens were sent over the Falls in canoes in a series of sacrifices that ended only when a favorite chief's beloved daughter was chosen as the Maid of the Mist and, heartbroken, he followed her to death.

The third, perhaps invented in bitter hindsight, tells how the erosion of the falls over centuries opened a passage to the deep, echoing ravine known as the Devil's Hole and loosed an evil upon the Indians that climaxed in the arrival of the white men.

The British blood that soaked into the soil of Niagara Falls that September day, just four years after French soldiers had fallen nearby at La Belle Famille, flowed for reasons as simple, and as complex, as that.

Pitted against each other by the French and the British, urged to raids and atrocities by both sides, pushed from lands that had been forever theirs, the Native Americans of the region were losing a battle of cultures. They had held the region at least since the days of the mysterious Hopewell Indians, who left 4,000-year-old mounds near the Lewiston landings; the Kahquahs or Neuter Indians, whose "queen of peace" had offered sanctuary to Indians of many nations, had held dominion over Niagara until about 1645, when the warriors of the Senecas had erased them from the map. But not even the Senecas could stand up to this new, overwhelming threat.

Joncaire's initial settlements at Niagara—and the small farm he started at the Riviere aux Chevaux (later the Buffalo River) the year before the Battle of La Belle Famille—were just the first of many white settlements. And the British, in the years before the Devil's Hole Massacre, were changing the rules of the game.

For one thing, rum—given freely to Indians

by the British to sow a note of discord in French territory—suddenly was banned, now that the territorial peace was in British interests. The widespread practice of giving generous gifts to Indian leaders declined. And British traders started driving harder bargains and forcing Indians to travel greater distances to trade, now that commerce was a monopoly.

Near Detroit, Indian unrest erupted into the Pontiac Uprising, and the passing of supplies over the Portage Road past Devil's Hole and the Falls took on new urgency.

But there, too, the British were changing the world the Indians had grown used to. Wagons rumbled where Indians had once hand carried loads. In 1763 a British army engineer named John Montressor built the first railroad in America, an inclined railway that carried freight up the escarpment at Lewiston on a windlass-powered system of counterbalanced cars with runners that slid along grooves cut in log rails.

Unemployment added to the rest of the woes confronting the Senecas, and they joined the Ottawas in the uprising led by Pontiac. But the attack at Devil's Hole, though it took a heavy toll in British lives, proved even costlier to the victorious Indians.

As the uprising collapsed, Indian leaders made the journey to Fort Niagara to sue for peace. Fearing retribution for the massacre, the Senecas sent a delegation to Sir William Johnson's home near Albany in 1764; Johnson asked for, and got, reparations in the form of title to the land on either side of the Niagara River.

The "Mile Reserve" on either side of the Niagara would forever cut off the Indians from their beautiful river. To be sure of controlling the vital portage, though, the British also had Montressor build a series of fortified blockhouses along the route.

Stedman, too, would argue a land grant—in vain. According to the portage master, visitor Ebenezer Mix would record in 1856, "The escape of Mr. Stedman, not only from the iron grasp of one of their most athletic and powerful warriors, but from the shower of rifle balls discharged at him from the rifles of their best and most unerring marksmen, confounded the Indians with wonder

Augustus Porter, a surveyor from Canandaigua, New York, built a water-powered sawmill above the Falls in 1805. In 1807, in partnership with his brother Peter, a lawyer and wartime general, he built a large flour mill. In 1808 he became the first judge of Niagara County. From 1822 on, he and his family and heirs sold land and water rights to industries that continued to develop Niagara as a leading industrial center. Courtesy, Buffalo and Erie County Historical Society

and fear, furnishing a subject whereon to feed their most absurd, superstitious whims. They at once pronounced him a favorite of the Great Spirit; and to appease its wrath, made Stedman a present of the tract of land he had encompassed in his retreat to Fort Schlosser. . . being a tract about two miles wide, and three and a half miles long."

No government recognized the claim, however, and apparently neither did the Indians—for the very next year they ceded the same tract to Great Britain during the meeting at Johnson's home.

British control of the region lasted through the American Revolution; Fort Niagara became a haven for up to 10,000 Tory or Loyalist refugees fleeing to Canada, and a staging point for raids by British troops or their Indian allies on settlements as far away as New Jersey.

Butler's Rangers, a force of Loyalists well versed in Indian warfare and language, brought fear to the hearts of settlers on the frontier. Led by Colonel John Butler, whose own wife and children had been captured on his Mohawk Valley farm and imprisoned by the rebel forces, the companies of green-clad rangers slipped through the forests with Indian raiding parties that destroyed supplies needed by the Continental Army and forced General Washington to divert troops from the seaboard battlefields.

Most infamous of the raids were those that took place in 1778 in the Wyoming and Cherry valleys. Butler's 1,000-man force for what became known as the Wyoming Valley Massacre included 500 Indians under Chief Joseph Brant; the raiders surprised and annihilated the American militia, destroyed 8 blockhouse forts and 1,000 houses, and drove off herds of cattle and swine. Two Rangers and one Indian died in the attacks that took the lives of about 300 defenders.

The summertime raid along the Susquehanna River in northern Pennsylvania quickly was followed by another on Cherry Valley, some 60 miles west of Albany. Captain Walter Butler, son of the Ranger commander, led a smaller contingent of Rangers and Brant's warriors in a surprise attack on November 11, 1778, that caught the American defenders of Fort Alden unprepared. Although the fort never fell, the settlers fell victim to an unchecked wave of slaughter. More than 30 persons died and more than 70 were taken prisoner during the Cherry Valley Massacre.

By 1779 General Washington was convinced that the frontier needed protection and the British and their Iroquois allies at Niagara should be destroyed. He sent General John Sullivan and a force of 5,000 seasoned Continental Army soldiers westward to take the fort.

Sullivan burned Indian crops and villages, defeating Brant and the Butlers at Newton on his approach toward Fort Niagara. But the army, low on provisions, stopped just 80 miles short of the fort and turned back.

Sullivan's scorched-earth advance through the countryside left thousands of Indians dependent upon the fort for food that winter, though, and the hardships weren't eased by word that the Peace of Paris had given the Americans the fort and all the land on the east side of the river. Butler's Barracks, built on the west bank in 1778, became the nucleus of a new settlement, but the British managed to keep control of the fort in what remained a wilderness.

It took 17 years and a new treaty negotiated by John Jay before the British colors would come down and the Stars and Stripes would be raised over Fort Niagara on August 11, 1796.

The following year American financier Robert Morris bought all the land west of the Genesee River for the Dutch investment group known as the Holland Land Company. The Indians received $100,000 and two square miles for Tuscarora settlement in Lewiston after a treaty was reached, despite opposition from the Seneca chief and orator Red Jacket and others, during the Big Tree Council in Geneseo.

The Mile Reserve, ceded by the Indians to the British, became New York State property after the war and remained state land until it was sold at auction in 1805 to the transportation firm of

Landing on the American Side, *an 1835 engraving by Charles Richardson, shows large rowboats used to transport passengers between the United States and Queenston Heights in Canada prior to the construction of bridges. In the background a monument to Sir Isaac Brock can be seen, which was destroyed in 1840 and reerected in 1853. Courtesy, Buffalo and Erie County Historical Society*

Porter, Barton & Co.

By then, Niagara Falls already was becoming a tourist destination even though the region was far from settled.

In 1791, with the area still in British hands, the west bank of the Falls was visited by Queen Victoria's father, Prince Edward, Duke of Kent. The prince made his way on horseback to the Falls, where "the only place of accommodation was a log hut for travellers of that day to refresh themselves," Colonel John Clark recalled. The royal party then followed an Indian path to Table Rock at the brink of the Horseshoe Falls, and the prince used an Indian ladder—a leaning tree trunk with notches cut for footing—to make his way down to the base of the gorge.

By 1800 those with time and money to spend on curiosity were travelling by coach from New York City up the Hudson to Saratoga Springs and Trenton Falls, and then westward to Niagara on what became known as the American "Grand Tour." The first recorded honeymoon couple arrived in 1803—Jerome Bonaparte, kin to the French emperor, and Elizabeth Patterson Bonaparte, daughter of a wealthy Baltimore merchant. Theodosia Burr, daughter of Aaron Burr, also arrived with her new husband, Joseph Alston.

Augustus Porter also was among the early visitors, arriving in 1795. In 1796, on his way to help survey what became known as the Western Reserve in Ohio, he stopped again—but his eye saw more than that of the average tourist.

When the state offered the Mile Reserve for sale in 1805, Porter and his associates—his brother Peter B. Porter, Benjamin Barton, and Joseph Annin—bought the land.

In the summer of 1805 Augustus Porter built a sawmill and blacksmith shop on the American side of the Falls—the first structures since the departure of the English. The following year he moved his family from Canandaigua to the Falls, to occupy Stedman's old dwelling near the ruins of Fort Schlosser.

"In 1806 little had been done to change the wild aspect of the country," Albert H. Porter would write 66 years later. "Bears and wolves were not uncommon in the forests. The latter were so numerous as to prevent the keeping of sheep, for many years. They would frequently approach by night within a short distance of the Stedman house, and their hideous nightly howlings were familiar sounds in all the regions around the Falls.

"Wild geese and ducks abounded in the river; eagles were common, and swans were occasional visitors."

Stedman, who incidentally also had introduced a herd of goats to what thereafter became known as Goat Island, also had cleared about 60 acres and planted the first orchard in the area. He had made use of Joncaire's old sawmill—the last remnant of the French complex that once included houses for Joncaire, Little Niagara's commandant, and the king's storekeeper, as well as a barn, shed, stable, and the king's storehouses. But all save the Stedman home were long since in ruin when the Porters arrived.

Porter & Barton also had leased the landing places at Lewiston and Schlosser, at either end of the portage route, and soon Benjamin Barton was living at Lewiston and Peter Porter at Black Rock, the lake port for the portage. With their own fleet of merchant vessels on Lake Ontario as well, they supplied the military posts of the region and shipped the goods of the fur trading companies.

In 1807 the firm built the first gristmill at the Falls, with the help of soldiers from Fort Niagara. Under the terms of the leases, the company also built storehouses at Fort Schlosser, Black Rock, and Lewis Town, named for Governor Lewis; the portage for salt and other articles formerly carried along the British shore shifted to the American side, where the road was better and two miles shorter. The seven-mile portage to Fort Schlosser went at the rate of 37 1/2 cents a barrel or 25 cents per hundredweight of merchandise.

The next year, Augustus built his own house near the Falls, and over the next few years local industry in what was laid out as "Grand Niagara" grew with the construction of a tannery, a ropewalk to make cordage for lake vessels from hemp grown along the Genesee River, and carding and cloth dressing businesses. A large log tavern and several more dwellings also were added to the growing community that Porter, with his eye toward commercial opportunities, soon renamed after the British industrial center of Manchester.

Manchester's growth would come to a sudden and tragic halt. War again came to the Niagara Frontier, in 1812.

Sparked by impressment of sailors at sea during the Napoleonic Wars, the War of 1812 would unfold some of its bloodiest chapters along the banks of the river that divided the young United States from the lands of its recent enemy, Great Britain.

The first shots on the Niagara Frontier came in October, when a force of American regulars and militia crossed from a ravine just above Lewiston to Queenston Heights on the Canadian shore. Poorly conceived and badly executed, the invasion immediately ran into trouble; the troops were pinned down along the riverbank under heavy fire, and many of the militia refused to cross and fight on foreign soil. A small force found a fishermen's path up the heights, though, and stormed a British gun position. In the counterattack that followed, British General Isaac Brock, the "Hero of Upper Canada" for his earlier victory at Detroit, was killed by musket fire, and the wounded commander of the American regulars turned his force over to young

Lieutenant Colonel Winfield Scott, who later would become the hero of the Mexican War and the supreme commander of American forces at the outbreak of the Civil War.

A more organized counterattack by the British and their Mohawk allies drove the ill-equipped Americans back to the river's edge, and the retreat down the embankment became a rout. Nearly a thousand were captured after the Battle of Queenston Heights.

The campaigns of 1813 saw the capture of York, now Toronto, and the American victory led by Commodore Oliver Hazard Perry at the Battle of Lake Erie. American troops occupied Canadian lands near the Falls, too, and late in the year General George McClure, in a misguided effort condemned on both sides of the border, ousted the civilian populace and burned the capital town of Newark, now Niagara-on-the-Lake, as American troops withdrew across the river for the winter.

Nine days after the burning of Newark during a December 10 snowstorm, British forces crossed quietly into the United States and took Fort Niagara. At Youngstown, where American soldiers were playing cards instead of keeping watch in the bitter cold, British troops burst through the doorway shouting "Bayonets are trump!" and slaughtered the American detachment. At the gates of the fort itself, a British sergeant following closely on the heels of an American sentry detachment wedged the gate open with his body, and the redcoats poured through to win a sharp but brief and one-sided fight. Some 65 American soldiers died as the fort fell, and another 15 were wounded and more than 350 captured along with a quantity of military supplies for the frontier.

The British then turned southward, burning Youngstown in retaliation for Newark. At Lewiston, the Poole Tavern and the dwellings and storehouses of the settlement were also put to the torch, and the small detachment at Fort Gray, a gun battery built on the site of one of Montressor's blockhouses, was driven off after a short resistance. The British climbed the escarpment and advanced on Manchester.

Lieutenant John Low and a few men met the British at the site of old Fort Schlosser, but the lieutenant was shot and his troops fled. Low's body was placed on a table in the hall of the old house at the site, and the building was torched.

A mile and a half from the Falls, at the crossroads of the portage and the Niagara Falls road, flames also consumed the Gad Pierce Tavern—where Pierce, a year earlier, had recruited a "militia" of locals and Tuscarora Indians to parade the riverbanks with "walking canes, sticks and ramrods" in lieu of muskets to convince the watching British that an army was on hand instead of the paltry single company of regulars defending the frontier. Pierce and three or four friends held off the enemy for a while, escaping out the back door as the British stormed the front.

Bates Cooke, fleeing with his brother Lathrop, a recent amputee, found himself pursued across the snow by Indians. Ignoring his brother's plea to save himself, Cooke paused and fired, killing his nearest pursuer; the brothers were saved from an attack by the rest of the band only by the arrival of a group of friendly Tuscaroras in the nick of time.

Broughton's Tavern, the building that once had been Stedman's home, also was burned, as was Field's Tavern, Augustus Porter's home, and almost all the rest of the little community. The British swept on to burn Black Rock, and Buffalo as well, on New Year's Eve.

At Manchester, Albert Porter wrote, "Buildings and property of every description were destroyed; many unresisting persons were killed, and others only escaping with their lives were in some cases reduced to extreme want and suffering. Nothing was saved, except two or three small dwellings and the log tavern, set on fire but extinguished by persons at hand after the hasty departure of the enemy."

The destruction of the Niagara Frontier was a disgrace for the American military and a disaster for the inhabitants of the region, but the war was far from over. The Niagara Campaign of 1814, in fact, was to prove bloodier still.

The Americans opened the fighting by crossing the upper Niagara to take Fort Erie, and then advancing along the Canadian shore toward

This engraving, drawn by Major Dennis, shows the first shots fired in the Niagara area in the War of 1812. American troops are crossing the Niagara River near Lewiston to storm a British gun position at Queenston in Canada. In the attack that followed, British General Isaac Brock was killed. Courtesy, Royal Ontario Museum, Toronto, Canada

FAR RIGHT: The Lockport Locks were an engineering marvel when the Erie Canal was completed in 1825. These 10 locks were constructed to keep the barge traffic flowing smoothly up and down the 70-foot escarpment. This photo was taken in 1900, showing the locks being repaired. Much of this masonry is still visible and in use to this day. Courtesy, J. Carl Burke Studio

Niagara Falls and Lake Ontario. There were major battles at Chippawa—where Scott and his "thin grey line" of regulars stood firm under withering British fire to win victory, forge a legend, and bequeath a uniform color to today's West Point cadets—and at Lundy's Lane near the brink of Horseshoe Falls.

Lundy's Lane, near the Portage Road on the Canadian side, included British troops who pushed south from Fort Niagara to take Lewiston before abandoning plans to sweep southward again along the American shore. Instead, the forces recrossed the river to join in a nighttime battle that ended with claims of victory on both sides and 1,700 men killed or wounded.

By August, American forces were concentrated once more at Fort Erie, opposite Buffalo; the campaign would end in the bloody fighting of the Battle of Fort Erie and a subsequent, failed British seige. Winter would end the combat, and the Treaty of Ghent would end the war with the borders unchanged, but not until nearly 5,000 men had died in three years of fighting on the Niagara Frontier.

In 1815 the British once more handed over Fort Niagara to troops of the United States, and two years later the Rush-Bagot Treaty demilitarized the border. Tensions would remain until mid-century and not fully ease until the Treaty of Washington in 1870, but centuries of peace along the world's longest unguarded border had begun.

"I have been at Lundy's Lane and at Chippawa," John Quincy Adams would say in 1843.

"I have seen no memento of that political era between these two countries—there I have been received as a friend with friendly greeting, and I ejaculate a prayer to God that this state of temper may be perpetual, and that the land of war and of garments rolled in blood may never again be exhibited."

With peace, came rebuilding.

The mills and the homes were cobbled back together, as the settlers who had been scattered by war returned to Manchester and Lewiston. In 1816 Augustus Porter bought Goat Island from

the state, and a year later built a bridge to connect it to the mainland. The bridge was partially destroyed by ice that winter, so in 1818—the year he rebuilt his house on its former site—Porter had a stronger bridge erected, and the island became permanently accessible.

A woolen factory was built in 1820, a forge, rolling mill, and nail factory in 1822. Augustus Porter opened his gristmill in 1822, and Jesse Symonds built his paper mill near the Goat Island bridge in 1823. In 1824 construction started on the Cataract House, to be followed 29 years later by the nearby International Hotel on the site of the log tavern that had survived the war.

In Lewiston, where the population hit 6,000 while Buffalo and Manchester were still in their village years, the still-standing Frontier House also was built in 1824 as a stagecoach stop and the finest hotel west of Albany. Now remodeled as a fast-food restaurant, the hotel once sheltered royalty, governors and presidents, and literary lights travelling the "Great Overland Route." Nearby, the famous Hustlers Tavern, another survivor of the war, touted its invention of the "cocktail," created when Catherine Hustler stirred a gin mixture with the tail feather of a stuffed gamecock.

In 1825 the portage route—mainstay of Niagara's early prominence and prosperity—became obsolete.

That year saw the opening of the Erie Canal, destined to become the major highway for the immigrants who settled America's heartlands and the commerce they sent back to the seacoasts. The western end of the canal was neither Manchester nor even Black Rock, but Buffalo—and that village would grow, in time, from a few hundred souls to a city of hundreds of thousands.

The portage, meanwhile, would lose its economic importance just as quickly. Goods could be shipped via the new canal at a fraction of the cost of the portage route. But Niagara's abundance of water power saved it—and the Porters—from economic disaster.

Pessimism, at any rate, was far from the order of the day as Manchester prepared in 1825 for a gala visit by a guest of the nation, the Marquis de Lafayette. Lafayette rode the pioneer Erie Canal boat *Seneca Chief* to the locks on the Tonawanda Creek, then travelled to the Falls by carriage. Bates Cooke, his narrow wartime escape now well behind him, gave the welcoming address at the new Eagle Hotel, where 100 guests enjoyed a June 5 dinner provided by General Parkhurst Whitney in Lafayette's honor.

Judge Hotchkiss of Lewiston presided over the dinner, aided by Judge Porter, the first judge of Niagara County, and Judge Samuel DeVeaux, as well as Major Barton. The elderly Lafayette

The Cataract House, seen in this vintage photograph from about 1870, hosted Abraham Lincoln and his family. Across the street was a large souvenir store built in the 1850s by Platt D. Babbitt, who started his career in tourism by taking daguerreotypes of tourists at Prospect Point. Courtesy, Local History Department, Niagara Falls, New York Public Library

The Port of Buffalo burgeoned with the opening of the Erie Canal in 1825. Buffalo was the western terminal of the canal, which provided an inland waterway from New York City to Lake Erie and on to the Midwest by way of the Great Lakes. Courtesy, J. Carl Burke Studio

visited Goat Island and the home of Judge Porter before spending the night at the home of Mrs. Kelsey in Lewiston.

At 5 a.m. the French hero of the American Revolution was up and en route to Fort Niagara and a 24-gun salute. After breakfast, a review, and an inspection, the general paused to express "admiration for the beautiful lake and the view of the country that he was privileged to see from the lighthouse."

By 1829, when 12,000 to 15,000 tourists a

"lighted a cigar and paced the piazza, minutely attentive to the aspect and business of a very ordinary village." Before succumbing, with a vengeance, to the majesty of the cataracts, he also paused to buy a souvenir walking stick made by a Tuscarora Indian.

By 1836 the "very ordinary village" had grown considerably, and by 1841 it included a large gristmill, two sawmills, the woolen manufactory, a trip-hammer shop, a furnace, two machine shops, two blacksmith shops, two cabinet

year already were visiting the Falls, Manchester was "the seat of the Honorable Augustus Porter, a brisk and thriving village with several mills and manufactories," noted one guest at Forsyth's Hotel. Included was the large paper mill built by Porter on Bath Island in 1826 and later sold to I.C. Woodruff, who enlarged it as the Niagara Falls Paper and Manufacturing Co. in 1855.

In 1834 author Nathaniel Hawthorne alighted from a coach and, refusing to rush to the Falls,

makers, one shop making railroad cars, four merchant shops, one public library, several hotels, three public houses, two public schools, one "classical institute," one "select school" for young ladies, 85 houses, and more than 700 residents—plus innumerable tourists in the summer months!

A railroad line to Buffalo opened in 1836, along with a small "strap" railroad linking Niagara Falls to the Erie Canal at Lockport. The first of a network of rail lines linking the village to

launched a four-year project to replace the span, using Ellet's cables to help build the two-deck Niagara Railroad Suspension Bridge. The first successful railroad suspension bridge in the world, the 822-foot span opened in 1855. The opening was spectacular—on March 16, a 28-ton locomotive pushing 20 double-loaded freight cars from Canada to the United States became the first train to cross a bridge suspended from wire cables. The first passenger train, three cars with people crowded on the cartops, quickly followed, and 20 trains made the crossing in the next 24 hours.

Colonel Roebling's bridge of wooden towers and 10-inch wire cables eventually got steel towers and wider decks, and in 1897 was rebuilt as a steel arch bridge. The names have changed, too, from Suspension Bridge to Lower Steel Arch Bridge to Whirlpool Rapids Bridge, but the historical significance remains—the span opened the international border to railroad traffic, spurring both commerce and tourism in the years to come.

On the American side, a new village grew around the "Suspension Bridge Yard" used by

FAR LEFT: In the 1840s "honeymooners" visited the Falls accompanied by their relatives, a custom that endured until the Civil War. At the turn of the century, Niagara Falls became the place for a romantic honeymoon, with businesses catering to newlyweds travelling alone, like this young couple. Courtesy, Ellen S. Comerford

nearby population centers, the railroads brought even easier access to the Falls, and tourism increased again. By the early 1850s the New York Central had taken over the smaller lines, and special trains to the Falls were leaving Buffalo, carrying cars of tourists from New York City, Philadelphia, and other cities.

By 1848 the mighty Niagara had even been bridged. Colonel Charles Ellet was the first of the bridge builders, choosing a site spanning the gorge just two miles below the cataracts. To get the first cable across, the local justice and ironmonger Theodore G. Hulett held a kite-flying contest—and a local lad, Honan Walsh, won the $5 prize for bridging the Niagara with kite-borne twine.

Ellet's $30,000 footbridge was just 7.5 feet wide, enough for pedestrians, horses, and carriages. Suspended on cables from wooden towers 240 feet above the river, the bridge opened when Ellet himself made the first crossing on horseback.

Just a few years later, the limitations of the footbridge were all too apparent. In 1851 bridge engineer John A. Roebling of New Jersey, who later would build the Brooklyn Bridge,

This view of the Roebling Bridge, which was constructed between 1851 and 1855, shows the railroad deck on top and the carriage floor below. Courtesy, J. Carl Burke Studio

the railroads. Originally Bellevue, laid out by the Bellevue Land Co., the community started in 1844 and incorporated as the Village of Niagara City in 1854 quickly became known simply as Suspension Bridge.

Other bridges followed, not always so successfully. The Lewiston Suspension Bridge actually was built in 1851 while Roebling was just getting started, but Edward W. Serrell's 1,000-foot span was destroyed by wind and ice on April 16, 1864. Samuel Kiefer built the 1,268-foot Upper Suspension Bridge close to the Falls in 1868, starting the project by having the first cable carried across the ice bridge that forms in the gorge each winter; its 10-foot-wide roadway was widened and improved in 1884, but it too was swept away in a gale in January 1889—just after Dr. John Hodge struggled back from a house call in Canada, along a roadbed rising and falling some 60 feet.

Rebuilt the same year, the suspension bridge was later dismantled and moved to Lewiston. Its place was taken in 1898 by a new steel arch bridge strong enough to support trolley cars, but that span known variously as the Falls View, Upper Steel Arch, or "Honeymoon" Bridge was destroyed again by ice in 1938.

Even stranger was the fate of the Michigan Central Railroad's pioneering cantilever railroad bridge near Roebling's span. It opened December 19, 1883, with 20 heavy engines and 40 loaded cars demonstrating its strength, but it was dismantled in 1925 and shipped to South Africa for continued use, its place taken by a still heavier steel arch railroad bridge.

Other bridges were being built in the middle of the nineteenth century in Niagara Falls—political bridges.

In 1848, the year Ellet set the boys of the villages to kite-flying, Manchester lost the name it had borne since 1810. Absorbing tiny Clarksville, dating from 1830, it was incorporated as the Village of Niagara Falls that July.

The first president of the new village was General Parkhurst Whitney, owner of the Cataract House and the provider of General Lafayette's civic dinner nearly a quarter century before. Upriver from the new village lay the community of

La Salle, settled in 1806; downriver lay Suspension Bridge, incorporated in 1874 with Colonel John Fisk of the Bellevue Land Co. as its first president. While all three would eventually become a single city, the three-village heritage would color local politics well into the twentieth century.

Augustus Porter, who had named Manchester, lived just long enough to see the start of the changes. Having issued unsuccessful calls in 1825 and again in 1847 for eastern capitalists to harness the power of Niagara, he died in 1849. Three years later, in 1852, another of the old guard died—Samuel DeVeaux, who had come to the area in 1816 to open the first store, at Main and Niagara streets, and whose writings offer some of the earliest history of the region.

More than politics was afoot, though, in the years in which Millard Fillmore of Buffalo held the U.S. presidency. The nation was moving toward the bloodiest chapter in its history, the Civil War, and the conflict would not pass Niagara Falls by.

In part, the war benefitted the region; industrial prosperity followed hard upon wartime production. But the price was steep, and paid in lives.

Colonel Peter A. Porter, a son of pioneer settler Peter B. Porter, died leading his regiment in a charge over the Confederate breastworks at Cold Harbor, Virginia, on June 3, 1864. Other Niagara Falls natives died with him, and at the battles of the Wilderness, Brandy Station, Petersburg, Murfreesborough, Hatcher's Run, Cedar Mountain, Saulsbury, Antietam, and Shiloh; still more died in the prisons at Libby, Salisbury, and Andersonville.

The sole attack on this area was a small one, mounted by a Toronto-based party of Confederate agents frustrated at the failure of their plans to capture the only Union warship on the Great Lakes and use it to free the prisoners at Johnson's Island and bombard Buffalo. Instead, John Yeates Beall and three other raiders crossed the border and tried unsuccessfully to derail freight trains near Buffalo; Beall and a companion were captured in a Niagara Falls railroad depot, where they had fallen asleep while waiting for a train to Toronto.

In 1863 the International Hotel—part of a

FACING PAGE: The Suspension Bridge at Lewiston was moved there from Niagara Falls, where it was replaced by the Steel Arch Bridge. This photo shows the span during the 1898 inauguration ceremonies at Lewiston. Courtesy, Local History Department, Niagara Falls, New York Public Library

A reunion of Civil War veterans is seen here at Old Fort Niagara in about 1890. Around this time, in an area adjacent to the historical fort, a permanent army base was established. During World War II it served as an induction center and prisoner of war camp. Today most of the brick barracks, mess halls, and officers quarters, and a training building, have been removed. Courtesy, J. Carl Burke Studio

complex that, with the adjacent Cataract House, could boast 1,000 rooms—served as the summer White House, with Mrs. Lincoln and her children in residence. And at war's end, rumors concerning the flight of the Confederacy's president were so common that local newspapers ran a daily column of "Jefferson Davis Sightings."

The post-war village was far different than the Niagara settlement of the first half of the century. Hotels and tourism flourished during the summer months, although shutting down for the winters; industry had a firm foothold, a transportation center had been born, and cultural institutions had begun to play a part in village life.

While in the 1840s the great Charles Dickens could simply hasten through to the Canadian side and in 1853 visitor William Chambers of London could see a simple village of "several streets in skeleton, with a large railway station in the centre, and a number of hotels stuck about for the accommodation of visitors," by 1871 novelist Henry James could be struck, not favorably, by "a multitude of hotels and taverns and stores, glaring with white paint, bedizened with placards and advertisements, and decorated by groups of those gentlemen who flourish most rankly on the soil of New York and in the vicinage of hotels."

Niagara Falls was growing from a village of a few hundred to a city of thousands in this era.

The New York Central had a stone depot in the village and a second at Suspension Bridge, with connecting lines along the top of the gorge; the Erie Railroad built its wooden depot at the Falls in 1871, and the brick and fieldstone Union Station opened in 1887 to replace the older wooden station of 1844.

Waterpower was being harnessed by industry, and even though the village still lacked pavement and sewers, there were civic water supplies—the Niagara Falls Water Works in 1868, the Suspension Bridge Water Works in 1876.

By the 1870s the handful of early nineteenth century churches had grown into a wide range of centers for spiritual needs, including the First Presbyterian Church (first organized in 1824), St. Paul's Methodist (organized in 1815), the First Baptist, St. Mary's of the Cataracts Catholic Church, the Church of the Epiphany, and St. Peter's Episcopal Church.

Among the schools, there were major institutions. The Union School of 1855, also known as the Fifth Street School, would become the city's first high school in 1885, and the Cleveland Avenue School built in 1872 in Suspension Bridge would become a high school in 1889. Judge DeVeaux, the early developer and philanthropist who had died in 1852, left most of his $200,000 estate to found a college for orphans to be run by the Episcopal Church, and the DeVeaux School complex—a military school until 1950—carries on his name today.

Niagara University, founded in 1856 as a seminary in Buffalo by Bishop John Timon and the Reverend John J. Lynch and moved to the town of Lewiston a year later, was incorporated as the College and Seminary of Our Angels in 1866 and gained its present name in 1877. In the village of Lewiston, the Lewiston Academy became one of the finest private schools in the nation early in the century but declined when the new bridges slowed business for the Lewiston-Queenston ferry, its source of revenue.

The growing community also had newspapers, including the still-published *Niagara Gazette*, originally named the *Niagara Falls Gazette*, and the former *Suspension Bridge Journal*. In his first issue on May 17, 1854, *Gazette* editor

William Pool backed the new Hydraulic Canal, hoped for completion of the Lewiston Road, and noted that a contract had been given to the Bidwell & Banta shipyards in Buffalo for a new Maid of the Mist tour boat.

Pool would sell the *Gazette* to Peter A. Porter in 1880 and start the *Niagara Courier* in 1884, and the *Gazette* would become a regularly published, year-round daily newspaper in 1893. The *Gazette* would take on a Republican bent, while the *Daily Cataract* in Suspension Bridge would counter with the Democratic viewpoint.

Twice-daily mail service came to be taken for granted, just half a century after government messengers would take days on horseback to reach Albany. Horsecars brought public transportation to the Falls' streets in 1882, the first Edison Telephone linked the Cataract Bank and the home of its chief cashier in 1878, and the village police department installed its first phone in 1882. There was even a short-lived race track, in 1887 and 1888.

Niagara Falls was beginning to look like a

city, even without the sewers and pavement. And soon, there was talk of a charter.

In 1890 the Businessmen's Association of Niagara Falls adopted a resolution by lawyer W. Caryl Ely, later president of the International Railway Co., calling for a city charter combining the villages of Niagara Falls and Suspension Bridge. There was a move to include the small community of La Salle as well, but it was soon dropped.

The plan drew strong support from Thomas V. Welch, the influential superintendent of the state's Niagara Reservation, and public meetings were held on March 4 and 5, 1892. Niagara Falls had grown from an incorporated village of 3,000 to 6,505 residents, and Suspension Bridge from 827 to 5,206; most favored the idea of a new, combined city.

The state approved, and the City of Niagara Falls almost was born on March 16, 1892. Welch, an Irishman, intervened with the governor and the official signing was delayed a few hours until early March 17—St. Patrick's Day.

The villagers on the American side became increasingly interested in harnessing the power of the rapids and the falls for industry. In 1825 the town was named Manchester for an association with the British industrial town. A little more than 20 years later, however, the name was changed back to Niagara Falls. Courtesy, J. Carl Burke Studio

"ould ye fain steal a glance o'er life's dark sea,
And gaze though trembling on eternity?
Would ye look out, look down, where God hath set
His mighty signet? Come—come higher yet,
To the PAGODA's utmost height ascend,
And see earth, air, and sky in one alembic blend!"

PAGODA is now open to visitors and perfectly secure
Admittance 25 cents 1st April, 1845

Like as not, the handbill would be pushed into your grasp by a small boy in the employ of the Pagoda, just one of many "perfectly secure" structures lining the gorge of the Niagara and offering a view of the Falls—for a price.

You could, if you chose, pay your quarter and take your chance on the Pagoda's views. You could also engage a cab—but that was even more of a risk, because the Niagara hackmen were legendary in their aggressiveness and their ability to separate the tourist from his or her dollar.

It was an era of excess, of honky-tonk and chutzpah, of showmanship and charlatanism that peddled the natural wonders of the Falls as so many oddities and curiosities worth the price of a peep. There were, in fact, peepholes—you could step up to the board fence lining the shore, pay your money and rent a wood-framed view of nature's awesome majesty.

The Clifton House on the Canadian side of the Falls offered an excellent view of both the American and Horseshoe falls. Built in 1833, it became a favorite spot for English tourists and Confederate plotters during the Civil War. Niagara Falls, Canada, also became important for the Underground Railroad, and many fugitive slaves found work as waiters and kitchen help at the Clifton House. Courtesy, J. Carl Burke Studio

FOREVER FREE

CHAPTER THREE

• • •

The great falls of the Niagara had become a commodity in the nineteenth century, and the struggle to free them from commercialism would set precedents for the scenic treasures of the entire nation in the decades to come.

There were tourists long before there were residents, at Niagara Falls.

Father Hennepin, led to the Falls by Indians, could be considered one; so, too, could any soldier or trapper of the French and English periods who strayed from his course or his Fort Niagara billet to gaze upon the cataract in the wilderness. Travellers' accounts come hard on the heels of the reports of the priests and explorers who first journeyed to Niagara.

"My first care, after my arrival, was to visit the noblest cascade in the world," the Jesuit Pierre Francois Xavier de Charlevoix wrote home from Niagara on May 23, 1721.

"Nothing but zeal for the publick good could possibly induce an officer to remain in such a country as this, than which a wilder and more frightful is not to be seen. On the one side you see just under your feet, and as it were at the bottom of an abyss, a great river, but which in this place is liker a torrent by its rapidity, by the whirlpools formed by a thousand rocks through which it with difficulty finds passage, and by the foam with which it is always covered; on the other the view is confined by three mountains placed one over the other, and whereof the last hides itself in the clouds.

"This would have been a very proper scene for the poets to make the Titans attempt to scale the heavens. In a word, on whatever side you turn your eyes, you discover nothing which does not inspire a secret horror . . . the soil of the three leagues I had to walk on foot to get hither seems very indifferent, it is even very ill-wooded and you cannot walk ten paces without treading on ant-hill or meeting with rattlesnakes, especially during the heat of the day."

Despite these accounts—or perhaps because of them—the Niagara continued to draw an increasing flood of visitors. And the visitors kept inventing new ways to see the Falls.

Some scrambled down the gorge by hand, or with the help of ropes, or were lucky enough to

This view from Goat Island, taken around 1900, shows the smaller Luna Island and in the background, the American Falls and the Honeymoon Bridge, built in 1898. The bridge collapsed in an ice jam in 1938. On the right is the observation tower atop the Moose Tower Hotel. Courtesy, Buffalo and Erie County Historical Society

The majesty of the Falls made the cataracts a stop on the "Grand Tour" in the nineteenth century. This drawing from a London newspaper shows people in their oilcloth coats enjoying a spectacular view. Courtesy, Buffalo and Erie County Historical Society

BELOW RIGHT: American William Lyon Mackenzie began a rebellion on Navy Island in 1837, proclaiming himself the head of a new Republic of Canada. Within two weeks he had 200 supporters and a one-boat Navy consisting of the paddle steamer Caroline. *The* Caroline *was used to bring artillery stolen from the U.S. Arsenal at Buffalo to the "New Republic." Captain Allen Drew, a Canadian commander, took over the ship and killed the watchman, who was a U.S. citizen. He then set the ship on fire and sent it over the Falls. Courtesy, Buffalo and Erie County Historical Society*

find the notched tree trunks known as Indian ladders.

Ralph Izard, an early tourist from South Carolina, was in a party of visitors that chanced upon an Indian ladder in 1765 and made their way to the bottom of the gorge. Unfortunately, they forgot to mark the return path and, wet with spray, spent three hours trying to find the way back up.

"The night approaching, gave us a comfortable prospect of staying there till morning, and the appearance of wolves' tracks in many places added much to our unpleasant situation," he reported. "We were informed that those animals frequently travelled about that place in companies of twenty or thirty at a time, and were so fierce as to attack men even in the middle of the day. As we had nothing with which to defend ourselves, nor flint and steel to make a fire, I think the odds were about five to four that no part of us except our bones would have ever got to the top of the hill undigested if we had not luckily found our way."

Hector St. John de Crèvecoeur and a friend named Hunter used a rope to descend into the gorge on the American side some 20 years later, and later journeyed to the opposite shore and

Table Rock—which at that time projected some 20 or 30 feet out over the abyss. Following a guide, they scrambled down the slope, added their names to those other travellers had carved in the trunk of a great tree, and climbed down an Indian ladder and across slopes of broken rock to reach the base of the Horseshoe Falls. Crèvecoeur's account of the exhausting, six-hour effort is the first of a journey behind the Falls—although presumably the guide had been there often, before them.

"The great force with which [the waters] are precipitated gives them an horizontal direction, so that at the bottom where we stood it left an opening between the water and the rocks," he wrote. "It was here we entered by slow and cautious steps. It soon became dark, which proves the immense body of water there must be betwixt us and the light . . . we had proceeded about 15 to 20 yards, when we found it so very sultry that we might be said to be in a fumigating bath. We hastened out of this dreary place, and once more congratulated each other with our safety."

In letters and books, the word about Niagara was spread. Newspapers reprinted travellers' accounts, as did such popular magazines of the day as the *Columbian*, which ran surveyor Andrew Ellicott's descriptions and measurements of the Falls in its issue of June 1790.

Some who came to the cataract were disappointed, in part at least because of the exaggerated claims of some of the earlier writers. Others indulged in raptures of their own. And, gradually, those who came to live near the Falls started making things easier for those who came to visit.

Mrs. Simcoe's Ladder was among the first of the improvements, a ladder route down the gorge that offered a more solid alternative to the Indian ladders on the Canada side. It was first put in place to accommodate the lady of Governor Simcoe, but soon proved not only a safer but a more popular way to descend the cliff.

Those who made the descent, though, were still relatively few. In 1796 La Rochefoucault Liancourt, in one of the best-known eighteenth

century accounts, lamented that "it is much to be regretted that the government of a people which surpasses all other nations for fondness in travelling and curiosity, should not have provided convenient places for observing this celebrated phenomenon at all possible points of view.

"It is pleaded in excuse, that the number of travellers whom curiosity leads to this spot is inconsiderable; that even they who travel this way on account of business, and stop here to view the falls, are few in numbers; that only hunting Indians and idle children form the idea of creeping down to the falls, and that consequently nobody would be benefitted by the money expended in providing an easy access. Yet all these pleas cannot justify a saving of thirty dollars, for which expense the greatest curiosity in the known world would be rendered accessible."

Considerably more than thirty dollars would be spent, and earned, in the years just ahead.

By the early 1800s, the newlywed Bonapartes had arrived to spend a week in a log cabin as the first of a long line of honeymoon couples. As the wilderness disappeared and access grew

Goat Island, looking peaceful here in a winter scene from about 1890, has long been considered a prime plot of real estate. In the early 1800s New York State planned to build a prison on the island—a seemingly impossible place to escape from. Instead, the land was developed for tourism. In 1869 famed landscape designer Frederick Law Olmsted, architect Henry Hobson Richardson, and lawyer William Dorsheimer began motions to preserve Goat Island as a natural park area. Courtesy, Local History Department, Niagara Falls, New York Public Library

This 1830 drawing is titled View of the Schlosser Fall. *Schlosser was one of the various names given to Niagara Falls in the early days. In the nineteenth century Schlosser was also the name of the docks where boats arriving from Buffalo landed. Courtesy, Local History Department, Niagara Falls, New York Public Library*

easier, the numbers increased—private carriages gave way to stagecoach lines, stagecoaches to the Erie Canal, the canal to railroads.

Samuel DeVeaux, in his 1841 *The Traveller's Own Book to Saratoga Springs, Niagara Falls and Canada,* names a Mr. Hooker as the first professional guide at the Falls, but claims no primacy for his little guidebook; in 1829 the pastor of the First Presbyterian Church already had published a guide to Niagara, and other pamphlets may have been earlier still.

The settlement at the Falls only had about 500 residents then, but several hotels were open for business, and up to 15,000 visitors were arriving each year. The number soared in 1827, for a spectacle that modern perceptions would view as sordid—the old and rotting schooner *Michigan,* cast adrift above the Falls with a load of wild and domestic animals, for the amusement of 30,000 to 50,000 spectators. Even then,

the stunt was "not generally approved," DeVeaux notes, and there were cheers when a bear and one or two other animals reached the Canadian shore as the vessel went to pieces in the rapids.

Nevertheless, promoters put the old *Superior* to the same use in 1829. Far fewer, though, would witness the fiery plunge of the *Caroline* just eight years later—British forces captured the boat at the Fort Schlosser dock, towed it to midstream, and sent it burning over the Horseshoe Falls on the night of December 29, 1837. The move was more strategy than showmanship, and created an international incident; the British claimed the vessel was being used to supply rebel forces on Navy Island during the Mackenzie Rebellion in Canada that year.

Visitors in the 1820s, though, already were paying fees to enjoy their views of the Falls. Judge Porter's bridge to Goat Island, in 1818, soon had sported a tollhouse—for 25 cents you could have access to the island for the entire season, and the caretaker could also sell you souvenirs.

In 1829 the Biddle Stairs were built at the gorge end of the island at the urging of Bank of the United States president Nicholas Biddle, who may have helped finance the venture. A 40-foot flight of steps leading to a steep, 80-foot spiral, the staircase provided access to fishing spots, the edge of the Horseshoe Falls, and the Cave of the Winds—once known as Ingraham's Cave for the first non-Indian to see it, although George Sims and Berry Hill White of Niagara Falls were the first to actually enter what was in fact a ledge sheltered by an overhang of rock behind Luna Falls.

By the 1870s, the price of the attraction was up to one dollar. In 1925, after nearly a century of service, the stairs finally would be replaced by an elevator; the "cave" itself was closed in 1955 after dangerous rockslides and some fatal accidents finally led to removal of the weakened stone overhang, but tourists still can ride the elevators to pathways at the base of the Falls.

Porter and his brother Peter, who had bought Goat Island from the state in 1816, kept Goat Island relatively undeveloped as industry began to cluster along the Niagara rapids above the American Falls. There were walkways and gardens, and where the island borders the Horseshoe Falls at Terrapin Point, the Porters in 1827 built a 300-foot walkway-type bridge over the now-vanished turtle-shaped Terrapin Rocks.

The bridge ended in a platform cantilevered 10 feet out over the gorge itself, a dizzying prospect for the casual tourist. It was made even more dizzying by Goat Island's most famous visitor, the "hermit," who arrived on June 18, 1829.

Francis Abbott was tall, handsome, educated, and "dressed in a long loose gown, or cloak, of a chocolate color" when he arrived in town, De-Veaux reports. He was carrying a roll of blankets, a flute, a portfolio, and a large book.

He was the son of a well-to-do Quaker from Plymouth, England, and he planned to stay just one week. He took a room in a local inn, took a

book from the library, borrowed some music books, bought a violin and guitar. And soon, he seemed to come under the spell of the Niagara.

The young man stayed for 22 months—2 of them in a hut on the mainland riverbank and 20 on Goat Island, first with the family of Porter's caretaker and then, for most of the time, alone. He kept largely to himself and to his music, poetry, and painting, with occasional walks out to the end of the Terrapin Point platform, where he would dangle over the edge doing chin-ups 160 feet above the churning river at the base of the Falls.

On June 10, 1831, he was seen bathing below the American Falls. In fact, boatmen saw him enter the water three times that day—and then noticed that he was no longer there, but that his clothing was still piled on the bank.

The body was recovered near Fort Niagara on June 21. His hut revealed no clues to the her-

Seen here around 1870 is the Terrapin Bridge from Goat Island. The span was constructed over the Terrapin Rocks, so named because they resembled turtle shells. Courtesy, J. Carl Burke Studio

The stone Terrapin Tower, reached via Goat Island, was built in 1833 and for 40 years gave visitors a thrilling view of the Horseshoe Falls, as well as a splendid view of Canada. Note that the bridge leading out to the tower has no railings. The tower was torn down in 1873 because it was a counter attraction to Prospect Park, which was owned by the operator's daughter. Courtesy, Buffalo and Erie County Historical Society

mit's background or life, and there was no written trace of his musings to shed light on his hopes or his dreams. His poetry and his paintings were gone, and some think his death was no accident. Francis Abbott died, by intent or by chance, at the age of 28.

After Abbott's time, the platform over the abyss was replaced by a tower at the brink of the Horseshoe Falls. Augustus Porter and his brother, who would move to the Falls from Black Rock in 1838, had the 30-foot viewing platform built on rock at the edge of the cataract, and visitors to Goat Island could gain a spectacular view of the waterfall from Terrapin Tower from 1833 until its demolition 40 years later.

Elsewhere in the gorge, too, there were "improvements." In 1836 financier and speculator Benjamin Rathbun started to build a road down the banks—a project that would be left incomplete, as his investments evaporated in the financial panic of 1837.

According to the Presbyterian guidebook, the people who came to the Falls early in the nineteenth century represented nearly as complete a cultural cross-section as the tourists of today—although then, travel was more costly and time-consuming.

"The fashionable, the opulent, the learned, congregate here from the principal cities of the country; from the southern and western cities, South America, the West Indies, the Canadas, all parts of Europe, and indeed from all countries," we are informed.

"Exiled monarchs, foreign ambassadors, Whigs, Tories, radicals, royalists, naval and military officers, governors, judges, lawyers, senators, etc., with a good proportion of female

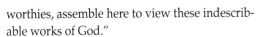

worthies, assemble here to view these indescribable works of God."

Indescribable, perhaps, because it was getting increasingly difficult to see them, at least without paying a price. Although the Presbyterians would excommunicate Augustus Porter for collecting his Goat Island bridge tolls on Sundays, the fact remains that the land around the Falls—and indeed the Falls themselves, for those claiming water rights—was private property, and few saw any reason not to profit by either using the power of the water or selling the view.

"Only a few buildings are yet seen peering from among the trees and shrubbery, and they have just begun to be a drawback on the stern simplicity and unstudied grandeur of the scene," traveller Thomas Rolph wrote in 1832. "I fear, however, they are destined to become a

positive nuisance, unless they are abated by the adoption of a more considerate course by visitors.

"This giving every other person who accosts you a few shillings to show some trumpery which you care not a straw for, may be the easiest way of ridding yourself of his obtrusive company and the interruption which it occasions to some cherished train of thought, but it is a riddance at the expense of the next comer, and directly calculated to ensure the perpetual and harrassing annoyance of all future visitors.

"I wish it were provided by law that no

Visitors could go to a photo gallery at the Falls to have a portrait taken, as this trio did in the 1880s. In a tintype studio a fabulous vista was available without the usual horde of fellow tourists or the mist, which dampened hair and clothes. Courtesy, The Knechtel Family

Since the Depression, the Falls have become a popular destination for bus tours. This group from Lackawanna, an industrial suburb of Buffalo, posed in 1931 in front of the Table Rock House on the Canadian side. A prominent attraction, the house has been featured in several films, including Niagara, *with Marilyn Monroe, and* Superman II. *Courtesy, The Knechtel Family*

building should be erected within sight of the little plot of ground immediately adjoining the cataract. As matters are now conducted, another twenty years may see the whole amphitheatre filled with grogshops, humbug museums, etc., etc.—who knows, but it may be profaned with cotton factories?"

Who, indeed? Rolph proved disturbingly prophetic. Some were already disturbed enough to protest—Edward Street Abdy called Porter a "vandal" for his bridge and tower, and two clergymen visiting American churches on behalf of the Congregational Union of England and Wales had even stronger words in 1834.

Andrew Reed and James Matheson, in their account of that journey, lamented that they "cannot say much for the taste either of the visitors or inhabitants of this spot. The visitors seem to regard the Falls rather as an object of curiosity than otherwise, and when they had satisfied their curiosity (which in most cases was very quickly done) and could report that they had seen them, the duty was discharged."

The residents fared even worse, in their estimation. "On the American side they have got up a shabby town and called it Manchester," they wrote. "Manchester and the Falls of Niagara! A proposition has been made to buy Goat Island and turn it into a botanical garden to improve the scenery—and such scenery! On the Canadian side, a money-seeking party have bought up 400 acres with the hope of erecting 'The City of the Falls,' and still worse, close on Table Rock, some party was busy in erecting a mill dam!

"One hardly has the patience to record these things. The universal voice ought to interfere, and prevent them. Niagara does not belong to them; Niagara does not belong to Canada or America. Such spots should be deemed the property of civilized mankind, and nothing should be allowed to weaken their efficacy on the tastes, the morals, and the enjoyments of all men."

In 1871 Henry James penned a portrait of Niagara for *The Nation*. He wrote movingly of the natural beauty of the Falls, but the encroachments of commercialism failed to escape his

notice as well.

"There is every appearance that the spectacle
you have come so far to see is to be choked in
the horribly vulgar shops and booths and catch-
penny artifices which have pushed and
elbowed to within the very spray of the Falls,
and ply their importunities in shrill competition
with its thunder," he lamented before wonder-
ing whether New York could yet buy the relatively unspoiled Goat Island, as California had
Yosemite.

Goat Island had, in fact, been offered for
sale a time or two, but a number of schemes
for its usage had come to nothing. By the year
after James' visit, the heirs of the Porters also
had organized the Prospect Park Co. and were
charging fees to the previously free Prospect
Point area on the mainland side of the American Falls opposite the island; a dance hall
pavilion, lighted fountains, tourist attractions,
and gardens would follow in the years to
come.

Tourism in much of the nineteenth century
was fundamentally different than it is today;
then, Niagara Falls was a resort community
and visits could last a week or more. Well-to-
do Southern families, before the Civil War,
would summer in the Falls or the beach communities on the Canadian shores of the lakes.
Even during the war, some prominent Southerners sojourned on the Canadian side of the

Falls; in 1864, famed *New York Tribune*
publisher Horace Greeley arranged "peace
talks" with a trio of Southern politicians staying at the Clifton House, with trusted Lincoln
aide Major John Hay shuttling back and forth
between that hotel and the Cataract House on
the American shore. (The talks fell apart when
it turned out the Southerners had no authority
from Jeff Davis, and both sides issued denials
when word leaked to the press.)

The railroads began to change that style of
tourism, making access easier and quicker and
opening the era of day trips to the Falls. The
number of visitors also increased, and that
added to the growing opposition to all-out
commercialism at the Falls.

A painting played a part in that opposition;
Frederick Church's glowing vista of the waterfalls, chief among the landscapes of the Hudson
River School artists who visited the area, gained
wide popularity and gave impetus to what became known as the Free Niagara Movement.

In August 1869 the Cataract House received
three guests who would play a major role in
efforts to return the lands bordering the Falls to
state control; Frederick Law Olmsted was
America's premier park and landscape
designer, H.H. Richardson was one of the nation's top architects, and William Dorsheimer
would later serve as lieutenant governor of
New York. More than a decade later, they

would help organize the Free Niagara Association, which would play a pivotal role in the preservation debate.

The state, aware of the complaints, already had taken some action. Lord Dufferin, governor general of Canada, had added his voice to the criticism of commercialism in the late 1870s, and in 1879 New York governor Lucius Robinson suggested development of a state park.

The state legislature ordered Olmsted and State Survey director James T. Gardner to ready a plan, and in 1880 survey board president Horatio Seymour recommended that the state buy the lands bordering the Falls to hold in trust for the people forever. Bills were introduced, but enthusiasm for the park concept wasn't universally shared; the cost drew strong opposition from farming communities and Grange associations throughout the state, and many felt that the federal government should develop what would inevitably be a national attraction. The threat to private property rights also raised fears in an era of strong capitalism, and many feared the precedent a state park at Niagara could set for the vast and still privately owned forest resources of the Adirondack Mountains.

Governor Alonzo B. Cornell, who had succeeded Robinson, had a simple reaction. The Falls, he told a Free Niagara supporter, "are a luxury, and why should not the public pay to see them?"

Under his administration, the bills got nowhere. But in 1882 Grover Cleveland of Buffalo was elected governor, and a month after the vote Olmsted and his friends met in New York City to organize the Free Niagara Association. The first president was Howard Potter, at whose home the group met; among the vice presidents was Cornelius Vanderbilt. More than 300 members, from as far away as London, were soon signed, and their dues formed the financial nucleus for some intense lobbying efforts.

Cleveland was a friend of the park concept, and quickly signed the Niagara Reservation Act passed by the legislature in 1883. A commission was formed to select the lands that would become part of the park, and state canal division engineer Thomas Evershed completed the survey.

The properties were appraised in 1884, and the sum proved hard to swallow. Even without water rights, a consideration rejected by the appraisers and the subject of consequent appeals, the bill came to $1,433,429.50—an appropriation request that state treasury officials regarded with horror.

Still, the landowners' claims had totaled nearly $4 million, and while attorney Ansley Wilcox of Buffalo led the legal fight to keep the claims down and successfully uphold the state's right to take private land through the process known as "eminent domain," the Free Niagara Association went about the equally difficult task of winning legislative votes.

The state, in 1885, was in no mood to withdraw such a huge sum from its coffers. Deputy Attorney General Isaac H. Maynard suggested an alternative, under which the state could issue bonds for the constitutional maximum of $1 million for a public purpose. The association sent its secretary, J.B. Harrison, around the state seeking the support of writers, editors, college professors, clergymen, professionals, and businessmen on a "think Niagara, talk Niagara" campaign. A citizens' committee also was organized at Niagara Falls, with committee member Alvah H. Gluck placing his Spencer House staff and rooms at the group's disposal; Frank Davidson of the International Hotel was hired as a clerk.

At the heart of the association's work was a massive letter-writing campaign, which reached thousands of friends and foes alike across the state. Addresses of influential citizens in every legislative district were sought and gained, and they in turn were asked to recruit others in their areas to join in the written and personal appeals to legislators.

Organized by former state assemblyman Thomas V. Welch, the campaigns were amazingly effective. Legislators were badgered, the opposition's inflated claims of massive tax hikes were countered with an argument that a free Niagara would cost each citizen only 28 cents, and votes were changed.

Many of those whose support was sought also wrote back to the association, and bound volumes of their letters were compiled. Comments both pro and con were received, with responses ranging from simple support to vehement opposition and even one suggestion from an embittered visitor that "if possible, to have a clause in the bill providing for the occasional hanging of a hackman of that locality."

The bill authorizing the creation of the first state park in American history passed the assembly and the senate in 1885, but it still had one more hurdle—the signature of yet another new governor, Daniel B. Hill. Hill was no friend of the measure—Welch, in a later report to the Buffalo Historical Society, says that a veto message actually was prepared—but there were other forces at work by now.

Hill could have either vetoed the measure outright, as the powerful Granges were urging, or simply allowed it to expire through a "pocket veto" as time ran out on the legislative session. But his mind was changed, apparently by a visit he made to Samuel J. Tilden, his political mentor, and by the strong intervention of former governor Cleveland—who by then was serving as president of the United States.

News of the signing on April 30, 1885, the last day allowed by law, was telegraphed by Welch from Albany to Buffalo, Niagara Falls, and New York City. Welch and O.W. Cutler, a movement supporter, then went to thank the governor in person, after which they adjourned to a Capitol Hill tavern for "refreshments."

Erastus Brooks, a legislative champion of the movement, later wrote in a letter that "it was the 'pull together' that put the bill through, and in the end only an intense and intelligent public opinion saved the bill in the Senate, and its clear defeat in the form of an executive veto. I was among those who pleaded with the Governor for his signature, and the President's urgency, I think, made assurance doubly sure in the end."

The Porters, who had claimed $1,000,000 for their lands, received the single largest award, $525,000. On the Canadian side, the Ontario legislature in 1887 passed its Queen Victoria Niagara Falls Parks Act, in an attempt to control

development and curtail abuses on that side of the border as well.

The New York act simply and forcefully set out its purpose: "The lands for the payment of awards for which this Act provides shall be known as the State Reservation at Niagara; they shall forever be reserved by the state for the purpose of restoring the scenery of the Falls of Niagara to and preserving it in its natural condition; they shall forever be kept open and free of access to all mankind without fee, charge or expense to any person for entering upon or passing, to or over any part thereof."

America's first state park was formally delivered to the people on Wednesday, July 15, 1885, in ceremonies attended by 75,000 people, the largest gathering up to that time in Niagara Falls—still a village of only 3,500 residents.

There was a 100-gun sunrise salute that day, and a parade with nearly 2,000 soldiers from the federal army, the state national guard, and the marine detachment from the warship USS *Michigan*. Bands from the Falls, Buffalo, Utica, and Cleveland took part, as did the Mexican National Band, and a 400-voice choir drawn from the singing societies of Niagara Falls and Buffalo sang the anthems and hymns. There were speeches by Governor Hill, commission president Dorsheimer, and others—and at noon, under clearing skies in Prospect Park, the papers were signed to free the lands of Niagara forever.

Welch, who would serve as the first superintendent of the Niagara Reservation and maintain that title for many years, must have felt a great deal of satisfaction as he watched the massive display of fireworks over the bunting-draped town that evening. Within days, workers would be tearing down the board fences and many of the 150 buildings that lined the water's edge, ripping out the illegal mill raceways and piers, and demolishing signboards.

Olmsted developed his landscape with an eye toward nature, blending necessary structures into the scenery and keeping in mind the total setting of parkland, river, and waterfalls. Canada would take a different approach, one of gardens and formal landscaping, and the differ-

ences in philosophy persist today; Olmsted's preference for natural beauty, though, provided a model for parkland throughout the state and the nation in years to come.

Debate, today, centers on the conflicts inherent in efforts both to preserve natural beauty and to enhance accessibility and enjoyment for tourists. Motor vehicle roadways and viewmobile routes, unforeseen in Olmsted's day, have been added; a section of the Robert Moses Parkway near the Falls was first opened to improve highway routes and then closed as an intrusion on the landscape. More recent efforts have been aimed at curtailing the noise and activity of helicopter tours from a Goat Island landing area.

And the Falls, too, has changed.

The area at Terrapin Point once bridged by the judge's walkways to platform and tower is now landfill, built up into a viewing area in 1954 after hydropower diversions left most of the Terrapin Rocks high and dry below Porter's Bluff. Rockfalls, part of the continuing process of erosion, also have altered the look of the waterfalls.

The single largest rockfall occurred on July 28, 1954, when 185,000 tons dropped from the cliff face at Prospect Point and the gorge next to the American Falls; on January 17, 1931, another 75,000 tons of rock had fallen from the middle of the American Falls crest. The collapses of undermined rock formed much of the huge rock pile, or talus, at the base of the cataract.

Other major rockfalls at the American Falls date to 1818, December 4, 1954, and May 11, 1967; at the Bridal Veil Falls, a rockfall at the Cave of the Winds on September 6, 1920, killed two visitors and injured three more. Sections of Table Rock on the Canadian side of the Horseshoe Falls fell in 1823, 1846, and 1850, and huge pieces of the crestline itself dropped in 1828, 1852, 1882, 1889, 1905, 1934, 1936, 1937, and 1963.

On July 8, 1983, humanity pushed the process of erosion along. Earlier geological studies had found that the bedrock at Terrapin Point was unstable, and the point had been closed to tourists. In 1983, 25,000 tons of rock were blasted off the point with more than 9,000 pounds of dynamite.

"The explosion sent one arrow-like thrust of rock and dust halfway across Niagara Gorge,

Tugby & Walker's stood by the entrance bridge to Goat Island and became the largest of tourist stores, selling popular curiosities including "petrified mist" (actually ordinary stones) and Indian artifacts. The store, and the shanties that lined the rapids, were later removed for the creation of the State Reservation. Courtesy, Local History Department, Niagara Falls, New York Public Library

This photo from about 1890 shows the Incline Railway covered with snow. The railway was built to replace the stairway to the ferry landing in 1845. Courtesy, J. Carl Burke Studio

and a second blast of dirt and dust shot 100 feet into the air," *Buffalo News* journalist Paul Mac-Clennan reported.

The dynamiting, witnessed by thousands and reported around the world, removed the rock overhang and stabilized the point well enough to allow the reopening of the viewing area. The effort, though, wasn't the only human intervention in the cataracts' history.

In 1969 the U.S. Army Corps of Engineers

constructed an earthenwork dam that diverted the flow of the river from the eastern channel and "dewatered" the American Falls. The purpose was to study the condition and strength of the rock in the Falls' crestline, and the talus below the Falls.

The work didn't mark the first time the Falls had gone dry; on March 29, 1848, a huge ice jam at the outlet of Lake Erie "dewatered" the entire Niagara River all the way from the lake to the Falls.

The sudden silence as the thunder of the cataracts was stilled drew thousands of onlookers to the banks. Hundreds explored the rocks of the riverbed, and War of 1812 musket barrels were picked from crevices as souvenirs.

"The preceding winter had been intensely cold and the ice formed on Lake Erie was unusually thick," *Scribner's Magazine* reported in 1876 in a remembrance of the national sensation. "During the forenoon of March 29, a stiff easterly wind moved it up the lake; a little be-

daughter a third of the way along the brink of the Horseshoe, where they wedged a little staff with her handkerchief for a flag in a crevice on the brink. During the night the ice jam broke and the water returned to again thunder over the brink, but the flag survived for a while.

Long periods of cold winter weather caused massive ice buildups and slowed the flow of the Falls in 1909, 1936, and 1947 as well, but the dewatering of the American Falls from June 12 to November 26, 1969, was strictly an engineering marvel. Congress had authorized the work in

In 1969 the U.S. Army Corps of Engineers stopped the flow of the American Falls by building a dam. The rocks and effects of the erosion were carefully recorded and studied. Courtesy, J. Carl Burke Studio

fore sunset the wind chopped around and blew a gale from the West. This brought the vast field of ice back with such tremendous force that it filled in the neck of the lake and its outlet so as to form a very effective dam."

With the American Falls reduced to a trickle and the Horseshoe almost dry for about 12 hours, visitors walked and drove carriages into the riverbed. Canadian miller and Member of Parliament Thomas C. Street took his youngest

1965, in part because of the 1950s rockfalls and in part because the buildup of rock at the base of the Falls had made it more cascade than cataract.

The studies resulted in some changes in the viewing areas, but the decision was made to respect the natural integrity of the Falls by leaving intact the talus, which in some places is piled halfway up the height of the Falls. The adjoining Bridal Veil Falls was dewatered with

For one dollar, visitors could ride the Great Gorge Route, which toured both sides of the Niagara River and traversed two bridges. The electric trolley cars were open on the sides for spectacular views, but continual crumbling of the rocks hampered trips. In 1917 a car derailed and slipped into the river, drowning 14 people. In 1935 a landslide covered the tracks with 5,000 tons of rocks, and the Niagara Gorge Railroad finally closed, boasting that it had carried 13 million passengers in 40 years. Courtesy, Local History Department, Niagara Falls, New York Public Library

a smaller coffer dam in 1972; drain holes were drilled in the cliff face to relieve groundwater pressure, and a system of rock bolts, steel pins, and cables and movement sensors was installed. The work allowed the reopening of Luna Island, which had been closed for safety reasons since 1954.

The old Gorge Route Railroad, an electric-car line that ran from Prospect Park down the side of the gorge near the Falls and then followed the river as far as Lewiston, also fell victim to rockfalls, leaving only a hiking trail where parts of its roadbed once ran. Built by Captain John Brinker in 1895, it saw tragedy in 1905 when a slide wrecked a car, killing the motorman and injuring passengers, and again on July 1, 1917, when the collapse of a portion of the riverbank threw another car into the river and drowned 14 of the 50 passengers.

On September 17, 1935, thousands of tons of rock again fell onto the tracks. No one was injured, but the line was abandoned the following year.

There are man-made tourist attractions, though, which have stood the test of time.

Early accounts by travellers note that canoes could safely navigate the deep pool below the waterfalls, and by the early 1800s ferrymen were boating passengers across the gorge. In 1846 the first of the famous "Maid of the Mist" tour boats was launched by James W. Buchanan, who also would be busy in the mid-century years selling building lots to the German immigrants who came to build the Suspension Bridge.

The *Lelawala*, named for the legendary Indian princess who became the Maid of the Mist, was a small, 150-foot steamboat that ran into financial troubles as well as turbulent waters. Buchanan was offered $25,000 for the boat, with just one hitch—it had to be delivered safely to the docks in Queenston, below the Whirlpool and the lower river rapids.

Captain Joel Robinson was offered $500 to make the dangerous run, and a fireman and engineer were offered $100 each. On June 6, 1861, Robinson and his crew made the nightmarish, roller-coaster ride through five miles of

monster waves and eddies in just 7 minutes and 45 seconds, at unheard-of speeds of more than 40 miles an hour. The *Lelawala* sustained only minor damage, and the Maid of the Mist Co. was soon ready with another tour boat.

Through the years the fleet, which has never had a serious accident, has been updated regularly, with new boats either lowered intact over the side of the gorge by heavy cranes or cut into pieces and lowered in sections for re-assembly in the gorge. The *Maid of the Mist VI*, a $1 million, 600-passenger vessel, received its traditional champagne christening in 1990 from

three-year-old Lauren Marie Fiore, the grand-daughter of fleet owner James V. Glynn.

New elevators also carry tourists to the company's docks on the Canadian side of the river, from a controversial $9.5 million tourism complex built into the side of the gorge wall facing the United States.

Equally controversial from a scenic standpoint on the American side is the 282-foot Prospect Point Observation Tower, which also houses elevators that go down to the bottom of the gorge and up to a viewing platform. Opened in conjunction with the Niagara Power Project in

1961, the structure also includes a bridge-like span that extends 376 feet over the gorge.

The tower draws streams of tourists, but the City of Niagara Falls in a 1985 report to the state called it a "visual blemish" and criticized the state for not considering alternatives.

A more time-honored scenic tradition is the use of light to illuminate the Falls at night—a practice that hinders the "moonbows" that gave Luna Island and the Luna Falls their names, but has proven very popular with generations of tourists.

The first illumination came in 1860, when a

The Maid of the Mist boat tours have provided visitors with a thrilling view of the Falls since 1846. At first the landing for the boats was only in Canada, but the venture became so successful that in 1892 a U.S. sister ship was added. Courtesy, Maid of the Mist Corporation

Mr. Blackwell of England used Bengal lights, colored and white calcium flares, "volcanic and torpedo lights," and fireworks to light up the cataracts for the Prince of Wales, later King Edward VII.

"The first view of the cataracts was when the Prince of Wales saw, as no man had seen them before, and as they will probably never be seen again—the Falls of Niagara illuminated first in silver, like cascades of diamonds, then in red like blood, then blue," the *London Times* reported in somewhat convoluted prose.

In 1879, 12 electric lamps powered by a 36-horsepower generating station provided a Fourth of July illumination. In 1892 Frank LeBlond tried an illumination using 4,000-candlepower lights installed on the Maid of the

Mist's Canadian docks, with gelatin plates for color. In 1901 the Great Gorge Road electric trolleys carried searchlights on their roofs during the Pan-American Exposition in nearby Buffalo, and in 1907 Mayor Anthony C. Douglass put up $5,000 of his own money to install billion-candlepower lamps for an illumination.

In 1924 the "Generators" club of the Niagara Falls Chamber of Commerce raised the money for two dozen carbon searchlights with color screens, to be mounted atop the Ontario Hydro overflow building in Queen Victoria Park on the Canadian side. The official inauguration of "permanent" illumination—which was to be interrupted by World War II blackouts and by power conservation needs—took place in 1925, opening five years of a "Festival of Lights," sponsored by the Chamber of Commerce through the Generators group and run by the Niagara Falls Illumination Board.

In 1958, while City of Niagara Falls mayor Calvin L. Keller was chairman of the Illumination Board, the 1925 lighting system was replaced with a 20-light, 4 billion-candlepower carbon arc system 10 times more powerful. The waterfalls glowed in white, pink, amber, blue, green, and magenta, and even with free power from the hydro projects, the costs shared by governments on both sides of the border top $100,000 a year. In 1981 the older carbon arc lamps were replaced with six-kilowatt xenon lamps five times more powerful still.

Queen Victoria Park on the Canadian side was augmented with a landscape illumination system in 1972. Lasers were used to provide special illumination effects for the Niagara Reservation's centennial celebration in 1985, and in 1989 a $250,000 lighting system was installed to illuminate the white-water rapids above the American Falls.

The centennial celebrations also saw the construction of a new visitors center near Prospect Point, with some of the parking areas near the cataract reclaimed to build a Great Lakes Garden. Niagara Falls entered the second century of its pioneering state park with the Falls drawing more than 3 million tourists a year, and with debate still intact over the twin goals of welcoming visitors and preserving the beauty of the cataracts for future generations to enjoy.

The 282-foot Prospect Point Observation Tower, seen here from Goat Island, has elevators that transport tourists between the viewing platform and the base of the Falls. The span extension provides visitors a view extending 376 feet over the gorge. This tower was opened in 1961 in conjunction with the opening of the New York power project. Courtesy, Carol Glaeser

mposing as the Great Falls of Niagara are, there have always been those who have viewed the thundering waters as so much wasted effort.

Soon after the arrival of the white man in the wilderness, the Niagara began to be seen not only as a scenic wonder, but as a source of stupendous power. Joncaire was the first to harness the mighty river, using French soldiers to help dig a tiny loop canal along the shoreline near what became the foot of Mill Street and then First Street, just above the American Falls; water running through the canal turned a wooden overshot wheel that powered a sawmill.

Joncaire managed to cut the planks for the chapel in Fort Niagara's "French Castle" and to turn out some lumber for shipbuilding projects before the British forced him to burn his mill and march to the aid of the main fort; John Stedman repaired the structure and resumed the pioneering harvest of waterpower from the cataract in the years that followed. But it would take the better part of a century before the promise of nearly unlimited power could be fulfilled.

The earliest uses of waterpower at Niagara, after all, were mechanical and not electrical; the story of Niagara hydropower is the story of emerging technologies at the cutting edge of human progress, and the names in its history include those of Edison, Tesla, and Westinghouse, as well as those of local visionaries whose dreams often outran the practicalities of engineering and financing.

This is the immaculate interior of the Schoellkopf Power Station circa 1905. A worker keeps watch over the machinery, in the center of the room. Courtesy, Buffalo and Erie County Historical Society

THE POWER OF THE FALLS

CHAPTER FOUR

• • •

In the beginning, Niagara simply outmatched its would-be masters.

Waterpower, in its most basic form, uses the force of falling water to turn mechanical devices ranging from ancient waterwheels to modern turbines. Key to the amount of power developed is the distance of the fall from one water level to another, the "head" that is harnessed by the man-made device.

Joncaire's waterwheel used a modest six-foot drop or "head." It would be years before engineers could build wheels that could master the full 314-foot head from the start of the upper rapids to the end of the lower rapids beyond the Falls; it would be years, in fact, before anyone could even dream of tackling the power potential of the waterfalls themselves, instead of just harnessing the 51-foot drop of the upper rapids.

But always, there was the lure of all that power. Survey after survey calculated the flows over the Falls and the horsepower that could be harnessed. In 1907 the United States Lake Survey estimated the volume of the Falls at 210,000 cubic feet of water per second and the theoretical horsepower at 8 million; in 1924 a Smithsonian Institution study reported 205,000 cubic feet and 6 million horsepower.

While the figures can vary with weather and wind conditions and with fluctuations in Great Lakes water levels, the overall message was clear: Niagara had power to spare, and riches awaited those who could control it.

The first major pioneers were the Porters, perhaps the single most important family in Niagara Falls history. Augustus Porter—surveyor and later first judge of Niagara County—built the first American water-powered sawmill and a blacksmith shop near the site of the old Joncaire and Stedman mills in 1805, and a year later brought his family from Canandaigua to the former Stedman homestead. In 1807 he built the first gristmill on the site of Joncaire's mill, with a separate canal intake from the Niagara River rapids just above Goat Island. Ropewalks and tanneries soon followed, as Niagara began to industrialize.

The aptly named Porter family was to found its fortune, though, on the old portage route while basing its dreams on the future path of power. In 1805 Joseph Annin and Benjamin Barton leased the old "carrying places" of the portage route from the state, and the firm of Porter, Barton & Co. was formed to haul freight by oxcarts and horse wagons.

The firm did well, loading freight on its Lake Ontario vessels at Oswego, off-loading onto its portage system at Lewiston for transport to Fort Schlosser about two miles above the Falls, and then poling it on a fleet of five cargo barges to Black Rock and the docks where larger company vessels waited to carry it farther up the lakes.

The most common commodity was salt, from 15,000 to 18,000 barrels a year, mostly destined for Cleveland. The cargo barges or "Durham boats" could carry 150 barrels, the oxcarts 12 barrels, and the horse wagons 7; Porter, Barton & Co. extracted a fee each step of the way, and for warehouse storage anywhere in between.

The wealth went toward other businesses, in the growing village near the Falls. Although the judge kept Goat Island fairly pristine, the banks of the mainland and of intervening Bath Island soon bristled with industry.

Judge Porter built a gristmill in partnership with his brother Peter B. Porter, a pioneering lawyer and wartime general. In 1822 he built a large flour mill that would eventually be sold to the Witmer Brothers, and in 1823 Jesse Symonds opened his water-powered paper mill near the judge's new Goat Island bridge.

In 1825 the brothers Porter issued a public "Invitation to Eastern Capitalists and Manufacturers" to form a company to harness the rapids' waterpower for industry. It was to be the first of the Porters' failed attempts along these lines, simply ahead of its time.

A year later, though, they extended the "upper raceway," or canal, built for their mill. Taking Niagara River water as far as the street leading to the Goat Island bridge, the raceway soon provided power for industries erected by Ira Cook, William G. Tuttle, and Capin & Swallow.

By 1831, riverbank industries included a trip-hammer nail factory, two gristmills, a

paper mill, a woolen factory, and a sawmill. On Bath Island, the largest of the scattered islands between the mainland and the large land mass known then as either Goat or Iris Island, Porter & Clark had built a large paper mill, later to be expanded by L.C. Woodruff. The first mill, built about 1825, was destroyed by fire in 1858; its replacement, capable of producing 500 tons of paper per day thanks to 400-horsepower turbines, also burned in 1882 and was replaced in turn by a mill that lasted three years before the state takeover of the island.

In 1845 a second canal, known as the "lower raceway," was dug from the river toward Prospect Point, crossing the approach to the Goat Island bridge. The second raceway provided space for still more factories dependent on "low-head" waterpower to turn the wheels that ran their machinery, but added to concerns that the scenic grandeur of the Falls was being walled off by a bleak manufactory landscape.

One way to preserve the vistas along the water's edge and still accommodate industries had already been dreamed of for years. A canal that would bypass the rapids and the Falls could provide waterpower and enable the fac-

The power of the Falls was first harnessed by people using huge paddle-wheels that turned grind-stones to process grain. The mills were later replaced by hydroelectrically run factories and the American city of Niagara Falls became an industrial center. Courtesy, Carol Glaeser

In 1876 Jacob Schoellkopf bought an unfinished hydraulic canal in Niagara Falls. Three previous owners had lost more than $900,000 in efforts to build a canal that would supply hydraulic power to plants to be located along its bank. Within two years hydraulic power was used by Schoellkopf to run his flour mills. Courtesy, Buffalo and Erie County Historical Society

tories to move inland, along its banks.

But two "Niagara Canal Companies," organized in 1789 and 1823, already had failed. Construction costs would be high, because of the hard limestone that would have to be excavated the entire six-mile length of the canals, and financing was never completed. National ship canal proposals designed to open navigation between the lakes also failed to gain support and were abandoned when the Erie Canal opened in 1825.

In 1847, though, Judge Porter once again issued a public invitation to the nation's "Capitalists and Manufacturers," offering a canal right-of-way through his extensive land holdings to anyone who would start work on a canal.

The invitation came three years after his brother Peter's death and just two years before his own, and led nowhere; it would be up to others, including some of their own descendants, to realize the Porter brothers' dreams.

It wouldn't take long. In 1852 Augustus Porter's heirs sold land and water rights to Caleb S. Woodhull of New York and Walter Bryant of Boston for a canal that would cut across the American side of the river from a point about a half mile above the upper rapids to the 210-foot "High Bank" along the gorge a quarter mile below the Falls.

The Niagara Falls Hydraulic Company, known popularly as the Woodhull Project, was formed the following year. Woodhull, who had been mayor of New York in 1849 and 1850, was president and Bryant was chief engineer. The firm began digging its Hydraulic Canal immediately, but ran out of money about 16 months later.

Next in line was the Niagara Falls Water Power Company, which took over the project in 1856 under the control of Stephen M. Allen. The canal entrance was finished in 1857 and the first water—unused by industry—flowed through the canal and over the "High Bank" on July 4 of that year. On the same day, three steamships churned their way from Lake Erie to Port Day, the small harbor at the canal entrance, to open steam navigation from Buffalo to the Falls.

The canal itself was still incomplete when Allen ran out of money in 1860. The property was sold to Horace H. Day, Allen's former vice president and the namesake of Port Day; he changed the company name to the Niagara Falls Canal Company, but it was known generally as the Day Project.

It lasted 17 years, part of it with borrowed money, and it resulted in an 8-foot-deep, 36-foot-wide canal, properly completed for only one mile of its length. The only mill built along the canal was a flour mill erected on the edge of the High Bank by Charles B. Gaskill in 1875; water flowed from the rapids across the village to a canal basin near the High Bank, where the Gaskill Flouring Mill diverted some of the canal water to its own "wheel pit," a vertical shaft sunk into the rock. Flowing first through wood flumes and later through iron pipes, the water dropped through the shaft to turn a turbine at the bottom.

Turbines still couldn't take the force of a 210-foot drop, though. At the Gaskill mill, the pit was only 25 feet deep; a short "tail-race" tunnel carried the flow from the bottom of the pit to a portal on the face of the cliff, where a new man-made waterfall plunged the remaining 185 feet to the river below.

Day's fortune had followed Allen's $300,000 and the Woodhull company's $550,000 into the churning waters. Foreclosure followed his project's inability to meet the interest due on its bonds, and in 1876 leather manufacturer Jacob Frederick Schoellkopf, a German immigrant then living in Buffalo, bought the whole thing at a sheriff's auction for $71,000. Even with an

additional $5,000 eventually added to the settlement Schoellkopf reached with Day, he thought it a bargain; when he came home that night, though, his wife reportedly moaned, "Jacob, Jacob, you'll bring ruin on us yet with your crazy schemes."

By 1878 Schoellkopf had changed the name of the canal firm to the Niagara Falls Hydraulic Power and Manufacturing Company, taking on Buffalo business partner George B. Mathews and installing his son Arthur Schoellkopf in Niagara Falls as manager of the canal properties.

Schoellkopf and Mathews spurred development by example, building their own large flour mill along the High Bank soon afterwards and using a 50-foot head and cast-iron turbines by 1881. The partners also were instrumental in the Central Milling Company, which set up shop nearby with 80-foot wheel

Seen here is a 1902 view of the Niagara Falls Hydraulic Power and Manufacturing Company (right center) surrounded by manufacturing mills, which derived their power from the old "Schoellkopf" canal. Among these were a brewing company, paper mills, and a silver company. Courtesy, J. Carl Burke Studios

pits. The earliest attempts to use deeper pits and thus increase the head failed when the turbine wheels broke, but stronger wheels soon followed.

Pulp and paper mills soon joined the new mill district. By 1882 the Hydraulic Company's water was powering not only the Gaskill and the Schoellkopf and Mathews mills, but also the pulp mills of J.F. Quigley and the Niagara Wood Paper Company, and the Cataract Manufacturing Company, the Oneida Community's silver plating factory, and the waterworks of the village of Suspension Bridge.

In addition to the raw horsepower—2,725 horsepower used to turn the factory rollers and machinery, to be exact—the company had hit upon another use for the falling waters. In 1881, Schoellkopf unveiled the future: electricity.

The first hydroelectric generating station was a modest affair, located in Quigley's Mill. The mill, later owned and run by the Cliff Paper Company, used an 86-foot head to turn water wheels that ran the pulp mill's rollers and the machines of several small shops. There was enough power left over, though, to run an arc light machine— and that quickly became a sensation.

Installed by the Brush Electric Light and Power Company—organized late in 1881 as yet another enterprise of Schoellkopf, Mathews, and their associates—the machine created an instant demand for electricity.

"No sooner was the announcement made through the columns of the Gazette that an electric light company had been formed in the village for the purpose of supplying our stores and manufacturers with light," that newspaper reported on December 14, 1881, "than applications began to pour in, and the company has been busy filling the orders.

"This evening, the company will furnish light for the Schoellkopf and Mathews grist mill, J. Quigley's pulp mill, Oneida Community Building, Marr & Duff's dry goods store, H.E. Griffith's drug store, S. Hirsch's dry goods store, and the Gazette office."

Sixteen 2,000-candlepower open arc lamps provided the street and shop lighting that launched the era of electricity in Niagara Falls.

A light was installed in Prospect Park at the edge of the American Falls and quickly became as much a tourist attraction as the Falls itself; "Electric Light Excursions" on the railroads brought thousands to see the light, and public interest in the novelty spurred public demands for the benefits of electricity.

Those demands couldn't be easily met, however. Lighting the streets of the little village was one thing; producing electricity that could be used at a distance from the Falls was quite another.

The technology simply didn't exist. There were schemes and theories, to be sure, but nowhere in the world, Schoellkopf and his friends found, did commercial use of electricity include any sort of useful distribution system.

Even as better turbines and better engineering increased the amount of horsepower humanity could wring from the falling waters of Niagara, hydroelectric power remained a curiosity or, at best, a local benefit.

In 1886, a year after the creation of the state park and the start of the gradual demolition of the eyesore manufactories on Bath Island and lining the Porters' old raceways along the rapids, competition emerged for the Hydraulic Canal in the form of yet another power scheme.

The Hydraulic Canal cut diagonally across the inland edge of the village, spanned by a number of bridges and losing only a few feet of elevation before reaching the forebays and basins of the Mill District, along the top of the High Bank. The power developed from the canal came from the drop down the cliff to the gorge—or as much of it as the turbines of the day could handle.

Now, Thomas Evershed of Rochester, a division engineer for the Erie Canal, proposed just the opposite approach to power. His scheme called for a tunnel that would start dropping immediately at its starting point 2.5 miles above the Falls, and discharge through a portal at river level at the foot of the gorge, near the Suspension Bridge.

Twelve connecting canals from the river to the tunnel route along the mile and a half between its starting point and Port Day would

FACING PAGE: The Board of Directors of the Consolidated Hydraulic Niagara Falls Power Companies gathered after their first meeting on November 1, 1918. Included are members of the Schoellkopf and Olmsted families. Courtesy, Buffalo and Erie County Historical Society

supply water to a series of wheel pits with gradually increasing heads of up to 124 feet, turning 238 wheels to supply power.

The "Evershed Scheme" would drastically increase the amount of land available for industrial development and keep the factories outside the boundaries of the new state reservation, and the idea quickly drew support. Special state legislation cleared the way for the formation of the Niagara River Hydraulic Tunnel, Power and Sewer Company on March 31, 1886, with mill owner Charles B. Gaskill as president and Evershed as engineer. It took three years to set up the financing; Evershed died during the attempt, and attorney William B. Rankine of New York emerged as a key negotiator. Eventually, with Francis Lynde Stetson of New York as the prime financial backer, the firm emerged as the Niagara Falls Power Company in 1889, with the newly formed Cataract Construction Company as both its land agent and the owner of all its stock.

The leaders of the new power company quickly offered a financial interest to a New York banking firm, which in turn sent one of its partners to investigate. That move had both immediate and far-reaching effects: Edward Dean Adams would not only launch an extensive scientific inquiry that had a great impact on power development at the Falls, but would head the Cataract Construction Company and build the major power plants over the next 20 years.

And the Evershed Scheme would be changed significantly, from a concept of a new industrial district with factories sitting atop wheel pits and a subterranean tail-race tunnel, to a vision of a hydropower generating system that would supply vast amounts of electricity.

Key to the concept was the realization that the village of Niagara Falls, with a population of about 5,000, couldn't consume enough power to justify the costs of miles of tunnel excavation through hard limestone. But Buffalo, a national manufacturing center of 256,000 souls just 20 miles away, could.

Unfortunately, no one had yet figured out how to transmit large amounts of power more than a mile or two. Schemes abounded, for transmission of power by compressed air, wire

ropes, electricity, or other means, but none had yet been proven. A group of 110 Buffalonians, keenly aware of the benefits that city could gain from Niagara power, offered a $100,000 prize in 1887 for a practical system. Despite a flood of proposals, models, and even tests during a fair in parkland along a city creek, no winner emerged.

No less an innovator than Thomas Alva Edison already was considering the problem. In 1886 Tunnel Company president Gaskill

The Pan-American Exposition, in Buffalo in 1901, demonstrated the power generated by the hydroelectric plant at Niagara Falls. More than 200,000 outdoor lights were placed on buildings. A staff was hired to change the bulbs, as the eight-watt bulbs had only a four-hour life span. Courtesy, J. Carl Burke Studio

had discussed the development of Niagara electricity with Niagara Falls native Gardiner C. Sims, whose Rhode Island engine company built the engines Edison used for his experiments. Edison, Sims told Gaskill, had even estimated the cost of transmitting power from Niagara to Buffalo.

Edison, therefore, was one of the first experts sought by Adams in his investigation of the Evershed Scheme. Asked by overseas cable about the practicality of power transmis-

sion to Buffalo, the Wizard of Menlo Park sent a succinct reply from Havre, France, in September 1889: "No difficulty transferring unlimited power. Will assist. Sailing today."

In 1886 the inventor had estimated that 6,800 horsepower could be sent the 22 miles to Buffalo with a 20 percent loss in the wires and a 6 percent loss in the dynamos and other apparatus—arriving as 5,000 horsepower in a 6,000-volt package. Unfortunately for his role in Niagara power, though, Edison was barking up the wrong tree. He was an advocate of direct current continuous transmission, in an era when the use of alternating current was beginning to take hold in commercial circles.

Edison's final recommendation called for a 14-mile cable buried in a trench across Grand Island and crossing the Niagara River at the Falls and at Buffalo on a pole suspension system. The Evershed tunnel, its turbines, a Niagara power station and three substations at Buffalo would cost $5,243,000, the inventor estimated. The cost of the distribution system would add more.

The Niagara Falls Power Company, which intended to fund the main construction project with the relatively modest income from power sales in the Falls village and mill districts, decided to keep looking. Edison declined to accept any payment for his work, and others turned their attention to the project.

Alternating current offered advantages in transmitting power over long distances with less loss, but the high voltages required were deemed unsafe, and the apparatus to reduce them to easily handled levels hadn't yet been perfected. But the promise of the new technology seemed bright enough to launch the tunnel project, anyway.

With Adams as president and Coleman Sellers as engineer, the Cataract Construction Co. in 1890 set about gaining rights-of-way, raising more than $2.6 million and buying 1,550 acres, including 368 acres for a new planned community to be called Echota. Also acquired was the Niagara Falls Water Works, to allow expansion and purification of the water supply for a growing population.

The streamlined plan, developed after a design competition judged by an International Niagara Commission chaired by Lord Kelvin in Europe, called for a shorter main tunnel and the development of a central power station rather than a series of canals and wheel pits to power individual factories. Since technology didn't yet exist for the safe and efficient transmission of power as far as Buffalo, the firm would try to cover costs and even turn a modest profit from local power sales while hoping

for a future bonanza.

Ground was broken for the new tunnel in October 1890. Preserved in a Niagara Falls power museum today is a shovel inscribed, "In our own respective ways he and I started the Niagara Tunnel. Therefore I belong to William B. Rankine."

The excavation of 600,000 tons of rock involved 2,500 men, and the project produced its first electricity in April 1895.

Schoellkopf's Hydraulic Power Company project, meanwhile, was building the Falls' first full-scale power plant, in 1895. The company's 15-turbine, 31-generator Power Station Number Two, far larger than the first plant in the Quigley mill, produced 34,000 horsepower in direct current and, for the first time, used the full 210-foot hydraulic head afforded by the cliffs of the High Bank. The only previous firm to use that high a drop was the Cliff Paper Company, which did it in stages—a 75-foot head to power its paper mill at the top of the cliff, and a second 125-foot drop for the same water to power horizontal wheels in its pulp mill at the base of the cliff.

Built in three sections and using both Westinghouse and General Electric generators, the Hydraulic Company power station supplied electricity to the Pittsburgh Reduction Company (later the Aluminum Company of America, ALCOA), the National Electrolytic Company's chlorate of potash works, the Acker Process Company, 50 small power users, and the Niagara Gorge Railroad.

Alternators producing AC power transmitted electricity up to two miles, including that used by the Buffalo and Niagara Falls Electric Light and Power Company for commercial and city lighting in Niagara Falls.

Schoellkopf died three years later, in 1899. His family continued the Schoellkopf companies, building the 132,000-horsepower Power Station Three-A (better known later as the Schoellkopf Plant) from 1903 to 1913 and restructuring as the Hydraulic Power Company of Niagara Falls and the Cliff Electrical Distributing Company in 1909 and 1910.

Adams and the tunnel companies weren't far

behind. Spurred by the pioneering inventiveness of Nikola Tesla and his innovations in alternating-current technology, and aided by the production advice of George Westinghouse, who was given the contract to build and install the generators, the Niagara Falls Power Company's Power House No. 1 went on-line not long after the Hydraulic Company plant in 1896.

Just after midnight on November 16 of that year, switches were thrown in what became known as the Adams Power Station, and a small lamp and motor powered by the waters of Niagara came to life in distant Buffalo. The Adams plant, a block-long complex of buildings designed by famed New York architect Stanford White, became the world's first large-scale alternating-current generating plant and set the standard for world development of hydroelectric power.

The 50,000 horsepower electrical station originally was to be mirrored by a 50,000 horse-power pneumatic power plant on the east side of the Niagara River inlet canal near Port Day, but the success of electrical power transmission was so complete by 1899 that Power House No. 2 also was built as a 55,000 horsepower hydroelectric plant—giving the station a peak capacity of 105,000 horsepower, or 80,000 kilowatts of electricity in more modern terms. A third power house was built in Canada, with all three plants interconnected and transmitting power to Buffalo.

Novelist H.G. Wells, recalling his visit to the Falls for *Harper's* magazine in 1906, decried the signboards and structures encroaching on the shores and the "Schoellkopf Company's untidy confusion of sheds and buildings on the American side, wastefully squirting out long tail-race cascades behind the bridge," but philosophically ascribed them to the "first slovenly onslaught" in the march of human progress.

"There are finer things than these outrages to be found," he noted. "These dynamos and turbines of the Niagara Falls Power Company, for example, impressed me far more profoundly than the Cave of the Winds; are, indeed, to my mind, greater and more beautiful than the accidental eddying of air beside a

downpour. They are will made visible, thought translated into easy and commanding things . . . When I thought that these two huge wheel-pits of this company are themselves but a little intimation of what can be done in this way, what will be done in this way, my imagination towered above me. I fell into a daydream of the coming power of men, and how that power may be used by them."

For a start, the industries of Niagara Falls and Buffalo were more than pleased to put to use a source of power much cheaper, and incidentally much cleaner, than coal. Buffalo gloried in electric street lighting, the first major city on the globe to do so; its Pan-American Exposition of 1901 focused world attention on the city and the international fair built around a "Tower of Light."

At the Falls, industry boomed as power output expanded rapidly from about 10,000 kilowatts in the mid-1890s to 40,000 at the turn of the century and 360,000 kilowatts by 1925. In 1918, by order of the secretary of war as a World War I emergency measure, the canal and tunnel power companies consolidated into a single Niagara Falls Power Company; production at that time was nearing 240,000 kilowatts and already had spurred a boom in electrolytic, chemical, abrasives, metals, and alloys companies.

"The development of Niagara power in 1895 marked the beginning of the electric furnace art," Carborundum Company president Frank J. Tone said in 1916.

"Up to 1895, when Charles M. Hall came to Niagara, the aluminum industry depending on steam power had given little promise of commercial success. Its almost incredible development has been due to the impetus of Niagara power.

"Dr. E.G. Acheson with a 150-horsepower furnace operated by electric power generated from steam had made a commercial failure of carborundum. Coming to Niagara in 1895 he was at once enabled to found the artificial abrasive industry.

"Willson, the inventor of calcium carbide, was working at Spray, North Carolina, with a 200-horsepower furnace. Today there are fur-

The Schoellkopf Power Station, built in 1920 and expanded in subsequent years, supplied electricity to United States industries. In 1956 a large segment of this plant collapsed into the gorge. Courtesy, New York Power Authority

naces at Niagara making as much carbide in a day as the former furnace produced in a year.

"With the technology of these great industries—aluminum, calcium chloride, abrasives, ferro-alloys, silicon and graphite—all are familiar, but few realize their economic importance or to what extent the industrial and the metallurgical arts are indebted to Niagara power for their development."

The industries were heavily dependent upon constant and abundant electrical power, and Niagara was the largest such source in the United States. Niagara Falls quickly became the center for the electrochemical industries that used power to combine elements into new materials, and the electrolytic industries that used power to create new elements by breaking down other materials.

The Niagara Falls Power Company's first local customer in 1895 was Hall's new Pittsburgh Reduction Company plant, later ALCOA, which moved from Pittsburgh to the Falls to produce the first aluminum by the electrolytic process on August 5 of that year. At one

time, the company had three plants in production at the Falls. In 1900 the company produced 7 million pounds of pure aluminum; Hall's home at 136 Buffalo Avenue was roofed with aluminum shingles that were still intact when the building was demolished in 1980.

Edward G. Acheson's Carborundum Company was another early customer, first built to make silicon carbide abrasives in electric furnaces and growing into a worldwide corporation with a patent for the manufacture of synthetic graphite. In 1900 Acheson—who lived in Niagara Falls, Ontario, because of water pollution on the American side—also founded the Acheson Graphite Company, later

a part of Union Carbide, to produce protective coatings for structural steel and the filler material for dry batteries.

The Niagara Electrolytic Iron Co. was formed to make seamless iron tubing by electroplating, and other firms produced iron alloys for the steel industry.

The Union Carbide Corporation's first plant was built at Niagara Falls to produce calcium carbide, which in turn produces valuable acetylene gas. Eventually, the firm would absorb not only Acheson Graphite but also the Electro Metallurgical Company and National Carbon.

Hooker Electro Chemical Company, much

This view of the Niagara Power Project shows the Robert Moses Niagara Power Plant, the forebay, the Lewiston Pump-Generating Plant, and the 1,900-acre Lewiston reservoir. At the Robert Moses plant, water flows through 24-foot diameter penstocks, made of steel-reinforced concrete, to 13 turbine-generators. Courtesy, New York Power Authority

later to become part of Occidental Chemical, was founded at Niagara Falls to produce chlorine and caustic soda through use of an electrolytic process. It, too, would absorb other local firms—the Oldbury Electro Chemical Company, which made phosphorous for matches, and Roberts Chemical, later Niagara Alkali.

DuPont's Niagara Falls plant developed from the Niagara Electro Chemical Company, makers of sodium; the Castner Electrolytical Alkali Works also was making caustic soda by electrolysis in the Falls before the turn of the century, later becoming the Mathieson Chemical Corporation which, in turn, merged with Olin.

The Titanium Alloy Manufacturing Company, later a division of the National Lead Company, was founded in 1906 and pioneered titanium and zirconium processing for steel alloys, paint pigments, and pharmaceuticals. The Niagara Falls Silver Company, later William A. Rogers Limited, produced silverware and cutlery.

John R. Carter and Samuel R. Moore used Schoellkopf electricity for their Carter & Co. paper products firm, which had started the American business forms industry and had printed the first double-leafed sales book in 1883. Later, the company became Moore Business Forms.

Other firms taking advantage of Niagara Power included the International Paper Company, Spirella (which produced spiral wire to replace the stiff whalebone and steel then used in ladies' corsets), the Pittsburgh Metallurgical Company, General Abrasive Company, Republic Carbon Company, United States Ferro Alloys, Gilman Fanfold Corporation, the Shredded Wheat Company, Certainteed Products Corporation, American Magnesium Corporation, the Norton Company, Ramapo-Ajax Corporation, the Phosphorous Compound Company, the Electro Bleaching Gas Company, Isco Chemical Company, and the Kimberly-Clark Company.

With all the diversion of Niagara water for power, public concern had centered on threats to the scenic value of the Falls. Even while me-

chanical power ruled, legal limitations were set on the amount of horsepower that could be drawn off from the river above the Falls; later, when electricity was king in the "Power City," the limitations were set by requiring a minimum cataract flow of so many cubic feet of water per second.

In 1950 the U.S. Senate ratified a treaty with Canada that provided more water for power.

The international treaty requires that at least 100,000 cubic feet of water per second, about half the natural volume, must flow over the Falls during daylight hours in the tourist season; the flow can be reduced to 50,000 cubic feet per second at night and during the off-season.

During the first half of the twentieth century, power production continued to expand, with the Schoellkopf family dominating the

Niagara Falls Power Co. after the tunnel and hydraulic projects were combined. The old Niagara Gorge hydraulic station, Three-A, was expanded with the construction of Three-B from 1918 to 1920 and Three-C from 1921 to 1924. The complex, generally known as the Schoellkopf Power Station, used six vertical shaft generators to produce 322,500 horsepower.

It died in spectacular fashion on June 7,

Visitors can learn how the Niagara Power Plant operates in clearly illustrated exhibits from the Power Authority of the State of New York. Photo by Anthony "Red" Glaeser

1956, and in its passing gave birth to a new era in power production far beyond the dreams of the hydropower pioneers.

At 5:15 p.m. on that date, the everyday trickle of water that normally seeped from the face of the High Bank and ran through the power plant at the foot of the gorge suddenly became a torrent, as the rock face gave way with a roar of stone, concrete, and twisted steel.

Two thirds of the Schoellkopf plant slid into the river, as workers ran for their lives. One man perished, as 120,000 tons of rock swept through the $100 million powerhouse and reduced it to rubble.

The catastrophe was worse even than the toll in life and property; in an instant, the Niagara region went from an abundance of power to emergency status.

Nature's destruction of the aging power station, though, brought a quick end to a political

impasse that had left Congress undecided whether to make future Niagara power development a public project or leave it to private enterprise. And it made the New York Power Authority, formed in 1931 to develop projects on the St. Lawrence and Niagara rivers, a major factor in the Niagara Falls area.

Within two years of the Schoellkopf disaster, construction would be started on the massive Niagara Power Project, the largest power complex in the Western world and only a shade behind the capacity of a Soviet power plant near Stalingrad.

President Eisenhower signed Congress' bill authorizing the public project in 1957, despite opposition from Niagara Falls and Lewiston. A second dispute, with the Tuscarora Indian Nation over the taking of lands for a planned reservoir, ended with a design compromise, and the first of four major construction contracts was awarded in January 1958. Excavations started that March.

The disruption in Niagara Falls was massive. Homes were relocated, highways and railroads were rerouted, population skyrocketed. The project itself constructed a major underground river and an enclosed waterfall half as powerful as the Falls itself.

"It was such a tremendously large project that the people working on the main plant wouldn't know what the people at the water intakes were doing," said Frank V. Roma, who worked on the construction project and later joined the staff at the authority's Power Vista museum and visitor center.

Construction sites were scattered from Niagara Falls to Lewiston in a $737 million, three-year effort involving 11,700 workers. Three "Hydro Cities," virtually self-contained communities, were set up to house workers and their families.

The power project built two massive underground intake tunnels, their inlets controlled by 400-ton gates in structures along the riverbank well above the rapids. Water courses through the 22,000-foot tunnels to Lewiston, bypassing the Falls on its way to the Robert Moses Niagara Power Plant. At the plant, a section of the gorge wall has been turned into a concrete cliff enclosing huge steel "penstocks," or vertical pipes that channel the fall of water to 13 powerful turbines at the river's edge.

Some of the intake canal water can be drawn off by the Lewiston Pump-Generating Plant, which fills a 1,400-acre reservoir with excess water at night when greater diversions from the river are allowed; during the day, the reservoir water flows back through the Lewiston plant, turning the pump blades in the opposite direction and generating electricity before rejoining the canal to the main power plant.

Statistics for the construction project are staggering. Spurred by Power Authority chairman Robert Moses, New York's "Master Builder," the project used the sale of investment bonds to fund contracts that moved enough dirt and rock to create a one-acre mountain higher than Mount McKinley (39

million cubic yards), poured enough concrete for a two-lane highway from New York City to Florida (3.65 million cubic yards), and laid enough reinforced steel for a double-track railroad line from Chicago to Nashville (284 million pounds).

A rock-crushing plant was built just to grind the rock excavation into ingredients for the concrete curtain lining 1,840 feet of the 389-foot-high cliff at the Moses power plant four and a half miles below the Falls.

Along the way, the project also created the Reservoir State Park, expanded the Niagara Reservation state park, constructed a 10-mile highway segment called the Robert Moses Parkway, built the American Rapids Bridge from the mainland to Goat Island, opened a park area now occupied by the Schoellkopf Geological Museum, allowed expansion of the city's Hyde Park on the land originally taken for the cut-and-cover construction of the inlet conduits, and developed Power Vista as a tourist draw.

And it took a human toll, as well. During construction, 20 men died.

On February 10, 1961, New York governor Nelson A. Rockefeller threw a switch starting commercial transmission of Niagara Power Project electricity. President John F. Kennedy called the project "an example to the world of North American efficiency and determination."

Completed in 1963 under the leadership of authority chairman Lawrence A. Fitzpatrick, the Niagara Power Project produced a dependable 2.4 million kilowatts of power—enough to light 24 million 100-watt light bulbs at the same time. In 1986, after a quarter century of operation, the project had produced 361.2 billion kilowatts of power and was still producing 14 percent of New York State's power, ranking second in the United States only to the Grand Coulee Dam project in the state of Washington.

Expansion is being considered, as the need for inexpensive energy and the desire to curtail oil usage continues. Neither the waters of Niagara, nor the demands made upon them by humanity, ever stand still.

Somewhere in the transition from sea green waters to lacy white foam, the plunging torrent of the Great Falls of Niagara calls to something deep within the heart of humanity.

Tourists stop and gaze, lost in thought, as the flashing liquid arcs gracefully over the brink and—free of the riverbed at last—curves unrestrained to the deep and turbulent pools far below. More than a few have been mesmerized by the sight and the constant, rolling thunder; some lose track of time, and some feel the irresistible pull of the water.

There are accounts of rare visitors so enthralled by the flood that they have walked, dazed, into the shallows—only to be rescued by others, or suddenly come to their senses. More common are those who welcome the call, and plan to find death in the falling waters.

Suicides are not uncommon at the Falls, and each year brings several. The peak number of suicides reported to police came, not surprisingly, during the onset of the Great Depression, but there are still enough each season, half a dozen or more in a normal year, to warrant the installation and maintenance of a series of suicide prevention and emergency phone stations in the parkland near the cataracts.

Disasters, too, have claimed lives along the Niagara—and there have been many, over the years, who have come to the Honeymoon Capital simply to flirt with death.

Sam Patch may have been the first, even before Francis Abbott—the Hermit

People held their breath on July 7, 1891, when Captain Dixon dared death by walking a tightrope across the whirlpool rapids at Niagara Falls. One of numerous daredevils who accomplished the feat, Dixon was distinguished by his costume, which included a Civil War forage cap. Courtesy, The Library of Congress

DISASTERS AND DAREDEVILS

CHAPTER FIVE

• • •

of Goat Island—practiced his chin-ups at the edge of the Horseshoe Falls and eventually disappeared in the raging water.

Patch was a diver, and an extraordinary one. According to early accounts, he made his living in a mill near Pawtucket Falls, Rhode Island, and joined his companions in diving from a bridge and from the mill roof into the river below. Eventually, he got so good he started touring the country and jumping from other high places.

"In September 1829 he found himself one of a big crowd attracted to Niagara Falls to witness the sending over the cataract of the condemned brig *Michigan* cruelly loaded with terror-stricken wild animals," writer and Niagara daredevil historian Orrin E. Dunlap recounted for *Cosmopolitan* magazine in 1902.

"Sam Patch was inspired to profit by the excitement that prevailed, and accordingly, he built a wooden tower ninety feet high at the water's edge at the foot of the Biddle Stairway on Goat Island. From a platform on top of this structure he leaped safely into the waters of the lower Niagara River."

The dive won him fame, but not much money. Shortly afterward, the 23-year-old adventurer tried to repeat the stunt farther east at the Falls of the Genesee—and died in the attempt.

Following Patch in pursuit of fortune or at least notoriety was perhaps the greatest of all the Niagara Falls daredevils. His full name was Jean François Gravelet, and his "stage" moniker was the Prince of Manilla, but he is best remembered simply as the Great Blondin.

Blondin was a tightrope walker, surviving more on skill than on the kind of luck that rode with the best of the barrel riders in future years. He was born in France in 1824, and he was just a few months past his 35th birthday when he arrived at Niagara in 1859.

At first, no one believed that Monsieur Blondin really would walk from Goat Island to Canada on a three-inch-wide hemp rope stretched high above the Niagara Gorge, as his agent had announced. But Blondin soon took to making casual strolls, puffing his cigars, along the guy ropes of the suspension railroad bridge, and folks began to take notice.

He was a showman, of the highest degree, brought to the United States by none other than P.T. Barnum in 1855. He had taken to the wires at the age of five, and had been performing in public since he was eight.

When the tightrope finally went up on June 23, though, it wasn't at Goat Island. Blondin chose a spot called White's Pleasure Grounds, about midway between the Falls and the Whirlpool Rapids. The 1,300-foot hemp cable was hauled across the deep gorge by a smaller rope that had previously been hauled across, and when the weight of the main cable appeared too great, Blondin simply tied a second rope to his body and walked out about 200 feet along the seven-eighths-inch guide rope to tie the second line to the cable.

"It was arranged that Blondin's first public performance should be given on June 30, 1859," Dunlap reported. "Previous to the river trip on the cable, he gave a performance on a rope in the Pleasure Grounds. He danced, turned over and over, leaped backward ten to fifteen feet, and bounded high in the air, showing astonishing skill."

A small man, about 5 foot 5 inches and 140 pounds, Blondin then walked out onto the gorge cable carrying a 38-foot pole for balance. About a hundred feet out, he sat down, then stretched out on his back, got up again, stood on one foot for a moment, and then set out again for the center of the river. Every few hundred feet, he repeated the performance until he reached the dangerously swaying center section of the cable, where about 40 feet of the curving hemp was unsupported by guy ropes from either shore.

"Then the steamer *Maid of the Mist* came up the river, her flags flying and loaded down with passengers," Dunlap recounts. "Blondin dropped a cord to the deck and pulled up a bottle, from which he took a long draft. He then leaped to his feet without touching his hands to the cable, and continued his walk to the Canadian cliff."

With the stop for champagne, Blondin was out on the tightrope for about 18 minutes. When he reached safety, his chronicler says, "the gorge rang with cheers." Blondin recrossed to the American side half an hour later, taking seven minutes and stopping midway to view the Falls.

The American Falls plunges more than 100 feet and makes a dramatic splash on the talus below. The Horseshoe Falls, seen in the distance in this view from 1900, plunges 170 feet without rock debris, making it a target for daredevils. Courtesy, J. Carl Burke Studio

Beginning in 1859 Jean François Gravelet, known as the "Great Blondin," performed more than 1,500 stunts for countless fascinated visitors, including Britain's Prince of Wales (later King Edward VII), who invited him to perform at the Crystal Palace in London. Blondin is seen here wearing the many medals awarded him for his feats. Courtesy, Buffalo and Erie County Historical Society

Collections were taken among the spectators on either side of the gorge, to compensate him for his efforts.

The canny Frenchman, though, had not left himself too tough an act to follow. On the Fourth of July he was back—this time with bigger crowds, and an even tougher act. He crossed the gorge successfully once more, with a sack over his head and body.

Ten days later, with Millard Fillmore in attendance, Blondin stepped out onto the cable again.

"On this occasion Blondin stopped in the center of the cable, and at a signal from the steamer *Maid of the Mist* in the river below he held out his hat and Captain Travis, a famous pistol-shot, sent a bullet through the rim of it," Dunlap reports.

After reaching Canada, Blondin ended his day's work by dressing as a monkey and returning to the United States pushing a wheelbarrow along the cable.

On August 3 Blondin treated yet another

huge crowd to a six-minute crossing, with a headstand en route. But it was his 45-minute fifth performance, on August 19, that really stunned the spectators in what was fast becoming Blondin's Summer.

"The horrors of the journey are best related by the man who sat on Blondin's back and participated in them—Harry Colcord," noted pamphleteer Justice Jarvis Blume, a friend of Blondin's manager.

Colcord himself notes that even Blondin wasn't too sure what effect his manager's extra weight would have on the rope.

"His earnest advice to me before starting was,'Harry, be sure and let yourself rest all the time like a dead weight on my back. If I should sway or stumble, on no account attempt to balance yourself,'" Colcord recalled after the trip.

"My first thrill occurred as we started; over the pine trees, whose sharp tops bristled far below us between the cliffs and the river, it seemed far more terrifying than out over the water.

"My heart was in my mouth as we began to descend the rope, which from its weight had a depression of fifty feet in the center; but it was a matter of life or death, and I resolved to follow Blondin's advice most implicitly."

Seven times along the route from Canada to the States, Blondin had to pause for a rest. Each time, Colcord had to climb carefully down from Blondin's back, feel for the swinging rope with his foot, then stand on it until Blondin signaled him to climb back up again. Not surprisingly, Colcord thought this the most dangerous part of all.

About a quarter of the way onto the unsupported middle section of the cable, Blondin lost his balance. The ends of his long balance pole semaphored in the air for an awful moment as he fought to stay on the cable, Colcord straining mightily not to make any moves at all. Suddenly, substituting momentum for equilibrium, Blondin sprinted along the cable and reached the first guy rope on the American side of the cable.

He stepped on it to regain his balance, and the guy promptly broke. The main cable whipped sideways, but Blondin somehow recovered just enough agility to run to the next set of guy ropes

and comparative safety.

"'Get off, quick,' he said, and I obeyed," Colcord related.

The incident, it turned out, was no accident. One of Blondin's rope handlers, who had money riding on the intense wagering that accompanied any Blondin feat, had become so incensed at the ropewalker's progress that he had cut the guy just as they reached it, fleeing through the crowd as spectators riveted their attention on Blondin's struggles.

"Again I got on his back, and by and by we toiled up the incline of rope toward the American shore, confronting a great sea of staring faces, fixed and intense with interest, alarm, fear," Colcord said. "Some people shaded their eyes, as if dreading to see us fall; some held their arms extended as if to grasp us and keep us from falling; some excited men had tears streaming down their cheeks.

"A band was trying to play, but the wrought-up musicians could evoke only discordant notes."

On August 31, Blondin was back out on the rope again, making his first night crossing, with a lantern on each end of his 45-pound balance pole. The lights gave out halfway across, and he finished the trip in darkness.

For his last act of a summer of feats that earned him a gold medal from the citizens of Niagara Falls, Blondin crossed the gorge to Canada with baskets on his feet and returned carrying a table and chair. The chair fell into the gorge when he tried to sit on it atop the wire, but the master simply perched on the wire itself to snack on cake and champagne.

Blondin had accomplished something that would stand the test of time as unique in Falls daredevil history. Others would survive their flirtations with death and even occasionally gain some fame, but Blondin was the only guy ever to make it pay.

The gold medal was as much for filling the hotels and tourist spas as for his heroics, but the following year Blondin would move his venue from Niagara Falls to Suspension Bridge. In 1860 he stretched his cable over the Whirlpool Rapids, to the delight of Suspension Bridge, then known as Niagara City, and the dismay of their rival villagers in Niagara Falls itself.

He opened his season by crossing the gorge backward. Then he walked blindfolded, did tricks on a rope hung from the cable, and on September 8 topped all of his performances by repeating the walk with Colcord on his back and then walking over on stilts, all in the presence of

the Prince of Wales. He offered to push the prince, later King Edward VII, across the cable in a wheelbarrow, but royalty wisely declined.

By this time, though, Blondin no longer had the gorge or the crowds to himself.

His first rival was Signor Guillermo Antonio Farini (actually William T. Hunt of nearby Lockport), who strung his own cable near Blondin's and the outlet of the Hydraulic Canal. Farini, who preferred a much slacker rope, would do a

headstand; Blondin would counter with a somersault. Farini would cross with his feet in a sack, Blondin would use foot chains. Farini would wash a ladies handkerchief in river water drawn up to the cable 200 feet over the gorge, and Blondin would counter by cooking a meal.

Farini even carried his manager, Rowland McMullen, over on his back, but he never won the same fame as Blondin. Farini followed the French master to London after their Niagara

After her stunt voyage over the Falls, Annie Edson Taylor left her barrel to rot in a pool of water. This was a mistake as most people were more interested in seeing the barrel than in hearing Taylor's story. She had a second barrel constructed and posed with it for sightseers. It is now on display at a Niagara Falls museum. Courtesy, Buffalo and Erie County Historical Society

Falls duels, but died in an accident over the river Thames. Blondin died peacefully in 1897, at the age of 73.

In 1865 the "American Blondin," Harry Leslie, repeated some of the ropewalking feats, and in 1871 the "Canadian Blondin," Andrew Jenkins, crossed in a bicycle-like vehicle with its seat under the cable. In 1873 Signor Henry Balleni, an Italian ropewalker, made three crossings with a twist—midway, he would fasten his balance pole

while drunk.

Samuel John Dixon made the next crossing on Peere's cable in 1890, followed by Clifford M. Caverley—who set off firecrackers and skipped rope on the wire in 1892—and D.H. MacDonald, Charles Cromwell, and James E. Hardy. Oliver Hinton, a young colleague of Hardy's already working professionally as "Zen Zeno," claimed to have sneaked across Hardy's cable in his stocking feet and without a balance pole on

to the cable, fasten himself to a 100-foot India rubber rope, and leap into the gorge.

A fan and helper, Stephen Peere of Drummondville, Ontario, got so carried away with the exhibitions that he grabbed a pole and ran out on the cable himself. Balleni was so mad at being upstaged that he tried to cut the cable, and had to be forcibly restrained.

Balleni practiced an early version of bridge-diving by leaping from the Upper Suspension Bridge on his India rubber rope in 1886, suffering three broken ribs in the process. He died two years later in a leap from London's Hungerford Bridge.

Peere crossed the Niagara gorge again on his own three-quarter-inch cable in 1887. A few days afterward he was found dead on the riverbank under the Canadian end of his rope, after apparently trying to walk at night in his street shoes,

September 16, 1897—when he was only 10.

There was also one female performer and crowd favorite who worked the high wire 200 feet over the gorge. Signorina Maria Spelaterini, described as a comely lass in flesh-colored tights, made several crossings in 1876.

She kept step to a waltz tune on July 8, crossed with peach baskets on her feet and recrossed blindfolded on July 12, made another blindfolded crossing July 19, walked the rope with ankles and wrists manacled on July 22, and made a straight-forward farewell appearance July 26 before heading toward an engagement in Buffalo.

Oscar Williams' crossing in 1910 ended the tightrope era. In 1947 The Great Arturo (otherwise known as Arthur Trosi), of Ringling Brothers and Barnum & Bailey fame, failed to win official permission for a performance. Several

Aware of the publicity that a Niagara Falls stunt could bring, Bobby Leach had this photo taken, made eyewitnesses sign affidavits, and had his trip over the brink filmed on July 25, 1911. Leach was so successful with the ensuing lecture tour that the original film wore out and he returned to the Falls to reenact and reshoot his feat. This time the barrel went over the Falls empty. Courtesy, Buffalo and Erie County Historical Society

In 1911 Lincoln Beachey flew his Curtiss biplane over the Falls and under the Upper Steel Arch Bridge, making aviation history. The Wright Brothers had successfully undertaken their first flight only seven and a half years earlier, and Beachey was the first to fly under a bridge. Courtesy, Buffalo and Erie County Historical Society

other tightrope artists unsuccessfully sought permission to perform in 1976; one, Phillipe Petit, returned in 1986 to play Blondin in a movie and walk a wire strung parallel to the cliff and suspended from crane booms 170 feet over the Canadian floor of the gorge.

Perhaps even more famous than the tightrope walkers, though, are those who have taken the ultimate plunge—Niagara Falls, in a barrel.

The turn of the century saw the start of the phenomenon, after earlier daredevils had tackled the lower river's rapids in barrels. The first and most famous of those to tackle the Falls themselves was an unlikely daredevil indeed—Mrs. Annie Edson Taylor, a plump 43-year-old non-swimming schoolteacher from Bay City, Michigan, who had taught or run rooming houses in a number of other places before visiting the Falls.

According to *Buffalo Times* reporter Marian Park, she "looked and acted as if she were more some plain, stout old woman on her way to Sunday morning service." Her legend has doubtless been enlarged by time, but the fact is she planned a perilous trip through three quarters of a mile of rapids and over the Horseshoe Falls—and then she carried it out.

Her motive apparently was financial, coupling a desperate need of money with a hope that fame would beget fortune on the lecture and show tours she was sure would follow. On October 24, 1901, her birthday, she climbed into an oak barrel four feet in diameter and four and a half feet high, with a 100-pound anvil strapped to the bottom to keep it upright. The barrel was towed from Grass Island into the Canadian current, pumped full of air, and cut loose at 4:05 p.m.

The barrel shot through the rapids, watched by a few thousand spectators as it tumbled and rolled through the rocks to the clear waters at the brink of the Horseshoe. "Just a moment it was visible on the brink," Dunlap recounts, "then with lightning-like rapidity it dropped, a distance of 165 feet, into the seething, foam-lashed waters below."

Far below in the gorge, the barrel bobbed to the surface and circled in the eddies until King Brady managed to hook it from shore. Carlisle D. Graham, who had shot the lower rapids in a barrel, pried open the lid, peered inside and gasped, "Good God, she's alive."

Mrs. Taylor's hand appeared, waving weakly, and the crowd cheered. Part of the top of the barrel was sawed off, and the bruised,

battered woman, bleeding from a gash behind her left ear, climbed out and was helped across a plank to land.

"I prayed every second I was in the barrel," she told reporters. "Except for a few moments after the Fall when I was unconscious."

Her first words on seeing her rescuers reportedly were a dazed "Did I go over the Falls yet?" and she later confided, "I'd sooner be shot from a cannon."

Fame failed to translate into fortune for the Falls' newest hero. Even when billed as "Queen of the Mist," she failed to draw crowds to her lackluster show appearances. In later years Annie became a familiar sight on Niagara Falls streets, posing with another barrel and selling photos while telling her story. It was a sad end-

ing, for a brave adventure.

Annie Edson Taylor died in 1921 at age 63, penniless, in the Niagara County Infirmary in Lockport. She was buried in a pauper's grave in the Oakwood Cemetery, Niagara Falls.

Ten years after Mrs. Taylor had survived the Falls, Bobby Leach of England became the first man to go over the Horseshoe in a barrel.

A veteran of two rapids barrel rides in 1898 and a parachute jump off the Upper Steel Arch Bridge in 1908, Leach had settled down to run a local restaurant. The successful rapids run of Swedish sailor Klaus Larsen in a motorboat prompted Leach to dust off and repaint his old steel barrel to tackle the rapids yet again.

The four-minute roller coaster of the rapids went according to plan, but the 46-year-old dare-

Industrious hawkers built wooden shacks from which to sell souvenirs on the Ice Bridge, atop 150 feet of frozen water. Liquor was a popular item and authorities were stymied about how to handle these entrepreneurs because they couldn't decide if Canada or the United States was responsible. Courtesy, J. Carl Burke Studio

devil found himself trapped in the swirling Whirlpool for nearly an hour. Finally, a 24-year-old riverman named Red Hill Sr. snagged the barrel and Leach was saved.

While the Englishman and his friends celebrated at his restaurant, Hill eyed the empty barrel. Fate took the form of another bystander, who bet him he wouldn't ride the contraption through the next set of Devil's Hole Rapids to Lewiston.

Hill would, and did.

"When I was offered a $25 bet to go through the lower rapids I took the offer up because I wanted to show I was game," Hill told the *Niagara Gazette.* "On the trip I struck three rocks and was badly shaken up. Near Queenston I lost the top of the manhole after shipping about a foot and a half of water."

He might have suffered more if he'd collided with Bobby Leach that evening. Upstaged and furious, the elder daredevil also was fighting mad that the loss of the lid would ruin his planned attempt to become the first man to run the rapids on consecutive days.

"Bobby's remarks yesterday would have melted the type if we had attempted to print them," noted the *Daily Record* of Niagara Falls, Ontario.

The rapids quickly became too little an arena for the rivalry. Each man publicly declared he would beat the other in the race to conquer the Falls.

On July 25, 1911, Leach rode an eight-foot steel drum to victory. It cost him two broken kneecaps and a broken jaw, and 23 weeks in a hospital. But he had beaten Red Hill.

Eventually, the two even patched things up. In 1921 both pleaded with a 58-year-old Bristol barber named Charles Stephens in an attempt to keep him from testing the Falls in a heavy Russian-oak barrel. Stephens, the father of 11 children, didn't listen. He went over the Falls inside his barrel, an anvil strapped to his feet for ballast; all that was ever found was the battered remnants of the barrel, with part of Stephens' tatooed arm still attached to the harness.

Joseph Albert Jean Lussier of New Hampshire was next, riding a six-foot rubber ball lined with inner tubes and ballasted with hard rubber. Some

15,000 spectators watched him bounce through the rapids and over the Horseshoe on July 4, 1928; Lussier emerged smiling, and waving both the Stars and Stripes and the Union Jack.

George Stathakis, a 46-year-old Greek immigrant chef from Buffalo, died two years and a day later in the home-built 2,000-pound barrel he rode over the Falls. Stathakis had taken only three hours' worth of oxygen, but the barrel had been trapped behind the Falls for 22 hours before an eddy released it.

The wood and steel barrel survived, and Red Hill Sr. rode it through the rapids and into the Whirlpool a year later.

The next barrel rider—and the Falls' next victim—was Red Hill Jr., nine years after his father's death of a heart attack in 1942. Red Hill Sr. had become a legendary riverman, credited with saving 28 lives and recovering 177 bodies in the treacherous river waters he knew so well.

Red Hill Jr. had begun developing a legend of his own, working with his father and even, on one occasion, swimming out to retrieve dad and his barrel after his last rapids run in 1934. Red Hill Jr. also swam from the foot of the American Falls to Canada twice, and shot the lower rapids twice to help raise money for his mother after his father's death.

Some 200,000 spectators watched the first run, which Red made in the same barrel his father had used. The second time, the crowd was half as big. Both times, his mother met him at the dock with a kiss, but the effort netted less than $500. A brother, Major Hill, made the trip with even less success.

But Red Hill Sr. had never attempted the Falls, and Red Hill Jr. was trying to add his own name to the record books when he went over the Horseshoe on August 5, 1951, in "The Thing," 13 large inner tubes swathed in netting and equipped with an inflatable mattress. The device broke open at the base of the Falls, to the screams of his mother, wife, and 10-year-old daughter; Red's body was found the next day, and his death wrote a sad ending to the saga of a legendary Canadian river family.

Equally legendary is the ironic end of Bobby Leach, Red Hill Sr.'s old rival. Bobby made some money off his exploits, touring North America and Europe with his barrel, and lived to the age of 70. He was on yet another lecture tour in Christchurch, New Zealand, when he slipped on an orange peel while taking his daily walk, and the fractured leg became infected. He died of shock during an operation to amputate the limb.

Nathan T. Boya, a 22-year-old New York City maintenance man whose real name may have been William A. Fitzgerald, became the first black to ride over the Falls, in July 1961. He did it in a six-foot steel and tin ball named the "Plunge-o-Sphere," and before spurning publicity and vanishing into obscurity he said simply that he did it for "personal reasons."

In recent years, there has been another spate of barrel riders. Five more men have survived the Falls since 1984, and others have been rescued from strandings in the upper rapids. But these riders no longer find a welcome ashore; the ride is illegal now and earns possible fines and jail terms, and the lives of rescuers have been risked in the attempts to save those who try the stunt. Some of the attempts have been little short of ridiculous; in 1990 a man died trying to "do" the Horseshoe Falls in a kayak, without even a life preserver or helmet.

The only sanctioned "ride" was done by magician David Copperfield, who created the illusion of a Falls plunge for a television special in that same year.

Other names, however, survive in Niagara River lore. Captain Matthew Webb of England, a famed channel swimmer, died in an attempt to swim the monstrous Whirlpool Rapids in 1883. He's buried in the Oakwood Cemetery, not far from Mrs. Taylor and Carlisle Graham, who made the first lower rapids barrel ride and four more just like it. William Kondrat, 18, survived an unexpected trip down the rapids and 40 feet into the depths of the Whirlpool during an attempt to swim across the gorge in 1933, and Ray Weaver shot the rapids in a 14-foot outboard motorboat in 1961.

William Potts and George Hazlett did a two-man barrel ride through the lower rapids in 1886, and Hazlett teamed with Miss Sadie Allen to duplicate the feat later that year. Mrs. Martha E.

Wagenfuhrer did the first solo rapids ride in a barrel in 1901, and soon afterward Miss Maud Willard died in a similar attempt.

In 1911 Lincoln Beachey piloted an early Curtiss biplane under the Steel Arch Bridges and buzzed the Falls; in more recent years, daring helicopter pilots have made at least two dramatic rescues of boaters whose craft have grounded in the rapids just above the Falls.

In 1912 natural disaster overtook three victims in the gorge. Scores of other visitors had been enjoying the winter scenery and the vendors' shacks on the "Ice Bridge" that forms from shore to shore below the Falls during the coldest part of the year, but on February 4 of that year a sudden growling heralded the unexpected break-up of the deep river's ice cover.

Red Hill Sr. was among the two dozen or so people on the ice at the time, and he knew what the sound meant. He helped shepherd all but four tourists to safety, as the ice broke into massive floes.

Hill yanked Cleveland businessman Ignatius Roth to safety and then had to jump a widening crack to save his own life, but those who were near the gorge that day could only watch in horror as a floe swept downriver with Mr. and Mrs. Eldridge Stanton of Toronto and Roth's friend Burrell Hecock, 18, of Cleveland.

The newlyweds stayed together, and vanished into the river. The youngster tried to swim to shore, but couldn't hold onto a rope hastily lowered from the Whirlpool Bridge; he, too, perished in the icy waters.

The river, though, has not always been so unkind.

On July 9, 1960, 7-year-old Roger Woodward of Pine Avenue in Niagara Falls was boating on the Niagara with his 17-year-old sister, Deanne, and a family friend, James Honeycutt. It had been a pleasant afternoon, but as Honeycutt headed his small craft north from Grand Island the waters of the Niagara were growing rougher—and suddenly, the motor failed.

Honeycutt's frantic efforts to paddle toward shore were no match for the beginning of the Niagara rapids, and the boat capsized. Honeycutt, 40, a co-worker of the children's father on

This steel scow, lodged in the rapids a quarter mile above the Horseshoe Falls, has been viewed by tourists since it became wedged there on August 6, 1918. The boat was being towed up the river with three men on board when its line broke and the swift current carried it toward the brink of the Falls. One man swam ashore as soon as the line broke. The other two men were rescued the next day by Red Hill Sr., a famous Niagara River daredevil, and the U.S. Coast Guard. Hill was awarded a Carnegie Life Saving Medal by the government for his feat. Photo by Anthony "Red" Glaeser

the Niagara Power Project construction effort, slipped under the waves and was carried to his death over the Falls. Deanne and Roger, buoyed by life jackets, swept through the raging waters and neared the brink of the Horseshoe as tourists watched in horror.

Deanne, screaming, was swept by the current toward the Goat Island shore, with the overturned boat. A pair of vacationing New Jersey policemen, John R. Hayes, Sr., and John A. Quattrochi, risked their own lives to climb over the railing at the water's edge and reach out to the struggling teenager. Hayes' fingers grasped the girl, and he managed to hang on and pull her to shore as the boat plunged to its destruction.

Roger Woodward went over the Falls—and survived.

Perhaps too light to be trapped by the main torrent of falling waters, he somehow hit clear water at the base of the Falls and was quickly carried to the surface. The crew of the *Maid of the Mist* couldn't believe their eyes when they saw the boy in the life jacket bobbing in the waters—but they reacted quickly, and Roger was pulled to safety.

The memories were still crystal clear when he talked to a *Buffalo News* reporter 19 years later.

"I can remember, like pictures in my mind, things that happened that day," the Florida businessman recalled. "That was really a traumatic thing that I went through, that our whole family went through. Pictures still pop into my mind, as clear as day.

"I remember being able to see the other side of the gorge, and thinking it looked awfully odd from where I was. I knew a drop was coming—but I didn't know it was the Falls.

"One minute I seemed to be up in the air, and the next I remember a wall of rock, and being thrown against it. It's almost like I can remember seeing people running up and down the shoreline—and then there was the Falls.

"The next thing I can remember was seeing the *Maid of the Mist*, and I wanted out."

Roger suffered only bruises in his miraculous 167-foot plunge down the thundering waters. "I still can't believe his luck," his sister Deanne said in 1979.

But the memories were terrifyingly clear for her, too.

"The fright that showed on your brother's face, the shape of his mouth as he yelled to you—that, you don't forget," she said.

Terror also toyed with two other victims of the upper rapids, before sparing them in a way that proved the Falls are always unpredictable.

It happened on August 6, 1918, when an iron scow broke its tow line in the Niagara River off Port Day and swept ever more quickly toward the Horseshoe Falls.

Gustave Lofberg, a 51-year-old Swedish sailor, and James H. Harris, his co-worker on an excavation project, were aboard the tug. Somehow, they shoved a one-ton concrete anchor over the side; it held briefly, and then the scow broke free. Steel rollers also failed to hold the doomed craft, and lines and wooden workbenches thrown from shore fell far short of the scow.

Finally, only about a thousand feet short of the brink, Lofberg and Harris managed to open the dumping hatch in the bottom of the old scow. The river rushed in, and the sinking barge ground to a precarious halt on the rocky bottom.

Frantic rescue attempts were launched im-

mediately. The Coast Guard Station in the shadow of the walls of Old Fort Niagara was notified, and a crew raced to the scene with a line-throwing Lyle gun. After a frustrating delay at the border, where officials balked at the idea of American servicemen rushing into Canada with a small cannon, the device was set up on the roof of a Canadian power plant just above the Falls, and the second shot put a line aboard the stranded scow.

Lofberg made the line fast, but in the fading light of the dying day the rescuers ruled out any immediate attempt to remove the men. Instead, working by searchlight and fearing that the barge could break free at any moment, they worked feverishly to rig a backup line and the breeches buoy that the sailors could ride to safety.

The lines became almost hopelessly tangled, adding despair to the emotions of the night. But Red Hill Sr. saved the moment, risking his own life to climb hand over hand along the lines and free them while he dangled above the foam of the rapids.

With Hill back ashore, the stranded men shivered through the night as the scow creaked and groaned under the onslaught of the current. Lofberg later told reporters the night seemed endless, and he feared that any moment the scow would break up, tear loose, and carry both of them over the Falls.

By nine the next morning, though, the breeches buoy had been rigged and sent out to the scow. Lofberg insisted that Harris, the father of five children, take the first harrowing ride to safety.

Thousands of spectators cheered as Harris reached shore. Still fearing that any false move could cause the barge to break loose, the crews ran the breeches buoy once more out to the barge—and Lofberg, the old Swedish salt, made it at last to shore.

As it turned out, it wasn't exactly in the nick of time. In fact, the scow is still there.

You can still see it when you visit the Falls—grounded on a reef, overgrown with vegetation, and slowly rusting away a mere thousand feet from the brink of doom.

iagara Falls' first motorcar rattled into town sometime in May 1898. B.F. Thurston's one-seat wonder was, appropriately enough, powered by electricity. Charging the battery was no problem at all in the Electric City, and it seemed natural enough that the Falls would be on the cutting edge of technology. It wasn't fully three years, in fact, before Niagara Falls would find a way to combine automobiles and stunting—a marriage accomplished February 27, 1901, when Buffalo Locomobile dealer F.W. Peckham drove across the bridge to Canada, down the gorge to the Maid of the Mist landing, and across the ice bridge back to the American side, where the Locomobile was winched part way up an ice mountain for photographs.

Soon Niagara Falls had Peter Lammerts' dealership and the Barclay and Sons service station, and Niagara Falls Boulevard was open as the main auto route from Buffalo to the Falls.

Thurston's motorcar, though, wasn't the only thing powered by electricity. So was the new city, by the Falls.

When the villages combined to form the city in 1892, Niagara Falls had 6,505 residents and Suspension Bridge had 5,206. The new city covered 6,970 acres, not counting the 412 acres in the State Reservation, and the assessed value of the whole community, unencumbered by such niceties as sewers and pavement, was some $8 million. The first city budget was just $79,000.

Within 20 years, thanks to the industrial boom spurred by the development

In 1992 the City of Niagara Falls celebrates its centennial. A gala dinner and period costume ball will open the festivities in February at the convention center. Activities will include a Great Gorge Kite Flying Weekend, an air show, a parade, and fireworks displays. Photo by Denise Wood

NIAGARA LIFE

CHAPTER SIX

• • •

This view of the Moose Tower Hotel dates from August 1934. Next door stood the Niagara Falls Museum. These buildings were razed between 1958 and 1959. Courtesy, Buffalo and Erie County Historical Society

of hydropower, Niagara Falls had 92 miles of sewers, 50 miles of paved streets, 114 miles of sidewalks, a new water supply and filtration system, and an assessed valuation of $100 million.

The first mayor, George W. Wright, expressed both the challenge and the optimism in his first speech to the newly seated aldermen when he said, "We have everything to do, and everything to make to do it with."

Wright, who had been the last village president of Niagara Falls, was elected on March 1, 1892, by defeating endorsed Republican candidate General Benjamin Flagler and an independent Republican, Suspension Bridge village president William H. Cornell. The Democrats, in fact, recorded almost a clean sweep—of the eight new aldermen, two from each of four wards, only one was a Republican.

The Republicans found solace, or at least editorial support, in the pages of Peter A. Porter's *Niagara Gazette*, which became a daily paper on March 17, 1893. For the Democrats, pats on the back came from the *Niagara Falls Journal* and the *Daily Cataract*, which opened April 27, 1892.

Three months after incorporation, Wright also appointed the city's first board of education. James F. Trott became the first board president, and N.L. Benham, who had headed the Village of Niagara Falls schools, was named as the first city school superintendent.

Student enrollment then included 757 pupils at Suspension Bridge Union, 133 at the Third Street School, 26 at Schlosser, and 659 at Niagara Falls Union for a total of 1,575. The city

This view of Falls Street at the intersection of Second Street, looking west, shows thriving business and traffic circa 1920. Courtesy, Melissa Dunlap, Niagara County Historical Society

would build Niagara Falls High School in 1903 at Pine and Portage, allowing the two village high schools to revert to elementary school status once more as the population increased.

There was a tragic link between two other facets of the growing city.

In the early 1890s, Niagara Falls had three railroad passenger stations—Union Station in the Suspension Bridge area, the Erie at Niagara and Second streets, and the New York Central at Falls and Second.

In 1894 the Niagara Falls, Whirlpool and Northern Railroad opened a single line to the Devil's Hole, and later merged with the Niagara Falls & Suspension Bridge line to become the International Railway Co. A year later the Niagara Gorge Railway would open its 40-year run along the edge of the Lower Rapids, from the Falls to Lewiston.

The old "surface line" of the Buffalo and Niagara Falls Electric Railway, headed by William Caryl Ely, linked the two cities for just 35¢ one-way or 50¢ round-trip in 1895, but in at least one key instance the link just wasn't fast enough.

In 1893, near one of the stations, a young

man was run over by a train. Carried into a baggage room and placed on a cot, he suffered for two hours while waiting for a train to Buffalo and the nearest hospital; he died before he could be moved to medical help.

Mrs. Thomas E. Clark and Mrs. Charles B. Gaskill, appalled at the tragedy, went house to house in the city seeking funds to build a hospital for Niagara Falls. Mrs. Clark soon became the treasurer of the Emergency Hospital Association, with Thomas V. Welch as president and E.T. Williams as secretary.

The city's resort and industrial contacts led

The Niagara Falls Armory, built in 1894-1895, is an outstanding example of Richardsonian Romanesque architecture, a popular type of building design from 1870 to 1900. This fortress-like structure is still in use for military functions. Photo by Gail Salter

LEFT: President William McKinley was in Buffalo in September 1901 to view the Pan-American Exposition. On the sixth of September he took the train to see the famous Falls. This photo was taken in the morning on Goat Island. McKinley is wearing the top hat, in the center of the path. Later that afternoon, he returned to the exposition and was shot by an anarchist. He died within two weeks. Courtesy, Local History Department, Niagara Falls, New York Public Library

Production of Shredded Wheat started in Niagara Falls in 1901. For decades, people eating breakfast would be looking at the Niagara Falls plant drawn on their cereal boxes. Photo by Gail Salter

to support from influential donors, and the new Emergency Hospital—forerunner of the Memorial Medical Center—opened in a home on Niagara near Fourth Street on September 1, 1893.

Beds soon were added in a second home, with Mrs. Clark, Mrs. Gaskill, and Mrs. Harry E. Woodford helping with patient care, while meals and assistance came from the women from whom the rooms were rented. Later that year, relatives of the late Mrs. James S. Townsend promised a hospital building as a memorial to her; land was donated to the Niagara Falls Memorial Hospital Association, and the new hospital took in its first patients on November 1, 1897.

Its earliest sister facility was the Quarantine Hospital, or "pest house," which started taking cholera and other cases in 1893; Mount St. Mary's Hospital, founded by the Sisters of the Third Order of St. Francis in Williamsville, opened in a house at 604 Ferry Avenue on August 28, 1907. Sister Superior Mary Cherubim's hospital soon expanded from 18 to 33 beds, and a new 188-bed hospital was opened on Sixth Street on November 14, 1914.

Business slowed a bit, at least for the pest house, when city water improvements cut into the typhus problem in the mid-1890s.

The Niagara Falls Water Works filtration plant opened in 1896, reducing the number of typhoid cases to just over 200 for the year. But that was still unacceptably high; when Niagara Falls logged 210 cases in 1900, only 211 were listed in nearby Buffalo, although it was 10 times larger.

William D. Robbins, who later would serve as an influential city manager in Niagara Falls for 18 years, was named as the engineer for a city water project that led to construction in 1912 of a new filtration plant that finally solved the typhus problem.

Burgeoning population also brought growth to the spiritual life of the new city. While the village of Niagara Falls had six congregations, and Suspension Bridge had seven just before incorporation, additions such as St. James Methodist, New First Baptist, Temples Beth El and Beth Israel, and a host of ethnic churches

helped swell the number of congregations to 52 by 1930.

As rosy as things were looking for the city by the Falls, however, at least one opportunity for glory—and perhaps for tragedy—got away.

The opportunity was the Pan-American Exposition, an international technology festival that seemed tailor-made for Niagara Falls. It was intended to showcase New World accomplishments in the nineteenth century and open the bright future world of the twentieth century; and at first it looked like it would be held just above Niagara Falls on Cayuga Island.

Niagara Falls certainly pushed for the honor, and in the summer of 1897 President William McKinley actually drove a ceremonial stake to mark the center of the proposed 1899 exhibition on the island. But in the end, as finances and the schedule slipped, the exposition site was shifted to Buffalo.

President McKinley returned to Niagara Falls, while the Pan-Am in Buffalo was the center of world attention in 1901, to visit Goat Island and lunch at the International Hotel. Later that day, while standing in a reception line at the exposition's Temple of Music, he was felled by an assassin's bullet.

Dr. Roswell Park, a renowned surgeon who would much later lend his name to the Roswell Park Memorial Institute and its cancer research center in Buffalo, was operating in Niagara Falls that day; a special train was sent to fetch him to the dying president's side, but he arrived in Buffalo too late to offer more than advice.

Not even the murder of a president could slow the growth of the Niagara Frontier, however. Both Buffalo and Niagara Falls continued to attract industry, and the industrial boom drew thousands of the European immigrants who arrived in the United States early in the 1900s. At the turn of the century, Niagara Falls had a population of 19,457—up nearly 60 percent from its incorporation just a few years before.

One of the companies most closely linked in the public mind to Niagara Falls opened its doors, in innovative fashion, in 1901. Shredded Wheat, which for decades pictured the Falls on its cereal boxes, started production that year.

Henry D. Perky's Natural Food Company didn't just open a plant, it opened a community. Perky, a health food enthusiast, designed an operation that didn't follow the usual practice of extracting work with no regard for the worker; his plant was clean, and his more than 1,000 workers were treated exceptionally well.

There were free noonday meals in a fifth-floor dining room overlooking the rapids, the plant's well-circulated air was cooled by being pumped through a water spray, workers were allowed an hour a week of bath or shower time in company washrooms, and female employees were given four rest periods a day.

The plant grounds were landscaped, and across the street, on the grounds of the old Peter Porter mansion, a playground and park for employees and the general public was maintained by the company. The public also could take plant tours and receive a free Shredded Wheat sample.

The cereal company later would become part of Nabisco, and part of its original plant would become the first home of the Niagara County Community College before NCCC built its own campus.

Also daring in concept was the neighborhood known as Echota, a pioneering "planned community" centered on industry and workers.

It was started in 1894 by the Niagara Falls Development Co., the holding company of the Niagara Falls Power Co., on 84 acres of company land along Gill Creek, about a mile upriver from the power plant construction site. Echota was a model residential area for the

working man, featuring a complete sewage and drainage system, water and the luxury of electric lighting, wide stone-paved streets, a coordinated color scheme, links to public transportation, a school, a fire hall, and other amenities.

Designed by renowned New York architect Stanford White, the community included single homes, duplexes, and row houses for 112 families. Rents started at nine dollars a month. There was a general store at A Street and Sugar, now Hyde Park Boulevard, and the store building also had room for bachelor apartments and a community hall.

The neighborhood gradually lost its unique identity after the company sold the property in 1910, and declined through the years until many of the remaining Echota structures were moved to the newer Veterans Heights housing

Henry D. Perky solved his digestive problems with a diet of milk and boiled whole wheat, and a major industry was born. This brick building was built in 1900 for the Shredded Wheat Company, and the central section later became part of Niagara County Community College. Courtesy, Niagara County Community College

area to make room for construction of the Niagara Power Project intakes in the 1950s.

The first government housing project started in 1918, to house workers who came to Niagara Falls for jobs in the area's World War I defense plants. Homes designed by the architectural firm of Dean & Dean went up in a complex planned by John Nolan on 23rd through 25th streets, between Ferry and Orleans avenues.

Housing of another sort also occupied the attention of the city in that year as well. The old, huge, and venerable International Hotel was destroyed by fire on January 3, 1918, in a blaze that rivaled the 1907 holocaust that consumed the Acker Process Co. caustic soda plant and left only its tall smokestack on the edge of the gorge.

The loss of the International and the declining condition of the adjoining Cataract House led to calls for new hotels, and the newly organized Chamber of Commerce tried to interest Frank A. Dudley in filling the void.

Dudley's United Hotel Corp., long headquartered in the tall United Office Building which still dominates much of the Niagara Falls skyline, was the center of a national chain that grew to include more than 50 centrally supplied hotels based on a standard design. Despite several proposals and a lot of work, though, the Hotel Niagara project had to be launched with a public stock subscription campaign, which proved highly successful.

Ground was broken in 1923 and the new hotel formally opened on April 8, 1925, as a community-owned business managed by United Hotel Corp. Despite the hardships of the Depression, the hotel was for decades the center of downtown Niagara life and wasn't sold to private interests until 1959.

The hotel was one of the earliest projects of the Chamber, organized in 1918 as a post-war effort of five earlier groups. Its parents were the Niagara Falls Businessmen's Association of 1890, the Board of Trade of 1903, the Greater Niagara Commercial Association, the Niagara Falls Real Estate Board, and the Rotary Club.

An earlier effort to organize a Chamber of Commerce in 1895 had been short-lived, but the 1918 effort proved more durable. The Chamber's first chairman was Fred Mason, president of the Shredded Wheat Co. and the Board of Trade.

While the Chamber became a force in civic life, there had been political changes as well. On November 3, 1914, six months after a new state law outlining various forms of city government, Niagara Falls became the 16th city in America to opt for a new format involving a city manager and city council.

George W. Whitehead won election in 1915 as the first mayor under the new system, and the first city manager here was Ossian E. Carr, who had held a similar post in Cadillac, Michigan. The format would survive three major legal challenges and into the 1980s, when more power reverted to the mayor.

There was work enough for the politicians in the years that followed. For one thing, there was Prohibition, which spurred the development of speakeasies and eventually made Niagara Falls the site of the national Prohibition Party convention of 1936. It also altered the flow of tourism, as Americans crossed the border to Canada for a legal drink, and the Canadian side's share of the tourist trade rocketed from about one tenth to one half.

For another, there was a surge in population. The number of Niagara Falls residents increased by 48.5 percent in the 1920s, and the school population nearly doubled. In the 1921-22 school year the Falls school system had 7,889 pupils; 10 years later there were 15,236.

When fire damaged the high school in 1922, the system was forced not only to rebuild but to open north and south junior high schools. By 1932 there would be two more junior highs, a vocational high school, four new elementary schools, seven elementary school expansions, and a new administration building costing more than $13 million.

Perhaps even closer to the politicians' hearts, though, even before governments tried to build their way out of the Depression with public works projects, was the creation of a city hall.

The fact that it took 33 years for the incorporated city to finally get around to opening a city

Niagara Life • **103**

hall doesn't reflect a lack of interest so much as it does the continuing rivalry between two old neighborhoods—the former villages of Niagara Falls and Suspension Bridge. In 1913 the city government compromised by investing $68,000 in a parcel of land right between the two villages, at Main and Cedar streets.

Construction started 10 years later, and the $439,203 City Hall was dedicated at last by Mayor Laughlin and other dignitaries on January 2, 1925.

Just two years later, Niagara Falls took another leap by voting to absorb the village of La Salle, along the upper Niagara River. La Salle's voters approved the merger by a vote of 2,170 to 1,661 on April 18, 1927, and city voters agreed in an April 28 referendum.

When the move became official on June 1, Niagara Falls instantly grew by 7,000 people and $5.6 million in assessed valuation.

Growth continued through the 1920s, and a 1928 survey found only 700 unemployed—mostly due to handicaps and lack of skills—in the city. But 1929 brought the stock market crash, and the start of the Great Depression.

On January 1, 1930, there were 15,645 work-ers at 92 companies in Niagara Falls. By January 1, 1931, that number had dropped more than 10 percent, to 13,729. Employment bottomed out at 9,605 in January 1933, but hydropower and the strong industrial base in the Cataract City helped it fare better than the average for both New York State and the country as a whole.

Progress continued on transportation links, as well. Americans were shifting from rail travel to the automobile in the 1920s and 1930s, and this meant changes for Niagara Falls. The Peace Bridge, linking Buffalo and Fort Erie, Ontario, opened in 1927, opening a route to Niagara Falls via the west bank of the Niagara River, and in 1935 the two Grand Island bridges offered an even faster, more direct roadway link between Buffalo and the city of Niagara Falls.

That meant the demise of the High Speed Line between the two cities, launched by the International Railway Co. in 1918 at a cost of $4 million. The IRC's low-slung yellow rail trolleys made the run in an hour, but just two years after the Grand Island bridges opened, the last train chugged into the trolley station on August 20, 1937.

Adding to its demise was the gradual public shift from trolleys to buses, which also was reflected on city streets. The first motor bus ran in the Falls in 1931, and the last streetcar in 1937.

Bridges may have been opening, but the limelight in the 1930s belonged to one that fell down.

The bridge was the Falls View Bridge, built in 1898 to replace a suspension bridge that had fallen into the gorge in 1889. Later, it gained the nickname "Honeymoon Bridge" —but only after reporters covering its wreckage applied a wry sense of humor to the disaster.

Locals knew it simply as the "upper bridge," a short form of its original designation as the Upper Steel Arch Bridge. It had been built a year after the Lower Steel Arch Bridge at Lewiston, a span that survives today as the Whirlpool Rapids Bridge.

The Falls View's steel frame and wood planking had rail lines, sidewalks, and a roadway, and the span had carried the first electric

The United Hotel Corporation built this Art Deco skyscraper in downtown Niagara Falls in 1929. At 230 feet, it is still the tallest building in the city. Photo by Gail Salter

trolley car from the United States to Canada in the year it was completed. But problems had been noted in ensuing years, and the swaying set up by a band marching in step during an early Festival of Lights had led to a ban on parading on the bridge.

Even more dangerous, the bridge's abutments sat on the river shoreline. And in the winter of 1938, weeks of frigid temperatures led to the formation of the the biggest ice bridge in the gorge in 30 years; massive mountains of ice, some towering 50 feet above water level, pushed against the base of the bridge supports.

One of the main arch cords and two reinforced trusses snapped under the strain. Engineers began measuring the bridge for slippage, and a "death watch" was set up by spectators and reporters from across the country, as workers tried in vain to break up the ice and reinforce the abutments.

On January 27, 1938, the day after the bridge was closed, the rivets holding the girders to the base began to snap, one by one. IRC crew foreman Forrest A. Winch went down into the gorge to take more measurements, and was hard at work when he heard another rivet pop.

Instinct made him run. He was 50 feet from the base of the bridge supports when the whole bridge came down.

"The sound of crunching steel and the reports of snapping rivets was a terrifying sound, but it was all over in five minutes," he told a reporter. "The bridge buckled in the middle, and as it dropped a huge cloud of snow lifted hundreds of feet in the air."

Ironically, when the bridge let go at 4:12 p.m. that day it fell almost unrecorded. The dozens of newspaper photographers and newsreel cameramen who had stood watch in the cold for days had chosen just that time to adjourn for their favorite hot or cold beverages, and the only picture of the actual collapse was taken by an amateur photographer.

The wreckage obligingly lay on the ice for the photographers, however, and drew tourists for the rest of the season. On April 12 the ice too gave way; some of the steel sank from sight and one section rode an ice floe a mile

downriver before it sank. On May 4, 1940, ground was broken 550 feet from the Falls View site for the construction of the replacement Rainbow Bridge, but this time the abutments were placed well inland.

Niagara Falls' industrial base, which by now included major chemical plants drawing on the abundant water source of the upper Niagara River, got another major boost during the years of World War II. Wartime production needs pushed vital manufacturing to new levels and brought new defense industries to the hydropower center.

Bell Aircraft, founded in Buffalo, built a major new plant at the Niagara Falls airport in Wheatfield, turning out thousands of Airacobra and King Cobra fighters for the allied forces. Its planes became a favorite of the Russian air force, and it was not unusual to see test flights of Russian fighters over the Falls.

Aviation history was made at the plant, where research would eventually lead to the construction of the Bell X-1 just after the war years; Air Force captain Chuck Yeager, the man who broke the sound barrier in the bright orange airplane, first saw its rocket engines fired in tests at the Niagara facility.

The Lake Ontario Ordnance Works, although never fully operational, also was built to turn out wartime munitions, and the most secret of all wartime efforts had a component here—the Manhattan Project's search for a workable atomic bomb included a facility along the Lewiston-Porter town lines and would leave the Niagara region a long-term radioactive waste legacy.

But the aftermath of war brought decline to Niagara Falls and its industries, and a slow erosion of the dreams that had helped build the city.

Some of the older industries withered and disappeared. National chains built newer and more efficient plants elsewhere, offsetting the advantages of Niagara power. In 1947 the ALCOA plant manager announced that the facility, one of the city's major employers and most important industries for half a century, would close two years later. Others followed;

Waterproofed participants in the exciting Cave of the Winds Tour explore the walkways at the base of Bridal Veil Falls. Photo by Kurt Ross/Imageworks

Rainbows are common sights in the mist-laden air of the Falls. Here passengers enjoy the view from The Maid of the Mist, *whose half-hour tours have thrilled visitors since 1846. Photo by Kurt Ross/Imageworks*

*ABOVE AND LEFT:
During the summer
months, the Niagara
Splash Water Park pro-
vides a refreshing place to
cool off. Photos by Kurt
Ross/Imageworks*

The frozen, ice-clad trees of Goat Island Park form a striking winter landscape. Located between the American and Horseshoe falls, Goat Island offers a great vantage point for an unobstructed view of Niagara's wonders. Photo by Kurt Ross/Imageworks

ABOVE: Colored lights and holiday decorations adorn a five-block area of downtown Niagara Falls during the city's Festival of Lights, one of North America's top tourist events. Photo by Kurt Ross/Imageworks

RIGHT: The wide open countryside and an abundance of farm animals make rural Niagara County a great place for children. Photo by J. Rocco Photo-Graphics, Buffalo, NY

This reenactment of the War of 1812 at Old Fort Niagara in Youngstown brings history to life. Photo by J. Rocco Photo-Graphics, Buffalo, NY

Set amid the landscaped grounds and inviting gardens of Prospect Park, the Niagara Reservation Information Center provides visitors with a diversity of interactive displays on the Niagara area, as well as a thrilling wide-screen film, Niagara Wonders. Photo by Kurt Ross/Imageworks

the 1950s were a period of decline, as heavy industry slumped at a cost of 10,000 jobs. The assessed value of property in Niagara Falls dropped $30 million, and the downtown area decayed.

The collapse of the Schoellkopf power plant in 1956 can be seen as a turning point, the end of one era and the beginning of another. It was the end of the years of power production by private industries, and the start of a future shaped by a massive public power project that altered the shape of the city forever.

Besides providing a massive boost in power generation, the Niagara Power Project had major impacts on city life. Three years of construction meant massive employment and an economic boom, but there also was a series of public works projects tied to the project.

Niagara Falls, which had completed its geographic growth by annexing a corridor of industries and motels leading toward the airport in 1955, found itself through the rest of the decade and into the 1960s at the center of new urban development set in motion by Power Authority chairman Robert Moses, New York's near-legendary "Master Builder."

New bridges were built parallel to the North and South Grand Island bridges, to double the traffic flow over the highway link to Buffalo. The Robert Moses Parkway was built from a new highway interchange on the Niagara side of the North Grand Island Bridge all the way along the river to Lewiston, and a new expressway from the same interchange provided an overland shortcut directly to the new Lewiston-Queenston Bridge opened in 1962 as a twin to the Rainbow Bridge.

By 1966 grade-level railroad crossings on city streets—a continuing source of accidents that had claimed more than 150 lives over the years—had been eliminated. Roads and highways were improved, there was a new Hyde Park golf course and a city recreation center, a new vehicular bridge reached Goat Island, state parklands had seen their own boom in building and renovations, and a new observation tower at Prospect Point provided elevators and views from the base of the gorge to a deck high above the Falls themselves.

Power Project construction cut, and then rebuilt, every highway artery into the city. Entire sections of the city were eliminated—either relocated or lost forever. The old Customs House disappeared; so too did houses, railroad tracks, freight yards, schools, businesses, apartment buildings, the old Shipston coal yard, and such familiar industries as the Niagara Wallpaper and Defiance Paper Co., which had incorporated the surviving landmark Acker Process smokestack into its complex, and the Byrne Warehouse, once home to the Niagara Falls Brewing Co. and its regionally famed Niagara Lager.

The project also provided land on the escarpment at Lewiston to the state parks system, and eventually Artpark was constructed as a unique performing arts state park on the slopes of the "three mountains" Father Hennepin had described so long ago. Nor was Hennepin's Catholic faith forgotten; the Our Lady of Fatima Shrine, built by the Barnabite Fathers on Lewiston land donated by the Walter Cuerczak family, was dedicated in 1965 and now draws more than 200,000 visitors a year.

Drawing international attention, too, was the little chapel built in 1913 along the river's edge just north of the village of Lewiston, near the Stella Niagara school founded by the Sisters of St. Francis of Penance and Christian Charity five years earlier. Built on the ruins of a small War of 1812 powder storehouse, the chapel's miraculous survival of several massive ice jams in the river, including a 1954 jam that destroyed everything else along the river but left 50-foot walls of ice protecting the tiny structure, was reported around the world.

Niagara Falls, though, needed more than an economic miracle of its own. It needed a rescuing knight on a white charger—and it found one, literally, in the person of one of the most remarkable political personalities in Niagara Frontier history.

The man riding the white steed at the head of countless parades was E. Dent Lackey, who won election as mayor in 1963. Formerly the public relations manager for the Carborundum

Niagara Falls remains a premier honeymoon spot for newly married couples. Photo by Kurt Ross/Imageworks

The new Lewiston Bridge is seen here under construction in 1962. In the foreground, work on the Niagara Power Project is in progress. In the background the old Lewiston-Queenston suspension bridge is visible. The bridge was erected at this spot in 1898 after being moved from the Falls when the construction of the Honeymoon Bridge was completed. Courtesy, New York State Authority

Co., he was an enthusiastic booster of Niagara Falls who saw how desperately the city needed to restore its pride in itself and reverse the years of decline.

He was an orator with a flair for dramatic action and a catchy phrase, promoting his city as the "honeymoon capital of the world" and performing thousands of marriages. While Carborundum president William H. Wendel

cofounded and chaired SPUR, the Society for the Promotion, Unification and Redevelopment of Niagara Falls, Lackey launched a concurrent "Operation Outbound" revitalization effort in 1965, traveled Europe boosting Niagara Falls as a tourist destination, and formed the city's Urban Renewal Agency to save the downtown area.

In his energetic 12 years as mayor, Lackey

arching design, but helped launch it by luring the Miss U.S.A. Pageant from Florida.

The Rainbow Center Project was only one of three major projects undertaken by the Urban Renewal Agency that Lackey chaired. The Allen-McKenna Avenue Project and the Highland-Hyde Park Industrial Project also were launched, but it was the Rainbow Center that had the most visual impact on the city by the Falls.

Its central building, formally titled the Niagara Falls International Convention Center, was started in June 1969, and opened in 1974 as the eastern end of a development corridor that extended 1,800 feet westward to Prospect Point and the Falls. Next came a Hilton Hotel, then the Wintergarden botanical complex in 1977, the turtle-shaped Native American Center for the Performing Arts, new corporate office buildings and the Rainbow Centre shopping mall.

An $8 million plaza, fountain, and skating rink now fronting the arched entrance to the center has been named E. Dent Lackey Plaza in honor of the colorful and dynamic mayor, who died in 1977.

His successor, former school administrator and Urban Renewal Agency member Michael C. O'Laughlin, was elected mayor in 1975 and has held the post into the 1990s. Lackey had turned the city around, but it would be up to O'Laughlin to finish the renewal efforts, retain the momentum—and weather some of the worst moments in the city's long history.

There were problems tied to the urban renewal. In retrospect, O'Laughlin and others described the changes as too sudden and too drastic. Much of the heart of the old city was razed to make way for the new; the project relocated 295 businesses, 200 families, and about 400 roomers.

The Pine Avenue business section became the main commercial area during the long years of demolition and construction, but much of the old downtown retail business shifted to the suburbs and new malls such as the Summit Mall in suburban Wheatfield.

But the major nightmare, the one that played out in the international media and im-

tore Niagara Falls away from an economic dependence centered purely on heavy industry and promoted tourism as well as civic pride.

He focused on a dramatic, central project—an 82-acre downtown development that would include a huge new $35 million international convention center. He not only won funding and backing for the convention center, which reflected the rainbow theme in its unique

pacted Niagara Falls tourism, wasn't retail—it was environmental.

In 1894 an entrepreneur named William T. Love had launched a scheme to dig a canal from the upper to the lower Niagara River, bypassing the Falls and allowing construction of a model city along its banks. The financial panic of 1897 torpedoed his plans, and the waterway he'd started digging inland a few miles above the Falls was abandoned.

Through the 1920s, the "Love Canal" was simply a neighborhood swimming hole in the village

areas in 1951, and in 1953, because a new school was needed and after threats of property condemnation, Hooker Chemical deeded the land to the Niagara Falls Board of Education for $1. The 99th Street School was built on the canal site in 1954, despite the soft spots and fumes encountered by contractors. The northern third went to the city for a park in 1960, and the southern third of the Love Canal was sold by the Board of Education in 1962 for housing development. Roads and sewers were subsequently built in the disposal areas

of La Salle. But soon industry found another use.

Industrial and municipal waste dumping at the site dates back to at least the 1930s, and intensified from 1942 through 1953 as the "organic chemical revolution" created new herbicides and pesticides that kept Niagara's chemical industry busy. The work was good for the economy, but the best of the day's disposal methods would return to haunt later generations; tons of residues were sealed in metal drums and buried at Love Canal.

Housing developments started in adjacent

despite notice contained in the deed that the area had been used for chemical waste disposal.

In 1976, chemicals began to ooze into backyards and basements.

In the years that followed, the Love Canal became a symbol of man-made environmental disaster. Life in Niagara Falls was dominated by testing, protests, legal action, evacuations, buyout plans, and eventually clean-up efforts.

President Jimmy Carter declared a national state of emergency at the site on August 7, 1978.

New York State bought out and evacuated 561 families from a 10-block area, and in 1980, after President Carter had declared a second federal emergency, the United States relocated 728 families from the surrounding area.

The federal government bought out another 550 homes later that year, and demolition of 227 houses began in 1982. Through the 1980s remedial work also took place, with federal Superfund money supporting the effort after levels of dioxin and other hazardous chemicals were confirmed at the site. The canal itself was capped with clay, and contaminated sewers were cleaned. Eventually, a controversial government decision allowed "outer ring" homes to be re-sold, and in 1990 families started moving back in to join the 84 residents who had refused to leave in the first place.

The Love Canal had far-reaching consequences. It heightened national awareness of the environmental problems left by industry, and set precedents for citizen action, protests, and responses everywhere in the country. Lois Gibbs, the young Love Canal mother who had led much of the protest and gained national prominence, moved to Washington, D.C., where she continues an active role in the national environmental movement.

A lump-sum settlement of $20 million was accepted by some residents of the site, and complex lawsuits, involving the city, the school board, the state and federal governments, and Occidental Chemical Corporation (which had purchased Hooker), for many times that amount continued into the 1990s. In addition, Love Canal's problems triggered a close look at other environmental problems in the Niagara Falls area, and other local pollution sites were identified.

Industrial discharges and leaking contaminants from the old disposal sites have made the upper Niagara, bordering the largest remaining industrial complex in New York State, one of 43 "toxic hot spots" identified on the Great Lakes by the International Joint Commission. And Niagara County remains one of the few spots in the nation allowed to accept hazardous wastes from Superfund clean-up

sites elsewhere, as well.

But progress has been made. Awareness of the problems led to efforts to slow the environmental impacts and clean up the wastes of past decades, and Niagara became the site of test projects in the forefront of technological solutions to pollution. Several of the chemical industry companies located in Niagara pursued research and implemented solutions

ranging from high-temperature kiln incinerators and improved oxidation systems to chemical pretreatment and the use of microorganisms.

Tighter governmental controls were used to slow the use of the area as a major national and state disposal site, as well. Despite the conflicts and problems of the past, industry has placed more emphasis on a role as "corporate citizens"

through participation in urban renewal and community activities. For example, in the largest joint public/private effort of its kind in the nation, Occidental agreed late in 1990 to contribute $64.9 million toward a $68 million drinking-water plant, to be built by the city away from the aging water works adjacent to the company's old "S-Area" dump site.

The 1980s, difficult economic years along the entire Niagara Frontier and throughout the industrial northeast, also saw plant closings in Niagara Falls. Nitec Paper Corp. went bankrupt in 1982, taking 700 jobs with it. Tajon Inc. closed the same year, putting 200 out of work. Carborundum laid off the 650 workers in its bonded abrasives division in 1983 and moved 275 jobs in its finishing operations to Texas in 1987, and in 1986 Union Carbide cut back by 650 jobs.

At the end of 1986, the state Labor Department put manufacturing employment in Niagara County at 23,600—down 1,000 from the previous year, and 12,100 from employment levels in 1978.

Population itself had peaked at 103,045 in 1958, dipping only slightly to 102,394 in the 1960 census. Just 10 years later, though, the 1970 census revealed a drop to 84,052. From 1980 to 1990, Niagara Falls' population dropped from 71,384 to 61,840.

Guiding the city through the decade of crisis was no small challenge for Mayor O'Laughlin, but he proved equal to the task. The census drop for the decade masked a period of recovery in the late 1980s, and Niagara Falls again has upward momentum.

There were triumphs, amid the gloomy economic prospects of the 1970s and 1980s. Niagara Falls gained the new Earl W. Brydges Public Library and, in 1972, the adjoining Harry F. Abate school complex. The city also became the first in the nation to be declared a "Bicentennial Community" in preparation for national celebrations in 1976, a salute to the area's spirit and patriotism. The Aquarium of Niagara Falls and the Schoellkopf Geological Museum became popular local attractions, as did the Power Vista visitors center and museum at the gorge power project. At the old DeVeaux campus, now part of Niagara University, the Buscaglia-Castellani Art Gallery became a center for fine art, until a striking new gallery could be built on the main campus.

A major barrier between the city and the Falls itself was conquered in 1977, when the long-recognized problem of the downtown

stretch of Robert Moses Parkway was solved by closing first one lane and then both.

The city even gained its own airline, when restaurateur John Prozeralik joined with businessmen Graham Harris, Les Price, and Thomas R. Johnston to launch Air Niagara in 1980. The airline's two Boeing-727 jets flew scheduled routes to New York City, Florida, and Mexico. Although foreign tourists arriving in New York listed Niagara Falls as their top-choice destination and the airline provided a needed tourist service, federal deregulation of the industry led to its downfall as a regularly scheduled airline and its sale to John Burns in 1983 for continuation as a charter flight business.

Niagara Falls International Airport continued to serve as a major charter airport, while on the other side of the huge airfield the Niagara

Falls Air Reserve base sustained a major military presence as the home base of the New York Air National Guard's 107th Fighter Interceptor Group and the Air Force Reserve's 914th Tactical Airlift Group—a combat support unit called to active duty for the Persian Gulf war, as was the Niagara Falls-based 365th Evacuation Hospital of the Army Reserve.

In the city itself, the Rainbow Project area gained new hotels and the renovation of older structures, and construction was launched on the Falls Street Faire and Falls Street Station projects. The Niagara Splash Water Park took over the former industrial lands behind the convention center, the Niagara Falls Rapids expansion team of 1989 revived one of the Class A NY-Penn League's original baseball franchises of half a century earlier, and a new visitor cen-

The Earl W. Brydges Library on Main Street in Niagara Falls is part of the NIOGA system, comprised of Niagara, Orleans, and Genesee county libraries. Designed by Paul Rudolph in 1974, it holds 210,000 items. Photo by Gail Salter

ter and other work brightened the approaches to the state parkland along the Falls.

There was increasing demand for efforts to restore the Falls lands to natural beauty and limit man-made intrusions, and to restore the city's identity by improving access to the Falls. Among the projects proposed were expansion of the park along the Niagara River and removal of the Prospect Point observation tower and the closed section of the parkway.

A new political era began in 1988 as well, as a new city charter, approved by voters in 1985, took effect. The changes incorporated a new "strong mayor" concept that had been sought unsuccessfully by Mayor Lackey, giving the city's chief executive more administrative power and removing him from the City Council.

The move marked the end of the city manager format, which had featured a five-member City Council that included the mayor. Under the new format, amended later in 1988 to make the post of mayor a full-time job, the number of council members increased to seven, and a new post of city administrator was created.

On January 2, 1988, Mayor O'Laughlin took the oath of office to begin his fourth term. Anthony F. Quaranto became the first chairman of the new seven-member council, and Barbara A. Geracitano became the first woman to serve as a council member. Mark R. Palesh became the first city administrator.

The mayor and council launched economic and light industrial development projects, began rewriting the city's master plan and zoning ordinances, and started housing initiatives; and in 1989 Mayor O'Laughlin could say that stability had marked the first year of operations under the new system.

With favorable economic conditions bringing thousands of Canadian shoppers across the border to Niagara's Factory Outlet Mall and other local retail centers in the 1980s and 1990s, there also was discussion and debate over a major project planned for the city's second century—a $110 million mega-mall to be built downtown in 1992, on a 100-acre parcel of land east of the convention center and water park. But Niagara Falls already had found a symbol of its latest

renaissance and a source of community pride.

Celebrations were nothing new to the Falls, but few had captured as much of the heart of the city and as much participation from its citizens as the Festival of Lights.

There had been an early series of such festivals, and mid-century had brought Maid of the Mist and Winter festivals and a Pride and Progress Week. But this was different—a festival that ran for 44 days, growing in size and scope each year as a boon to winter tourism and a chance for volunteers to shine as brightly as the thousands of Christmas lights illuminating the Rainbow Center area.

Organized in 1981 by Niagara Falls Area Chamber of Commerce/SPUR executive vice president Henry Kalfas and other community leaders, by 1989 the festival had been designated the "Number One Event in North America" by the American Bus Association. Fireworks, more than 100,000 holiday lights, and a full program of concerts, parades, and other entertainment highlighted the 10th annual Festival of Lights in the winter of 1990-91, as buildings displayed computer-controlled lighting patterns, colored floodlights illuminated the rapids, and animated displays brightened the spirits of children.

Attendance at the annual festival, which draws visitors from around the world, has climbed steadily from 200,000 in 1981 to 970,000 a decade later. Volunteer chairman Charles P. Steiner, president of the Chamber and SPUR, joined other leaders of the community and the festival board of directors in envisioning a 1991-1992 festival passing the million mark in attendance.

That festival, though, would serve as prelude to another party planned by and for the citizens of Niagara Falls itself. On March 17, 1992—the 100th anniversary of the incorporation of the city—a Centennial Birthday Party and Mayor's Ball will launch a six-month "family celebration" of the city's history, ethnic heritage, business growth, and quality of life.

The second century of the city's existence is being met with renewed energy, by those who live near the ceaseless thunder of the world's most spectacular falls.

*N*iagara Falls has been drawing admirers of natural beauty since the 1800s and continues to attract record numbers of visitors from all over the world.

By the turn of the century, the area's vast resources of hydropower lured many industries eager to harness the energy for manufacturing. Industrial growth brought prosperity to Niagara Falls and, until the Depression, the city proved to be the fastest growing in New York State.

The 1930s and 1940s brought a leveling-off period after decades of incredible industrial expansion. Growth resumed during World War II as Niagara Falls industries joined the war effort.

When industrial growth began to decline, the importance of Niagara Falls as a tourist attraction rose proportionately. By 1992 tourism is expected to become the city's number-one industry as millions more people discover the attractions of Niagara Falls.

The organizations whose stories are found on the following pages have chosen to support this important literary and civic project. They illustrate the many ways in which individuals and their businesses have contributed to the city's development. The contributions of Niagara Falls' businesses, institutions of learning, and local government, in cooperation with its citizens, have made the community an excellent place to live and work.

There were many proposals to harness Niagara as a source of power, including one plan for 200 new factories around the Falls. A group of businessmen formed the Niagara River Hydraulic Tunnel, Power, and Sewer Company. In 1889, after a lack of investment capital, the company reorganized as the Niagara Falls Power Company, as advertised by this group of men from about 1890. Courtesy, Buffalo and Erie County Historical Society

PARTNERS IN PROGRESS

CHAPTER SEVEN

• • •

NIAGARA FALLS AREA
CHAMBER OF COMMERCE/SPUR, INC.

ABOVE: Among the chamber's many concerns is the promotion of the vast Niagara Falls tourism industry. Each year millions flock to enjoy panoramic views such as this.

RIGHT: Thousands of outdoor lights illuminate the night sky during the 44-day Festival of Lights, first organized by SPUR in 1981.

The 1918 resolution that marked the birth of the Niagara Falls Area Chamber of Commerce stated, "Niagara Falls should have one strong, well-organized central commercial organization representing all the business, professional, and civic interest of the city."

Today it has that and more. The "more" is its alliance with an organization called SPUR, the Society for the Promotion, Unification, and Re-development of Niagara, Inc. Composed of and funded by citizens from industry, commerce, the professions, and government, SPUR serves as a catalyst to coordinate and accelerate private and public efforts to improve Niagara. Although separate, the two organizations are symbiotic. They share office space and even leadership.

The roots of the chamber go back to 1890 when the Niagara Falls Business Men's Association was formed. Although the association was unsuccessful in its attempt to establish a chamber of commerce, it was not without accomplishments. It played a major role in the merger of the villages of Niagara Falls and Suspension Bridge to form the City of Niagara Falls.

In its early years, the chamber focused on traditional activities such as industrial and economic development, government relations, and promotion of the tourist industry. Today new business development, government relations,

economic development, and tourism are its key focus, but it is also very involved in housing and environmental issues.

An active Small Business Council, Plant Managers' Association, Industrial Liaison Committee, and Environmental Liaison Committee help the chamber serve its entire membership.

SPUR was formed in 1964 by William H. Wendel, Carborundum Company president. The society "believed that a new approach to redevelopment is required, an approach that will demand of public and private leadership a greater degree of unselfish concern for the welfare of the total area."

Among SPUR's early achievements were the

establishment of the City Management Advisory Board, Niagara Food Bank, Niagara Beautification Commission, the development of the Music School of Niagara, the Horticulture School at Niagara County Community College, and others.

In 1979 the chamber and SPUR formed an alliance to develop and promote what has become one of the Falls' greatest tourist attractions, the wintertime Festival of Lights.

Under the leadership of Henry J. Kalfas, past executive director of both SPUR and the chamber, the Festival of Lights blossomed from a grass-roots undertaking into a major contributor to both the local economy and spirit. The 44-day festival attracts hundreds of thousands and involves hundreds of volunteers from every segment in the community.

With SPUR's ability to gather resources to focus on specific projects, and the expertise of the Niagara Falls Area Chamber of Commerce in issues related to "the big picture," the private sector's future in the Falls is bright, indeed.

SMITH BROTHERS CONSTRUCTION COMPANY

The family name "Smith" is one of the most common in America. The family business called Smith Brothers Construction Company, on the other hand, is a most uncommon organization.

Looking at the dozens of shopping malls, school buildings, supermarkets, and apartment complexes the company has built, one could safely say the firm has left an indelible mark on the Niagara Falls area. But when the company was starting out in the 1950s, a job such as fixing and enlarging a porch was more of a typical undertaking.

Although it takes its present name from brothers Donald and Gordon Smith, the company was actually begun by their father, Harold, under the name Harold J. Smith & Sons. Smith senior worked days as a carpentry foreman for another company while his sons were working toward their engineering degrees

at the University of Buffalo. To earn extra money, they began working together part time, doing general carpentry work.

When Donald and Gordon graduated, they formed a partnership to continue the construction enterprise full time. For the first two years, they built houses in Niagara Falls, Lewiston, and Grand Island. Sensing greater potential in commercial and heavy construction jobs, however, they decided the branch out.

With the help of their uncle, George Fischer, a former construction superintendent whom they coaxed out of retirement, the company put in a successful bid on the city parks' maintenance garage on Hyde Park Boulevard. This job quickly led to others, including the construction

of a number of schools, which has proven to be a very significant area for the firm. Beginning with the Thomas Marks and Ransomville elementary schools, Donald and Gordon went on to build many local schools, including the 60th Street and Millgrove elementary schools and LaSalle and Jamestown high schools. In 1962 Smith Brothers moved to its present location at

Haseley Drive in Niagara Falls, the former site of the Mioska Dairy Farm, where Harold Smith used to buy milk for his family.

In addition to schools, Smith Brothers has been responsible for constructing hotels, roadways, bus terminals, restaurants, office buildings, and even the athletic facility for Niagara University. The company also has 35 Tops Supermarkets to its credit, built over a period of 15 years.

To complement the construction partnership, Donald and Gordon established the Smith Brothers Development Company, which is responsible for a number of impressive projects. Notable among these are the Rainbow Industrial Center, adjacent to the Niagara Falls International Airport, and the 27-acre Witmer Industrial Park, a multiuse office complex.

Today Smith Brothers Construction Company, which began with a father and two sons working part time, now has more than 100 full-time employees, including a number of Harold's grandchildren. Thus continues a tradition of uncommon work by the family named Smith.

ABOVE: The company was actually begun by Harold Smith, under the name Harold J. Smith & Sons.

LEFT: The Smith Brothers: Donald (left) and Gordon.

FAR LEFT: Smith Brothers is responsible for the construction of Schrafft's Restaurant and Motor Inn at Rainbow Bridge in Niagara Falls.

WASHINGTON MILLS
ELECTRO MINERALS CORPORATION

RIGHT: This building, part of the company's New York facility constructed in 1949, now holds company offices and serves as a shipping and distribution center.

ABOVE: Smaller tilt furnaces like this one manufacture Washington Mills' premium products.

If history is a river, then Washington Mills Electro Minerals Corporation represents the confluence of two major arteries: the Washington Mills Emery Manufacturing Company formed in Ashland, Massachusetts, in 1868, and The Carborundum Company, founded in Niagara Falls in 1891.

Like many local industries, Washington Mills owes not only its location, but also its existence, to the power generated by the Falls. Its business is the production of artificially made, "electro-fused" grains such as the silicon carbide discovered by Dr. E.G. Acheson in 1891. Today Washington Mills Electro Minerals Corporation is not only a major supplier of silicon carbide in North America, but the largest manufacturer and supplier in the world of aluminum oxide and a number of specialty grains.

Just four years after his discovery, timed to take advantage of the inexpensive hydroelectric power just-then coming on line in Niagara Falls, Acheson's newly formed Carborundum Company built its first silicon carbide plant just off Buffalo Avenue.

For more than 80 years, abrasive grain production at the Carborundum plant continued smoothly. But the 1970s ushered in a series of ownership changes that would permanently alter the course of this company's history.

In 1977 The Carborundum Company was purchased by the Kennecott Copper Corporation. In turn, Kennecott was acquired by Standard Oil of Ohio (SOHIO) in 1981. The plant on Buffalo Avenue became part of the SOHIO Electro Minerals company.

While expert in the oil industry, SOHIO lacked the know-how to manage its new electro minerals capability, and in 1986 SOHIO decided to sell off this part of the business. Ironically, the purchaser was the smallest entity in the abrasives industry at that time—a Massachusetts-based company called Washington Mills. Although small, Washington Mills had a long history of success, and with it, the confidence to turn around its new acquisition.

Founded in Ashland, Massachusetts, by five men—Oliver Ames, Charles Alden, N.J. Pike, Willard Smith, and Bradford L. Crocker—the company was the first U.S. producer of abrasive grains, predating Acheson and silicon carbide by more than 20 years. Originally known as the Washington Mills Emery Manufacturing Company (in 1940 it changed its name to Washington Mills Abrasive Company and in 1988 to Washington Mills Company), the firm moved to North Grafton, Massachusetts, in 1878. The site chosen by the company proved propitious: the Nipmuc Indian name for the new location near the Quinsigamond River, "Hassanamisco," means "place of small stones." Over the years Washington Mills' growth was steady, if unspectacular. Looking ahead, it poured its profits back into the company, modernizing existing facilities and continually improving the reliability of its processes and products.

Just across the Niagara River, a new Canadian corporation, Washington Mills, Ltd., was formed in 1980 to run the company's newly built aluminum oxide fusion plant. When SOHIO's electro minerals plant came on the market, Washington Mills saw it as an opportunity to further expand its holdings in a geographical area where it already had a significant presence.

The first task facing the new owner was to turn around the fortunes of the newly purchased plant, and this it did by immediately cutting overhead and unnecessary costs and putting profits right back into the firm. The success of this strategy is reflected in two figures: 250 employees and an annual production of 85,000-plus tons of abrasive grains. In fact, the Buffalo Avenue facility is today the largest of all of the Washington Mills Electro Minerals Corporation's plants.

Included in that annual figure of 85,000-plus tons are several types of grains, one of which is silicon carbide—the "granddaddy" of electro-fused minerals and the plant's original product.

The power of silicon carbide lies in its abrasiveness—when mixed with water, for instance, it can cut granite. Among other applications, it is used in the making of steel, as well as in electrical circuits and lightning arrestors because of its low conductivity.

Aluminum oxide is another grain produced at Washington Mills with exceptional abrasive and corrosion resistance properties. This has led to its use in the manufacture of grinding wheels and sandpaper. It is also used to fabricate refractory products and to provide insulation and corrosion resistance in steel-making mills.

As befits the largest producer of electrofused

grains in North America, Washington Mills also owns two of the largest electric tilt furnaces in the world—the "Queen" and the "Princess." Every four hours, these two-story-high furnaces pour 20 to 25 tons of molten material into aluminum molds. And besides its significant capital investment in equipment, Washington Mills has also made research and development a top priority. Through its research, the company has developed a number of important new products, many of which are already on the market. Over it all, however, is a simple but powerful company philosophy: to manufacture quality products to meet its customers' needs.

The company's customers and its vendors now come from all over the globe. Washington Mills has a broad market base in Europe; buys the bauxite it needs to make its fused aluminas from China, Australia, and South America; and has recently been qualified for business in the Far East.

When Dr. Acheson invented silicon carbide, he had no way of knowing that Niagara Falls would one day become the host of not only the single greatest concentration of electro mineral producers in North America, but its single largest producer as well—Washington Mills Electro Minerals Corporation.

ABOVE: Washington Mills' New York manufacturing facility.

INSET: The silicon carbine grain plant at the New York facility was constructed in 1966.

LEFT: At first much of the grain production had to be performed manually (photo circa 1930s).

NUTTALL GEAR CORPORATION

R.D. Nuttall, founder.

If a company's history can be captured in an adage, Nuttall Gear Corporation's would be, "The more things change, the more they stay the same."

What has changed since its founding in the late nineteenth century have been its ownership, location, and manufacturing sophistication. What has remained the same have been its basic products (gear drives, speed reducers, and speed increasers), its attention to detail, and its commitment to quality. From a small company that began by making gears, pinions, trollies, and bearings, Nuttall has evolved into a corporation whose products can be found in every industrial, commercial, utility, and transportation application imaginable.

Founded in 1887 by R.D. Nuttall with one gear cutter, five men, and a combined capital of $500, the company originally manufactured supplies for trolley systems.

As the young R.D. Nuttall Company prospered, it contributed numerous "firsts" to the gear industry: flexible gearing for transportation applications, forced feed lubrication for large industrial enclosed gear drives, and the first integral type gearmotor. Its development of single helical gears was one of the most significant contributions to the field of gear engineering.

In 1916 the R.D. Nuttall Company called together the nine leading United States gear companies to found the American Gear Manufacturers' Association (AGMA), which focused on writing engineering standards for the gear industry.

Nuttall remained privately held until 1928, when it was purchased by Westinghouse Electric Corporation. For the next 55 years, the only ripples in an otherwise steady stream of gear production and innovation were a move to Buffalo in 1960 and changes in the name from the R.D. Nuttall Company to the Nuttall Works of Westinghouse to the Westinghouse Gearing Division. All that would change dramatically, however, in 1983.

Like many American companies during the early 1980s, Westinghouse's business was affected by a slowing economy. The result was a decision, in 1983, to sell the gearing division.

Westinghouse chose to sell the gearing division to its management employees in a leveraged buyout transaction. The risk factor was high, but four division executives decided to accept the offer and formed the new Nuttall Gear Corporation: Christopher Collins became president with W. Charles Kolkebeck as vice president of marketing and sales, David Ashman as vice president of manufacturing, and A. Carl Becker as vice president of engineering and purchasing.

Under the terms of the sale, Nuttall purchased all of Westinghouse's gearing assets, including machinery, engineering designs, patent rights, patterns, tooling, and inventory. Financing was the key to this leveraged buyout, and on April 4, 1983, Nuttall Gear's Industrial Revenue Bond, issued by the Niagara County Industrial Development Agency, was purchased by Merrill Lynch. Having revived the original founder's name and having moved the operation to the town of Wheatfield, the "new" Nuttall Gear Corporation was in operation manufacturing high-quality gear drives, speed reducers, and speed increasers.

Despite a tough economic and competitive environment, Nuttall's success was immediate. The company remained focused on providing the highest-quality products and superior customer service. Niche markets were targeted that emphasized the strengths of Nuttall to provide customized gear drives as well as standard gear drives to a variety of demanding applications. New products were developed to enter new niche markets that provided steady, repeat orders. Customer relations were strengthened and the ability of Nuttall to be a broad line gear supplier was emphasized. Market share grew as the new markets were successfully penetrated.

Nuttall did more than just develop new products for niche markets. The company also positioned itself for the future by investing in new machinery and computer systems to ensure a competitive company in a global marketplace. Computer systems were installed to manage the company, and computer-aided design (CAD) was added to reduce development time for new products. The company computer systems were completely integrated from order entry to engineering, purchasing, inventory control, shop floor control, material requirements planning, and accounting.

New computer numerically controlled (CNC) machines were purchased to increase productivity and ensure high quality. Nuttall invested heavily for the future.

This success was prelude to what could be called Nuttall's "declaration of independence." On April 15, 1990, just seven years and 11 days after securing its original financing, Nuttall was able to retire its bond debt.

Nuttall took another dramatic turn in owner-ship when the Nuttall Gear Corporation Employee Stock Ownership Plan (ESOP) was formed on January 1, 1991. Under the terms of the ESOP, the employees of Nuttall now own a significant portion of the company and will share in the future success of Nuttall. The ESOP reinforced the commitment of the founding shareholders to share the success of the company with the employees. As an employee-owned company, Nuttall should enjoy even more success as employee-owners work to provide customers with the highest-quality products.

Times, products, and markets have changed since Nuttall first began making trolley parts when Grover Cleveland was president. Today the employee-owned company services every industry in the United States, including paper, steel, petro-chemical, bulk material handling, electric utilities, grain elevators, sewage treatment, and crane and hoist markets.

Although it will surely change in the future, Nuttall Gear Corporation will just as surely stay the same—making sure the various operations of the company continue to mesh smoothly through innovation, service, and attention to detail.

ABOVE: A customized gear drive developed for a particular customer's application.

LEFT: The original R.D. Nuttall Company factory in Pittsburgh, Pennsylvania.

OHMTEK

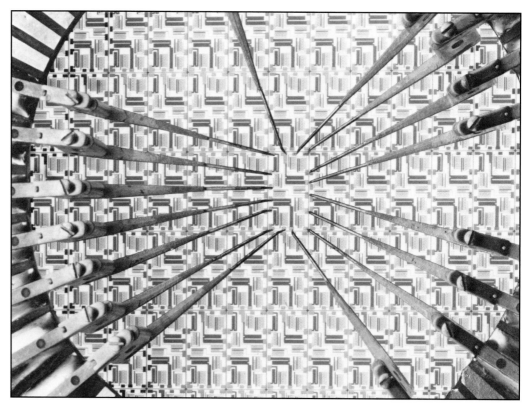

Most people associate the word "resistance" with the phrase "path of least." At Ohmtek it is the key concept behind one of western New York's most successful high-technology businesses.

The company's name is an amalgam of "ohm," the standard unit of electrical resistance, and "tekhne" the ancient Greek word for art or skill. And what Ohmtek skillfully makes are resistor networks. Resistors are nichrome or tantalum nitride components that control the amount of electrical current that flows through an electronic product; these resistors are custom designed and then applied to ceramic or silicon substrates in (literally) thin films in order to create what amounts to a "network" of electrical pathways. Ohmtek's products are used in computers and instruments of all kinds for a wide variety of applications.

Although the company began in 1978, its history actually goes back to the early 1960s, to another company, and to a young Ph.D. in physics named Dr. Franklyn Collins, Ohmtek's founder.

Fresh from his studies at the University at Buffalo, Collins went to work in the research

and development department of the former Niagara Falls company Airco Speer. In short order he was appointed manager of resistor research. Under Collins' leadership, Airco Speer in 1972 produced one of the first custom-designed resistor network on the market. This marked the first of many advances in thin film technology that Ohmtek continues to this day.

Mindful of the strides taken by Collins and his team, a number of large clients brought their business to Airco. The defense giant Litton put resistor technology to use in military applications, including an internal guidance system for missiles, which depend upon the precision of the resistors for their accuracy. Another example is IBM, which used Airco resistor networks for mainframe computer applications.

Despite this success, Airco Speer decided to withdraw from the electronics market. In 1978 it put its resistor division up for sale. From this decision, Ohmtek was born.

Collins and Allan Wiegley, a certified public accountant from Tonawanda, New York, formed a group of private investors, and purchased the resistor operation. Wiegley became

vice president of finance and Collins the new firm's president. From the beginning, Ohmtek has been a company characterized by both ingenuity and progressive thinking.

In an industry in which high employee turnover is the rule, Ohmtek built in a human relations "resistor network" of its own. One way it did this was by making a conscious decision to hire employees almost exclusively from western New York, counting on the area's strong work ethic and the strength of local ties to encourage long-term employment. A second example is Ohmtek's profit-sharing plan. Established in 1981, it pays benefits quarterly (rather than annually) based on company performance to reward its employees' dedication and reinforce their loyalty. Such innovation also can be found in Ohmtek's products.

The year the company was founded, it developed and patented the Tamelox process, which today accounts for 75 percent of its business. Tamelox forms a multilayer film structure that provides superior resistor reliability and stability—and a higher-quality product.

Ohmtek also pioneered the use of cathode sputtering for laying down resistor films, a move that paid off in both expected and unexpected ways. Expected because the process quickly proved superior to the evaporation method that had previously been used. Unexpected because, inside the "previously owned" sputtering machine Ohmtek acquired through a broker, it found a platen of platinum (used in the sputtering process) which more than paid for the purchase.

Another area of thin film technology in which Ohmtek has made significant advance is substrates, the surfaces upon which film is actually deposited. Because the quality of the "base" has a direct effect upon both production efficiency and product characteristics, Ohmtek changed from ceramic to glass substrates in 1978.

A milestone event in Ohmtek's history took place in 1981. Amdahl, a large California-based computer company, wanted to switch from a Japanese supplier of resistor networks to one

from the United States. It searched across the country for a supplier that could meet its stringent requirements for exceptionally precise resistor networks in the state-of-the-art surface-mount configuration and found Ohmtek, which was not only able to produce a higher-quality network than the foreign competitor, but also do so at a lower cost. Today Ohmtek is sole supplier to Amdahl of more than one-half million of these resistor networks per year.

Success has also led to well-deserved recognition for Ohmtek—as well as other rewards. In 1982 Dr. Collins accepted the New York State Small Business Administration's Innovation Award. The following year, Ohmtek was named Supplier of the Year by Amdahl, further publicizing the firm's accomplishments.

Perhaps the clearest signal of Ohmtek's prowess was its 1986 purchase by the French firm Sfernice. This not only gave Ohmtek an international perspective, but also richly rewarded the company's owners for their drive and innovation. Sfernice, in turn, was acquired by the Pennsylvania-based firm, Vishay Inc., in 1988. Ever the innovator and still very much master of its own destiny, Ohmtek most recently entered into a joint project with its new parent, with the result being yet another new product, a metal foil chip resistor.

In its brief but illustrious history, Ohmtek has found the path of least resistance lined with gold.

FAR LEFT: Tiny electronic circuits are produced by patterning using photolithography within the class 100 clean room.

BELOW: Computer-operated lasers are used in calibrate miniature electronic components to exact electrical specifications.

BOTTOM: Operators examine microscopic circuitry under high magnification for defects.

DU PONT

The origins of Du Pont's Niagara plant can be traced back to 1896, when the Niagara Electro Chemical Company built and operated a facility to manufacture chlorine and metallic sodium along the banks of the Niagara River. As it was for many of the pioneering industries of the day, cheap electricity was the lure that drew the company to the Falls.

Today, as Du Pont, the plant continues to make those products, as well as caustic soda, Terathane®, and precious metal pastes. Employment has increased from a handful to more than 800 people, and the site itself has undergone many changes. One thing, however, has remained constant: Du Pont's philosophy that it will not make, handle, use, sell, transport, or dispose

ABOVE: State-of-the-art membrane technology is used in the NIACHLOR facility.

RIGHT: The original sodium plant (1914), which is still in existence today. The site now covers 52 acres. (Robert Moses Parkway was added later. The section that appears as river in this picture was filled in to build the road.)

of a product unless it can do so safely and in an environmentally sound manner.

Niagara Falls Electro Chemical Company merged with the Roessler and Hasslacher Chemical Company in 1925, and Du Pont purchased the facility five years later. Historically, the sodium produced at the site has been primarily used in the manufacture of agricultural chemicals, specialty lightweight metals, and in processes to produce dyes. The Terathane® made there is used in urethane formulations for everything from roller skate wheels to hockey rink sideboards, as well as in Spandex for textile

manufacturing. The Niagara plant's precious metal pastes are used in the electronics industry.

Although chlorine has been made at the site since 1896, even greater quantities of the widely used element have been produced there since the 1987 addition to the plant of the NIACHLOR facility. This joint venture between Du Pont and the Olin Corporation uses the latest membrane cell technology to convert brine ($NaCl$ and H_2O) into caustic soda ($NaOH$) and chlorine (Cl). At a cost of approximately $200 million, NIACHLOR represents the largest capital investment in the area since the 1950s.

Du Pont's commitment to the Niagara Falls area goes beyond mere economics, however. As a good industrial neighbor, the company operates its facility in a manner that protects the safety and environmental integrity of the community. And whether working in the oldest or the newest part of the facility, Du Pont employees are committed to a guiding plant principle:

"Every employee performs every task in a manner that ensures the safety and health of himself or herself, fellow workers, the community, and the environment."

This effort and commitment to work safely together has been recognized with numerous safety awards from such organizations as the National Safety Council, the Chemical Manufacturers Association, and the Chlorine Institute.

A good neighbor, a major employer, and a manufacturer of products that touch nearly everyone's life, nearly every day, Du Pont is proud of its place in the history of Niagara Falls.

TAM Ceramics, Inc.

When TAM Ceramics was named Company of the Year by the Niagara Falls Chamber of Commerce in 1989, it received a well-deserved moment in the sun. For more than 80 years, this quiet local giant had been one of the world's leading innovators in the field of ceramics, a role it continues to play today.

Originally called the Titanium Alloy Manufacturing Company (the first three initials of which make up the company's modern-day name), TAM was founded in 1906 by Dr. Auguste Rossi, holder of the patent for the technology that extracts titanium metal from its ore. It established its operations in Niagara Falls on Hyde Park Boulevard in order to take advantage of the electric power required to manufacture ferro titanium alloys—its original product line. As the company matured, however, it put its research and development capabilities to work to develop new products, including the specialized ceramic materials that are the company's mainstay today.

One early example of TAM's research and development prowess involved titanium dioxide. In a joint venture with the National Lead Company, TAM used this compound as a key ingredient in the world-famous line of Dutch Boy Paints. Other early technical innovations including milled zircon (used as opacifiers for ceramic glazes), weld rod fluxes, and zirconium oxide for refractories, are still in use today.

Another ceramic powder, barium titanate, was first produced commercially by TAM during World War II. It is used extensively to make ceramic capacitors, which are basic components of almost every electronic device made. Today

TAM is the world's largest producer of this essential powder.

Such success in product development and marketing did not go unnoticed. In 1979 TAM was acquired by the British firm Cookson Group plc. Cookson is highly supportive of TAM's R&D capability, which continues to make important strides in the ceramics field.

For instance, in 1988, TAM achieved yet another technological breakthrough when it produced exceptionally pure (99.7 percent) zirconia—used in camouflage paint to prevent detection from infrared sensors. Another recent advance, and one for which TAM holds an exclusive worldwide license, is the development of mold and ladle powders that purify steel early in its manufacturing process.

TAM's management team, led by Robert A. Rieger, president, emphasizes the importance of maintaining the "leading edge technology" that has made TAM Ceramics an important player in the world market. Approximately 25 percent of its sales are made outside the United States, including Japan, where TAM's dielectric powders hold an unusually high (15 to 20 percent) share of the market.

With a record like this, there's little reason to doubt that this redoubtable Niagara Falls "company of the year" will continue to be honored for the excellence that has made it a worldwide power.

LEFT: Furnace room with Thompson, Dr. Auguste Rossi, and Hassley Sr. circa 1910.

BELOW: TAM's management team.

BOTTOM: TAM Ceramics was named Company of the Year by the Niagara Falls Area Chamber of Commerce in 1989.

OCCIDENTAL CHEMICAL CORPORATION

More than 2,000 tons of household-type wastes are processed daily at the company's Energy-From-Waste plant located in Niagara Falls adjacent to the company's main manufacturing complex. In addition to converting the BTUs in these wastes into steam and electricity, the EFW plant recovers and recycles 12,000 tons of ferrous metals annually.

Potassium sulfite, a chemical used in making photographic materials, is produced in these facilities recently built at OxyChem's Niagara Falls plant. The unit was custom designed to meet the needs of a major supplier to the industry.

The bigger the tree, the deeper the roots. For the oak named Occidental Chemical Corporation, the depth of its attachment to Niagara Falls can't be measured in mere years. Several of this giant's more than 100 worldwide facilities are in the area, and 1,800 of its approximately 14,000-plus employees work there.

The seed that began this mighty enterprise was planted in 1903 by a then 33-year-old entrepreneur named Elon Hooker.

Young Hooker originally created what was essentially a venture capital firm, The Development and Funding Company, with a goal of providing financial backing for undercapitalized enterprises.

After investigating more than 250 "projects," Hooker decided to underwrite a large-scale application of the recently discovered Townsend process, which used electric current to produce elementary chlorine (Cl), sodium hydroxide (NaOH), and hydrogen (H) from ordinary table salt (NaCl) and water (H_2O). This first enterprise was such a success that Hooker never followed his plan to undertake other funding ventures.

The firm's first facilities were built in 1905 on the site of a former pear orchard on Buffalo Avenue, an ideal location for its proximity to both the power generated by the Falls and to raw salt resources. The early plant, like others of its day, operated with two 12-hour shifts, seven days a week, year round, with no holidays or vacations. Fifteen cents was the average hourly wage.

Elon Hooker soon realized that a larger plant meant greater profits, and so the facility's capacity was quadrupled. Production increased steadily until World War I, when demand for chemical products suddenly escalated. The company established a research department in 1914, and by the time the war ended, had increased the number of its products more than sevenfold.

Hooker also played an important role during World War II, winning many commendations

from the government for its increased production. When the Japanese cut off the world supply of natural rubber, U.S. petroleum, rubber, and chemical companies stepped in. Of the nationwide chemical industry's total wartime synthetic rubber production, Hooker accounted for more than half.

During the postwar years, the company expanded rapidly through mergers and acquisitions. In 1955 it acquired Durez Plastics in North Tonawanda and the adjacent Niagara Alkali Company in Niagara Falls. The following year it bought Oldbury Chemical Company. In what was the largest acquisition up to that time in American corporate history, Occidental Petroleum purchased Hooker in a stock transaction valued at $800 million in 1968.

Occidental placed its worldwide holdings of chemical operations under the Hooker Chemical name in 1973, with the Niagara Falls operations continuing as Hooker Chemicals & Plastics Corporation. Then, in 1982, Occidental Chemical Corporation (OxyChem) was established. All of Occidental's chemical operations, including the Niagara Falls and North Tonawanda plants, were placed under this name.

Today OxyChem operations in western New York are located in Niagara Falls, Lockport, North

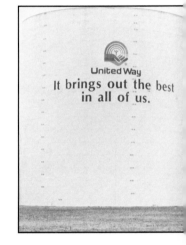

LEFT: The Occidental Chemical Center building in downtown Niagara Falls serves as a headquarters facility for a number of corporate and regional support groups for the company's operations. Its unique design features captured a national award for energy conservation in 1980.

ABOVE: While the temporary storage of raw materials or process chemicals is the main function of holding tanks at the company's Niagara Falls plant, this one provides a billboard-type background for a timely message to motorists moving along the Robert Moses Parkway.

Tonawanda, and Grand Island. The Niagara plant, which employs more than 700, still produces the chlorine, caustic soda, and hydrogen it began making back in 1905, plus a wide range of specialty chemicals. The Lockport facility became an OxyChem holding in 1986 and presently serves as a regional bulk silicate terminal.

OxyChem's Durez Division began in 1921 as the Industrial Molded Materials Company, Inc. Its founder, Harry Dent, saw the potential for a then-new product called "plastic." In 1926 the rapidly growing firm, then called General Plastics, Inc., moved to its present site on Walck Road in North Tonawanda.

Today OxyChem is the world's largest producer of phenolic molding compounds and the North Tonawanda facility is responsible for a significant percentage of that production.

The Durez-Niagara plant was part of Oxy-Chem's 1989 acquisition of the phenolic resins business of the former BTL Specialty Resins Corporation. Located on Packard Road in Niagara Falls, the plant has an annual capacity for more than 50 million pounds of specialty resins.

The company's Corporate Technology Center is located on a garden-type 32-acre site on Grand Island. There, 200 employees support OxyChem's existing business through programs geared to waste minimization, cost reduction, and new product development. In addition, at the Development Center in Niagara Falls, chemists and engineers investigate ways to take new projects from bench scale to large scale. An on-site pilot plant allows engineers to test processes in designing safe, cost-effective facilities.

The Energy-From-Waste (EFW) plant adjacent to the main Niagara can convert 2,000 tons a day of municipal and household refuse into steam and electrical energy. Operational since 1980, it is the largest privately owned plant of its kind in the United States, offering area municipalities an environmentally acceptable alternative to landfills.

OxyChem's newest local facility is the distinctive Occidental Chemical Center office building in downtown Niagara Falls, regional headquarters for a number of the company's worldwide and area operations.

Deep rooted, many-branched, and enduring, OxyChem is continuing a well-established tradition of more than 80 years of responsible community involvement in western New York. Perhaps it is fitting that Elon Hooker began his enterprise in a pear orchard, for over the years OxyChem has been truly fruitful.

MOORE BUSINESS FORMS

RIGHT: The Paragon Black Leaf counter checkbook, the simple idea to "let one writing serve many purposes," was the beginning of the business-forms industry.

BELOW: Founder Samuel J. Moore.

BOTTOM: Moore's first United States manufacturing facility, located in Niagara Falls, started production in 1883.

The success of Moore Business Forms bears out the axiom that the best ideas are the simplest ones. In this case the simple idea was "let one writing serve many purposes," and its first materialization was in 1882, when the company produced a sales book containing a bound-in sheet of carbon paper.

Emigrating from England to Canada in 1861, young Samuel Moore worked as a reporter, editor, publisher, and entrepreneur, and by age 22 he was a partner in the Grip Printing and Publishing Company of Toronto. When a sales clerk in a nearby store suggested the usefulness of a book that could produce an identical record of sale for both merchant and customer, Moore quickly recognized the idea's business potential. The result was the Paragon Black Leaf counter check book, which revolutionized business recordkeeping and the business forms industry was born.

In 1883 Moore established the world's first plant devoted solely to the production of business forms in Niagara Falls, a city he liked for both its readily available electric power and its proximity to Toronto.

Moore's ties to the Cataract City strengthened when it acquired a manufacturing building at 1001 Buffalo Avenue in 1925. The 112,144-square-foot plant at one time utilized some of the largest presses in the East, as well as in the entire forms industry.

In 1929 Moore established a re-

search subsidiary, early evidence of its continuing emphasis on developing new products. Over the years it had come up with such innovations as the 1926 Speediset® snap-apart form, and it continues to be an innovator today, with such products as Moore Clean Print® carbonless paper and the Midax® electronic imaging system for the printing of variable data on forms.

Just after World War II, Moore established an administration center at 900 Buffalo Avenue, directly across the street from its manufacturing facility. The building was expanded in 1968 by a two-story, 14,400-square-foot addition, doubling its original size. Today Moore's Niagara Falls facility houses financial activities vital to operations in their U.S. Divisions, serving the entire country. Specific responsibilities include credit and accounts receivable, invoicing, sales use tax, and various support services.

Another key Moore facility on the Niagara frontier is its ultramodern research center, located on Grand Island and built in 1978.

Moore Business Forms was one of the first companies to see the potential of doing business in Niagara Falls. This potential has actualized into a company with a worldwide presence, close to $3 billion in annual sales, and a local work force of more than 300 people—all starting with the simple idea of "one writing serving many purposes."

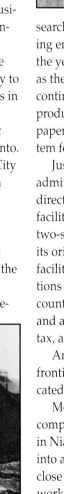

EMPIRE BUILDERS SUPPLY CO.

The great pyramids of Egypt are proof that concrete lasts. Empire Builders Supply of Niagara Falls is proof that a company that sells that substance can do the same.

The company began in 1919 as the successor to Mitchell's Builders Supply, whose primary

products were coal, ice, brick, and dynamite. Originally officed in the Gluck Building with a location on Sugar Street, now Hyde Park Boulevard, Empire continued to supply these products to local contractors, branching into concrete production in the mid-1930s.

The original principals of the business included such well-known citizens as Paul Schoellkopf, John Broderick, and Burton Mitchell. As Niagara Falls grew, the firm grew with it, until it attracted the notice of a pair of investors, Don Coe and Gene Truslow, who purchased the company in 1947.

The Niagara Power Project signaled boom times for Empire, which landed the dynamite contract for the massive undertaking. But, ironically, the project also forced the firm to move to its present location on New Road, as its previous site stood in the way of construction.

Empire's ownership changed in 1965, when it was bought by a group of local general contractors, and again in 1974, when it was purchased by Paul A. Schmidt, owner of Clarence Materials Corporation. Today Empire operates two Niagara County locations as a separate division of CMC under the leadership of Martin L. Segarra, president of Empire since 1985. Throughout these ownership changes, however, Empire's primary focus has remained on the mixing and supplying of concrete.

While the substance itself—a mixture of ce-

ment, stone, water, and sand—has basically remained the same since the time of the pharaohs, the mixing and supply process has become more sophisticated—a fact reflected by Empire's plant. Complete modernization of the plant took place over the past decade, and it features a storage area with space for up to six different types of aggregates, full computerization, and push-button loading of the batch trucks that carry mixed concrete.

Empire has also built a reputation over the years for production of special concrete including refactory concrete, acid resistant concrete (used primarily in local industry), as well as ar-

chitectural and specially colored concretes. These have provided both structure and style for such local landmarks as the Castellani Gallery, the Niagara Parks Visitor Center at Prospect Point, and E. Dent Lackey Plaza. It has also supplied standard concrete for practically every major building in the area, including St. Mary's Hospital, Artpark, Rainbow Mall, Niagara County Community College, and Summit Mall.

Today 60 percent of Empire's business is concrete (bricks and building supplies account for the rest), and on a normal day the company runs 18 to 20 trucks. The plant itself has the production capability of more than 1,000 cubic yards of concrete per day, and the company employs approximately 40 people.

And like its long-lasting product, Empire Builders Supply sees itself as a permanent resource for the future of Niagara Falls.

FAR LEFT: Since branching into concrete production in the 1930s, Empire has supplied concrete for practically every major building in the area.

LEFT: Since it began in 1919, Empire Builders Supply has grown with Niagara Falls.

CERTO BROTHERS DISTRIBUTING COMPANY

Albert J. Certo

In the 1950s Certo Brothers operated out of the Old Spray Brewery Building at 750 Third Street, the site of the present-day Aquarium of Niagara Falls.

In the world of beer and soda distribution, brand names come and go faster than the fizz in a bottle of pop. Even so, one family name has remained a constant in this ever-changing picture: the Certos of Niagara Falls.

Innovators, survivors, and entrepreneurs—any of these labels would aptly describe this close-knit family and its family business, Certo Brothers Distributing Company. But to understand the success of this enterprise—now the largest beer distributorship not just in Niagara Falls, but in all of western New York—one must go back a century and across an ocean.

The year was 1888, and the place was San Pier-Niceto, Sicily. This was the birthplace of family patriarch Peter Certo, and with it, the beginning of the American dream that Certo Brothers lives today.

At the age of nine, Peter arrived in America, and soon afterward his brother followed him to the coal country of western Pennsylvania. A tragic accident claimed his brother's life, and Peter quit the mines for a better life in the city called Niagara Falls.

A butcher by trade, young Peter soon opened a small grocery store at 19th and Niagara streets in his newly adopted hometown. Quick to answer opportunity's knock, he soon noticed the popularity of soft drinks, and thus was born Certo Bottling Works, a small soft-drink bottling plant.

In the beginning, Peter produced the popular flavors of the day, but in short order took on outside brands, including Hires Rootbeer, O-So-Grape, and Nesbitt Orange.

After the repeal of Prohibition, Peter Certo applied for a license, and in 1933 became the first beer wholesaler in Niagara Falls. Peter Certo remarked, "To say that we were the first beer wholesaler in the area is not completely true. We were just the first legal one." Although he received the very first boxcar shipment of beer in Niagara Falls after the ban was lifted, not a single drop made it to the warehouse—the entire delivery sold out at the railroad siding.

It was during this time, the 1930s, that three of Peter's sons—Ken, Albert, and Hank—would begin to play the active part in the business that they would continue throughout their adult lives. A fourth son, Anthony, would distinguish himself as a lawyer and then as chief city court judge of Niagara Falls. Peter's three daughters, Margaret, Elizabeth, and Mary, also had active roles in the company. Today, almost 60 years later, Betty, Mary, and Hank are still very active in the business.

In 1947 it could be said that Certo Bottling Works "went modern" by taking on the distributorship of Lord Calvert's ginger ale and club soda. Little did the Certo family know, however, that this would prove an almost fatal move.

Around this time, Lord Calvert ran a successful "buy one, get one free" marketing campaign. In fact, it was too successful. Canny customers ordered Lord Calvert by the thousand, which proved to be the label's undoing. Lord Calvert was forced to file bankruptcy, and Certo was left holding the bag for the insolvent company. As a result, Certo was also forced into bankruptcy.

If the ability to recover from misfortune is a measure of a company's character, Certo

Brothers has character to spare. Although it did not operate as a distributor again for six months, it did survive—thanks to help from fellow distributors, friendly customers, and helpful business associates.

From a marketing point of view, Certo kept alive by allowing other Buffalo distributors,

Regal Beverage and BeeDee Distributing, to carry its brands while it was reorganizing. Legally, it made the important step of incorporating as Certo Brothers Distributing Company Inc., in 1949. And financially, its former customers pitched in, going so far as to pay their bills in advance.

Signs of Certo Brothers' recovery came as early as 1951, when it won first prize in a national contest sponsored by Schlitz Brewing Company for the highest increase in sales by a distributor. (The prize given by Schlitz—a 1951 Oldsmobile '98—transported Hank and his new bride on their honeymoon to California in 1952.) Just a few years after its 1947 bankruptcy, Certo Brothers was able to pay back its investors and begin operating independently again.

Until 1959, that meant operating out of the Old Spray Brewery Building at 750 Third Street, into which the company had moved some 10 years before. While meeting Certo's needs during its period of recovery, the space and operational limitations of this building led the company to seek new headquarters. A 13-acre parcel of land on Porter Road was purchased, and a custom-designed building was erected.

Completed in December 1959, the 24,000-square-foot building was the first clear-span structure (that is, it had no supporting posts) in the country used for beer distribution. It pro-

vided for easy storage without wasted space and enabled forklifts to move entire pallets of beer at one time. The purchase of 16 side-loading "palletized" trucks went hand in hand with the move into the new building, with the result that the same warehouse staff improved the efficiency of their operation by more than 33 percent.

In the 1960s Certo Brothers grew dramatically. In 1962 it purchased a Buffalo firm, BeeDee Distributing, renaming it J&M Distributing Company. One year later Dotterwych Sales of Olean, New York, was purchased and renamed Allegany Beverage Corporation. These acquisitions allowed the company to ex-

pand both geographically and financially. Prior to these acquisitions the company had begun to diversify their holdings. To handle their vehicle and equipment requirements Niagara Leasing Corporation was formed in 1956 and in 1957 the Peter Certo Corporation was formed as a land and building development company and currently owns all of the facilities that the companies operate from.

Through the 1970s and early 1980s the company's growth was constant but limited. The year 1987 brought the first of two major additions to the organization. The Coors Brewing Company entered the New York market and appointed the Certos as its distributor for the

ABOVE: Certo Brothers employees receive their pay in silver dollars.

TOP LEFT: In this picture from 1956, Peter and Catherine Certo pose with their sons and daughters (from left) Al, Tony, Betty, Margaret, Mary, Ken, and Hank. All of the Certo's children had active roles in the company.

five western New York counties. The addition of the Coors brands helped strengthen the company's position in the marketplace, and in November 1990 in a dramatic and surprising move, the Genesee Brewing Company appointed J&M Distributing Company as its new distributor for most of Erie County. The addition of the Genesee brands doubled the volume of J&M Distributing.

Since the very beginning, Certo Brothers has pioneered a number of innovations. It was one of the first firms in the country to adopt a pre-order sales system. Although this was a radical move in the early 1960s, today more than 95 percent of all beer distributors nationwide are now preorder operations. There were many other innovations pioneered by the Certos, such as merchandising, electronic data processing, and side loading beverage delivery trucks. Continuous updating and modernization has been an important factor of its success.

The company's 24,000-square-foot headquarters was completed in December 1959.

As one might expect from such leadership, the firm has been very closely associated with its trade group, the New York State Beer Wholesaler Association. Albert J. Certo served two terms as president, and Peter I. Certo, Hank's son, held the office of chairman for three years, until 1990. The New York State Beer Wholesalers Association honored both Al and Hank in naming them the recipients of the "Sammy" Award, recognizing their commitment and contributions to the beer distribution industry. Al received his award in 1969 and Hank received his 20 years later.

Over the years there have been many changes in the industry, as well as its distributors. Brands of beer have faded and breweries have closed, but the one thing that has not changed, especially in this very close-knit business, is family involvement and loyalty. Unity has always been a key in the firm's success. Each of the three sons who entered the business developed expertise in different areas. Ken was president of the business from 1949 to 1954, and

later earned a reputation within the brewing industry as a draft beer specialist. He passed away in 1989. Albert served as president from 1954 until his death in 1980, and was in turn succeeded by brother Hank, who continues as president today.

Besides the three sons of Peter and Catherine Certo who were active in the business, three of their daughters also took an active role. Betty Pfleger continues as secretary/treasurer, while Mary Rolle and Margaret Serianni both served as office managers. Today there are 10 members of the third generation serving in various capacities of the company and as the firm enters the 1990s the fourth generation of the redoubtable family are now becoming involved in the business.

Another important ingredient to their success has been the dedication and loyalty of their employees. It has always been the philosophy of the company to treat their employees as "family." This was evident as Certo Brothers was one of the first employers in the area to provide medical coverage and also a pension plan for their employees.

From a small bottling plant on Walnut Avenue, Certo Brothers has grown to become an organization that includes three beer distributorships servicing all of western New York, a leasing company, a freight transportation company, a land development company, a fleet of more than 150 vehicles, and more than 250 loyal and hard-working employees.

Peter Certo died in 1974, but his dream lives on.

BRODA MACHINE COMPANY

Walter Broda (LEFT) and Martin Broda (RIGHT) were cofounders of Broda Machine Company and co-owners of the Plantation restaurant.

Broda Machine Company began in 1935 as a part-time wire coat hanger manufacturing business, after brothers Martin and Walter Broda perfected a machine to produce coat hangers. After several years in this business, working from a garage behind their home on 22nd Street in Niagara Falls, they gradually expanded into more general machining. By the time World War II broke out, Martin and Walter were out of the coat hanger business and full time into the production of parts for aircraft, machine guns, and other war-related items for companies such as Bell Aircraft, Curtis-Wright, and Buffalo Arms. The brothers officially incorporated as Broda Machine Company in 1942, with Martin as president and Walter as vice president.

In January 1946, Martin and Walter constructed a new building on the corner of Packard Road and Pine Avenue. The high quality of their machined parts work continued, as did their loyal following, with customers recommending Broda Machine to their business associates.

Looking to diversify, in 1951 the brothers bought the Plantation, a one-time Prohibition-era night spot located at the corner of Pine Avenue and Military Road. Under the direction of Walter Broda, who excelled in his dual roles as host to guests and talent scout for musical and

comedy groups, the Plantation got a new lease on life as a nightclub and restaurant. Later it became well known as a banquet facility for large parties and weddings. The Plantation's smorgasbords, three live bands, and a unique 12-foot-in-diameter "revolving banquet table" built by Broda Machine were special touches that combined to make the Plantation a Niagara Falls favorite. The family closed the Plantation in 1965, although it continued to own the site for many years.

Broda Machine had also had a closing of its own to contend with several years earlier, when New York State condemned its building to make way for Power Project construction in 1959. Rented space on McKenna Avenue served as home for the company for the next nine years. Continuing to dream of owning their own shop, the brothers purchased land on Lockport Road in the town of Niagara and moved into a new, 10,000-square-foot facility in July 1968.

Still in this location today, and under the leadership of Tom Broda, Walter's son, the 25-employee firm continues to produce high-quality, limited production parts for area and national customers. Given the Broda family's penchant for quality and hard work, that record of success will no doubt continue for many years to come.

The Broda brothers owned and ran the Plantation restaurant, located at Pine Avenue and Military Road.

HELMEL ENGINEERING PRODUCTS

Founder Erwin Helmel displays a prototype Checkmaster in its first trade-show appearance.

To Helmel Engineering Products, "paper thin" is actually pretty thick.

That's because the company's three-dimensional coordinate measuring machines (CMMs) can accurately measure as fine as .0001 of an inch—1/40th the thickness of a piece of paper. Invaluable to quality control, as well as to many other manufacturing processes, Helmel's CMMs provide fast, reliable, accurate dimensional information for companies throughout the world.

While measurement itself is as old as human endeavor, CMMs are a fairly recent innovation. Erwin Helmel, company founder, began working on the devices in the early 1970s as a project engineer for a Rochester-based firm. Recognizing the product's market potential and believing he could design and build a better device than his employer, Helmel incorporated in 1973.

Moonlighting with original partner Jim Whitlock in Whitlock's garage, the pair built an improved three-axis CMM and sold it to a division of General Electric. From there it became a full-time operation working at 12 Industrial Park Circle in the Town of Gates, its headquarters from 1973 through 1979.

Early on, Erwin Helmel had decided to move away from Rochester. One factor in this decision was his belief that the Niagara Falls area offered the company both a better labor pool and a more favorable economic climate. On January 1, 1980, Helmel opened the doors of its present location on Lockport Road in the town of Niagara.

The company developed its first computer-

assisted CMM, the Checkmaster, in 1981. A device introduced in 1988, the Microstar, goes a step further by being computer controlled. While the marketplace for CMMs is still primarily oriented to manually controlled machines, the firm estimates that the demand for computer-driven machines will account for more than 60 percent of its future sales.

Awareness of the need for computer support led to Helmel's 1985 purchase of Geomet, a computer software company in San Carlos, California. Geomet produces a universal CMM language software that allows machines to perform a variety of complicated tasks. As such, the inclusion of Geomet with Helmel CMMs represents a significant value-added feature.

Value-added also applies to the hardware in Helmel Engineering Products' machines. An example that symbolizes the company's quality-conscious approach to the business is its use of premium mechanical bearings, rather than air bearings, for their superior durability and dependability.

If the advances made since 1973 are any gauge, machines able to measure to the millionth of an inch will one day bear the Helmel name—and that will make this page look thick, indeed.

Helmel Engineering Products as it first appeared when it was built in 1980.

DCB ELEVATOR CO., INC.

Although Newton would have interpreted the phrase, "what goes up must come down," in terms of the laws of gravity, Dan and Dana Brockway would be more likely to think of it in terms of a potential new contract for their bustling firm, DCB Elevator Co., Inc.

Elevators have been in the DCB family (the initials stand for both Dana Cattarin Brockway and Daniel Clinton Brockway) since 1941, when Dana's father, Alfred Cattarin, started an elevator-maintenance business called AAC (his initials). Alfred Cattarin's first office was on Chippewa Street in Buffalo, a location that permitted him to bid on jobs in that city. In 1970 Cattarin opened a Niagara Falls branch office of AAC, and he started the AC Elevator Company in Rochester. The following year he purchased a competing firm called Elevator Maintenance of Buffalo.

In 1985 Alfred Cattarin retired, and rather than just hand the business over to his children: Anthony, Matthew, Tara, Dana, and Dana's husband, Daniel Brockway—Alfred decided it would be better for them if they went out and solicited AAC's clients themselves. This they did, regaining every one of AAC's clients under the new name of DCB Elevator Co., Inc.

Part of DCB's success can be tied to the fact that it is a family business that offers personal service. That includes making repair and service calls at all hours under all circumstances. One notable example was rescuing an elevator of 22 college students stuck between floors during the wee hours of a Sunday morning.

While the majority of its clients are in Niagara County, it still does a significant amount of business in Buffalo and Rochester. It also maintains a considerable number of high

rises, including the city's Veterans Administration hospital, U.S. courthouse, Dunn building, and the federal office building in Buffalo, and the 18-story Niagara Towers in the Falls.

Specialty work, which often includes the modernization of an existing elevator, is another important aspect of its activity. For instance, the company updated elevators manufactured in 1925 in Buffalo's old city courthouse, installing new controls while keeping the mechanical components intact.

For the future, DCB Elevator has formed a partnership with a manufacturer and set up a separate company called GTS (Gorge Transportation System) Associates to build and operate a "people mover" monorail system connecting downtown Niagara Falls with the river gorge. Dan and Dana Brockway call the system the opportunity of a lifetime—servicing and maintaining what is essentially the first "horizontal elevator" in Niagara Falls history.

ABOVE: (From left) Anthony Cattarin, Daniel C. Brockway, Dana C. Brockway, Tara Walker, and Matthew Cattarin.

LEFT: DCB's current project at New York State Power Authority.

WASTE TECHNOLOGY SERVICES, INC.

RIGHT: Waste Technology Services moved to 640 Park Place in 1985.

BELOW: (From left) Craig Avery, vice president; Judy Sahr Cline (seated) office manager; Gary Hall, president; and Mike Oliver, director of operations.

A literally sticky situation proved to be the perfect first job for Waste Technology Services, Inc.

A defunct molasses company had abandoned tanks with residual product in the construction path of an interstate highway. There was only one hitch: What had been estimated as a 100-ton cache of the slow-moving stuff turned out to be 11 times that size. Undaunted, WTS literally scooped it out and added sawdust and kilndust until the entire 2-million-pound problem was solved.

This choice of headquarters proved propitious when their previous employer sued them for $40 million after they had hired away Michael C. Oliver as their third partner. Although the suit was eventually dismissed, the "David vs. Goliath" case actually helped WTS gain recognition within the industry.

WTS' knowledge of the law goes far beyond lawsuits, however. As the 1980s brought forth a host of new rules and regulations regarding the handling and disposal of waste products, WTS responded by creating an ongoing environmental audit and compliance program to aid its clients.

Another notable aspect of Waste Technology Services is its yearly symposiums. These meetings bring together individuals from every level of their customers' businesses, and they have resulted in lively exchanges of information and a number of good, new ideas.

Since its beginning in November 1982, solving waste disposal problems has been WTS' specialty. It functions as an expert waste coordinator—a description that includes analyzing, indentifying, labeling, and packaging waste materials of all kinds, coordinating their transportation, and making arrangements for disposal. WTS' in-depth knowledge of the industry and its myriad regulations saves its more than 300 clients—including many *Fortune* 100 companies—hundreds of thousands of dollars each year.

WTS founding partners Gary P. Hall and Craig E. Avery had both the experience and the enthusiasm needed to get a new business off the ground in 1982, having just left jobs at a large, local waste disposal company. Their first offices were in space leased from their law firm at 730 Main Street in the Falls.

In October 1985, the company moved to its present location at 640 Park Place, a former funeral home. True to character, the old house had a few surprises in store for the new owners, including a casket in the basement that later served as the centerpiece for a combination housewarming/Halloween party.

Western New York natives and Niagara Falls boosters, WTS' partners believe that a small, well-run organization such as theirs need never leave the area in search of growth. And with its knowledge of the waste industry and regulatory climate and its "roll up your sleeves" philosophy, there's little reason to doubt that Waste Technology Services will be in the Falls for many years to come.

MAID OF THE MIST CORPORATION

The Prince of Wales boarded it in 1860, becoming the first in a long line of the rich and famous to do so, and it was a princess—the legendary Lelawala of the Ongiara native American tribe—for whom this oldest of Niagara Falls tourist attractions was named.

Sent over the Falls in a birchbark canoe to appease the gods as a sacrifice to end the scourge afflicting her tribe, she has reigned as the Maid of the Mist from that day forward.

The reign of the boat by the same name began in 1846. After two years of service as a steamboat ferry, the *Maid*'s owners instituted the trips close to the Falls that continue today.

A larger, more luxurious *Maid* was launched in 1854, but financial difficulties forced its owner to sell it by auction in 1861; a condition of the sale was that it would be delivered into Lake Ontario. The dangerous journey to Lake Ontario required a trip through some of the most treacherous whitewater rapids in the world. Captain Joel Robinson safely guided the *Maid* through the hazardous rapids in only 17 minutes, but the the captain's wife said Robinson looked 20 years older when he came home.

In 1884 R.F. Carter and Frank LeBlond of Clifton, Ontario, invested $10,000 in a *Maid of the Mist*, adding a sister ship in 1892. Carter and LeBlond were partners until Carter's death in 1917. The LeBlond family continued to operate both ships until 1971.

The boats miraculously survived a great ice jam in 1938, the especially cold year when the seasonal freezing of Lake Erie caused the ships to be encased in ice—even though they were on shore for the winter. The ice that crept up on the river banks threatened to crush the boats, but in the spring the ice melted and unbelievably left the ships undamaged. Seventeen winters later, again while the boats were out of the water and not in service, an errant welder's torch set both *Maids* ablaze while he was replacing some planks on the boat's hull. The fire damaged the boats beyond repair.

Just three months later, however, on July 28, 1955, a new, all-steel *Maid* was launched. In 1956 it was joined by an identical sister ship. They were christened *Maid of the Mist I* and

Maid of the Mist II, although they were actually the fifth and sixth vessels to bear the name.

In 1971 James V. Glynn of Lewiston, New York, who began working for the Maid of the Mist Corporation when he was 16 years old, purchased the company from Frank LeBlond and other stockholders, and beginning shortly after this purchase, the "fleet" grew steadily. *Maid of the Mist III* began operation in 1972; *Maid IV* in 1976; *Maid V* in 1983; and *Maid VI* in 1990. *Maid I* and *Maid II*, meanwhile, were removed from service in 1983 and 1990, respectively.

Besides the Prince of Wales (later King Edward VII), other notables who have been aboard the *Maid of the Mist* include Teddy Roosevelt, who praised it in an early-1900s guidebook; Marilyn Monroe, who rode it during the making of the movie *Niagara* in 1952; and Roger Woodward, who was rescued by the *Maid* after a boating accident that caused him to drop over the Falls wearing only a life jacket in 1960. Woodward, along with his sister and his uncle, had moved close to the brink of the Falls when the boat experienced engine failure. Woodward's sister was rescued before being swept over the Falls by the strong currents, but Woodward and his uncle were not. His uncle tragically did not survive the accident, but Roger Woodward, at 7 years old, weathered the fall to be pulled aboard the *Maid of the Mist*. Woodward has recently come back to Niagara Falls and has taken his son aboard the *Maid* that rescued him as a child.

ABOVE: Maid of the Mist *ships have toured the Falls since 1846.*

TOP: Maid of the Mist IV, *which began operation in 1976, and* Maid of the Mist VI, *the most recent addition to the fleet, tour Niagara Falls.*

JOHN W. DANFORTH COMPANY

Michael Adams (left) and Martin Adams, Jr.

Consider the following list of names. Many, if not all, will be familiar to anyone who has ever been to Niagara Falls: Model City, Du Pont, Summit Park Mall, Goodyear, St. Mary's Hospital, Occidental Chemical, Bell Aerospace, Niagara Hilton (Radisson), NIACHLOR, Rainbow Mall, and Memorial Medical Center.

What these companies have in common is a company named John W. Danforth. Closely associated with the construction of many of the largest projects in Niagara Falls and western New York for more than a century, Danforth's client roster is a true "who's who" of Niagara County business and industry.

Founder of the firm was John Willison Danforth, an engineer who started the company that bears his name today and was incorporated in 1884. Today, working from offices in both Niagara Falls and Buffalo, the John W. Danforth Company's many specialties include industrial process piping, central heating and power systems, nuclear reactors, plumbing, and fire protection—a long way from its beginnings.

By the turn of the twentieth century, the company had begun to concentrate on the installation of high-pressure boiler and heating equipment in larger buildings—including such Buffalo institutions as the Twentieth Century Club and Westminster Presbyterian Church. A newer Buffalo institution—Pilot Field—also ties

into both Danforth's recent and past history. Not only did the company install the new baseball facility's heating, air conditioning, plumbing, and sprinkler and irrigation systems, but it also did so on familiar ground: the area around third base at Pilot Field is the exact location of Danforth's original Buffalo office, at 72 Elliott Street. Today the company's Buffalo address is 1940 Fillmore Avenue; in Niagara Falls, it is located at 560 56th Street.

John W. Danforth was a firm believer in unionization, a tradition the company continues in its second century. In 1889 he became a charter member of the Master Steam and Hot Water Fitters Association of the United States, which evolved into the Heating Piping Contractors National Association of America, Inc. Today the company is still a proud union contractor, working with Local 129 of the United Association of Journeymen & Apprentices of the Plumbing & Pipefitting Industry.

John W. Danforth's leadership of the company continued until his death in 1911. Under the leadership of his son and successor, N. Loring Danforth, the company continued its rapid growth.

A graduate of MIT, N. Loring Danforth immediately broadened the company's scope from residential to industrial/commercial work by soliciting work as a general contractor. This contributed greatly to the company's growth, as it

One of J.W. Danforth's largest Niagara Falls projects was the design and construction of the desulfurization test center at the NYS Electric & Gas facility in Somerset.

took on projects throughout the eastern United States, including power stations, hotels, and numerous government and municipal buildings.

Upon his death in 1936, N. Loring was succeeded by Leo N. Hopkins, previously vice president of the company. As N. Loring had done before him, Hopkins also added new specialities to the company's repertoire, notably the installation of process piping for area and national manufacturers of chemical, rubber, and steel products. It was this specialization, in part, which led to Danforth's long list of projects in the Niagara Falls area. Among the company's early clients were the Pathfinder Chemical Corporation (today known as Goodyear), Hooker Chemical Corporation (now Occidental Chemical), Stauffer Chemical, and Bell Aircraft Corporation.

Business in the Falls was extensive enough to warrant the opening of a regional office there in 1946, located at 234 12th Street under the direction of Clifford J. Carroll. Carroll joined the John W. Danforth Company in 1946, after completing two years on the Manhattan Project in Oak Ridge, Tennessee.

Carroll developed a strong relationship with the area's chemical and food processing industry. Upon his retirement in 1980, he was succeeded by the current branch manager and company vice president, Karl M. Bykowski. In 1985 the office was moved to its present 56th Street location.

As John Danforth had been succeeded by his son N. Loring, Leo Hopkins was also succeeded by his son, L. Nelson Hopkins, Jr., in 1964. The company had prospered under the tenure of Hopkins and would continue to do so under his son.

A number of new opportunities immediately presented themselves to the company's fourth leader. Danforth's involvement in the cleanup of Love Canal, still an ongoing project in the early 1990s, enhanced its reputation for environmental expertise. The company was also one of the first in the nation to obtain a license from the Atomic Energy Commission to use radioactive isotopes to do leak-detection work.

Another specialty Danforth developed was work for "white rooms"—dust-free, controlled research environments for such companies as

Bell Aerospace and Westinghouse. Fire protection, which called upon the company's long experience in installing fire pumps and sprinkler systems, was yet another new field opened up to the company at this time.

Danforth's innovative and thorough approach to the business has not gone unnoticed.

One of its many projects in the Niagara Falls area has been the design and construction of the desulfurization test center at the NYS Electric & Gas facility in Somerset. For its work there, which began in 1984, the company received the prestigious American Academy of Environmental Engineering's 1989 Award for Excellence in Environmental Engineering.

Today, under the direction of Wayne R. Reilly, its fifth CEO and chairman; Donald V. Brown, president; and aided by the Niagara Falls leadership of Karl Bykowski, company vice president, the company has continued to grow. During Reilly's tenure, annual revenues increased to $32.9 million. Today total employment includes more than 250 skilled trade workers and 60 professional and support staff. And geographical expansion has included the acquisition of Rochester-based Dineen Mechanical Contractors, Inc., in 1980 and Syracuse-based Nova Mechanical in 1988.

Building upon these impressive numbers, the John W. Danforth Company is well under way on its second century of excellence in construction.

ABOVE: Karl Bykowski is the company vice president and part of the Niagara Falls leadership team.

TOP: Clifford J. Carroll (center) has always kept a helping hand in the community.

THE CARBORUNDUM COMPANY

Luiz F. Kahl, president of The Carborundum Company.

The William H. Wendel Technical Center in Niagara Falls is a center of research and development.

The tiny sparkling crystals were not exactly the synthetic diamonds he had hoped to create, but they proved to be a "diamond in the rough" nonetheless.

The year was 1891, and Edward Goodrich Acheson, an energetic young inventor, had just created silicon carbide, the first man-made abrasive. Erroneously thinking he had mixed carbon with corundum (aluminum oxide), he named his product and his company Carborundum. Thus began a tradition of inventiveness and innovation that has remained strong for more than 100 years.

While the crystals Acheson had made were not the diamonds he was looking for, they were hard enough to cut diamonds, and the inventor recognized their commercial possibilities. Gem cutters became his first customers, and soon dentists were also taking advantage of the super-hard substance. Sales to such clients were brisk but not profitable, and Acheson turned his attention to another market: manufacturers who used grinding wheels in their production processes. In 1893 he secured a $7,000 contract from Westinghouse Electric for 60,000 wheels to be used to grind parts for light bulbs. This venture yielded Carborundum's first profit.

In 1895 Acheson learned of the abundant, inexpensive power available in Niagara Falls—power he needed to produce large volumes of the silicon carbide crystals. Carborundum became one of the first companies to sign a contract with the New York Power Authority. Soon after, Acheson moved Carborundum from Pennsylvania to Niagara Falls and received funding from prominent financier Andrew W. Mellon.

Acheson left Carborundum in 1899, but before he did, he pioneered yet another important business trend—international expansion. He accomplished this with the formation of Carborundum's first international subsidiary in Niagara Falls, Ontario. By 1906 Carborundum had sales operations in seven countries and had opened its first overseas plant in Germany.

Mellon continued to support his investment after Acheson's departure from the company, hiring engineer/inventor Frank J. Tone to add his skills to the Carborundum operation. Tone, who was to serve as the company's president from 1919 to 1942, pioneered the mass production of silicon carbide and the use of synthetic abrasives to grind wood commercially. He is credited with recognizing that electrically heat-fused materials such as silicon carbide might have application in the refractory industry. However, the full realization of this market's potential was to wait many years and two world wars. Under Tone's guidance, the market for The Carborundum Company's abrasive products continued to expand at a remarkable pace.

The production demands of World War I pushed Carborundum to expand its operating

capacity, and by the war's end, the company's annual sales reached $11 million. A steady expansion followed. In 1927 Carborundum bought the American Resistor Corporation of Milwaukee and entered the nonmetallic electric heating and resistor business. The new acquisition was moved to Niagara Falls and renamed the Globar® Division, after "globar" heating and resistor elements. By producing Globar® silicon carbide heating elements, Carborundum introduced improved products that quickly gained worldwide prominence as a clean, efficient means of controlling temperatures in a wide variety of furnaces. The company's Electric Products Division continues to manufacture Globar® heating elements today at its manufacturing facility on Hyde Park Boulevard in Niagara Falls.

World War II brought another production explosion to Carborundum's abrasives area. Sales reached $52 million in 1943, with Carborundum supplying more than 100,000 different abrasive products to the war effort.

The postwar period called for major internal restructuring and further diversification. Tony Clark, Carborundum's president from 1947 to 1952, announced a $20-million improvement plan 20 minutes after his first election to that office. Among his planned projects was the much-needed refurbishing of the Buffalo Avenue complex following the demanding war years. Clark's program modernized Carborundum plants and streamlined production.

Following Clark as president, Clinton Robinson began an aggressive worldwide expansion program that continued throughout his tenure, from 1952 until 1962. Carborundum plants were established in Mexico, Brazil, Argentina, Puerto Rico, South Africa, Australia, India, and France, and subsidiaries and interests were purchased in Europe and Japan.

Robinson was also instrumental in expand-

ing Carborundum's influence into new product areas as well as new marketplaces. In 1952 he created Carborundum Metals Co., Inc., which contracted with the Atomic Energy Commission to produce zirconium and hafnium for use in nuclear reactors. Robinson also brought the company into the ceramic-based electrical materials market and the polishing and buffing materials industry by making key acquisitions in these areas. His establishment of the Electro Minerals Division to manufacture and market raw silicon carbide, fused alumina crudes, and abrasive grains firmly established the company's market position.

After Robinson's death in 1962, William H. Wendel became president of Carborundum, which by then had become the world's largest abrasives operation. Wendel recognized that with the maturation of the abrasives industry, Carborundum needed to shift its focus in order to grow.

The potential for sales to the refractory market, targeted by Frank Tone in the 1920s, came to fruition through Wendel's emphasis on diversification. A ceramic fiber called Fiberfrax® was discovered in 1942 when Carborundum scientist J.C. "Charlie" McMullen poured aluminum oxide past a directed air stream, forming ceramic fibers. By adding sand and other materials to McMullen's original substance, Carborundum's development team created a fiber finer than human hair, one that could retain its chemical and physical identity at 3,000 degrees Fahrenheit (a temperature high enough to melt iron). By the early 1960s, Fiberfrax® ceramic fiber was lining furnaces, kilns, and ovens throughout the world. Although abrasives still represented more than two-thirds of Carborundum's revenue, Fiberfrax® ensured the company's place in the fast-growing market for new ceramic technology.

Wendel took a systematic approach in expanding Carborundum's product base. He supported a concept called "vectored growth" by which the company made acquisitions and developed new materials by building on established skills and resources. Following this "like complements like" approach, Carborundum

LEFT: The silicon carbide crystals Acheson had made were hard enough to cut diamonds, and the inventor sold them to gem cutters, dentists, and manufacturers who used grinding wheels in their production processes.

BELOW: In 1891 Edward Goodrich Acheson created silicon carbide crystals, the first man-made abrasive. He named his product and his company Carborundum.

Carborundum's Combat® boron nitride is produced in solid, powder, liquid, or spray form.

Products made of Hexoloy® silicon carbide are easily shaped, can hold that shape under stress, and are less expensive to produce than similar ceramic products.

bought the Lockport Felt Company, a felt hat maker, in 1965. With this new acquisition, Carborundum obtained the weaving techniques necessary to manufacture new products using its ceramic fibers. Another acquisition was the purchase of Spode China, the English manufacturer of fine ceramic dinnerware. Carborundum, with its expertise in manufacturing heat-resistant products, improved Spode's products by matching Carborundum's skills with the production capabilities of an established and related industry.

During this period the team concept of customer-driven product development was cultured. A project team managed the company's responses to changes in customer requirements, developing a new product and then following that product from research and development into the marketplace. The company's support for R&D brought it 28 awards for its work in the development of technically significant products.

Near the end of the "Wendel years," Carborundum scientists invented another breakthrough product. Under the trademark Hexoloy®, the silicon carbide-based material heralded the company's entry into the field of structural ceramics. Products made of Hexoloy® silicon carbide could be easily shaped, could hold that shape under stress, and were less expensive to produce than similar ceramic products.

Anticipating public concern for the environment, the company entered into the pollution control and energy conservation markets. The company acquired a major filter supply company, developed activated carbon compounds for wastewater treatment, and developed and manufactured a silicon carbide igniter to eliminate energy-draining appliance pilot lights. Carborundum also distinguished itself as one of the top three global producers of bauxite proppant, a product that reduces the amount of time required to obtain oil and gas from the deeper, high-pressure wells upon which the world would increasingly depend. Carborundum had long been active in the affairs of the Niagara Falls community, and in 1964 Wendel followed that tradition with the founding of the Society for the Preservation and Urban Renewal (SPUR) of Niagara to promote economic progress in the area. Under his leadership SPUR was the driving force behind such major urban renewal projects as the Niagara Falls Convention Center, the Hilton hotel (now the Radisson), the 82-acre Rainbow Center, and Carborundum's six-story corporate headquarters.

By the mid-1970s Carborundum's operating and financial record had made it an attractive target for acquisition. In 1977 Kennecott Copper Corporation purchased Carborundum. Four years later Kennecott itself was acquired, by Standard Oil of Ohio (SOHIO). SOHIO provided support for Carborundum research and development, focusing on meeting the demands of the growing ceramic business rather than those of the mature abrasives business. To support this change in emphasis to ceramic technology, Carborundum's abrasive-related divisions were sold in 1983, and its electro-minerals operations in 1986.

Today, under the leadership of Luiz F. Kahl, president of Carborundum since 1984, the company has made significant incursions into promising new ceramics markets with advanced structural and electronic applications. In 1987 Carborundum established two new electronic ceramics facilities: a production plant in Sanborn, New York, to manufacture computer circuit platforms from aluminum nitride, and a plant in Amherst, New York, to manufacture boron nitride-based products. And in 1990 its latest investment in electronics was opened in Phoenix, Arizona, for the development of highly advanced microelectronic com-

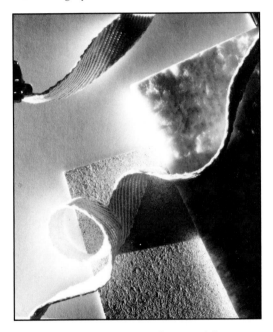

ponents. Through the manufacture of these advanced products, Carborundum is shaping its own future.

Continually modernizing manufacturing operations to maintain the company's competitive edge in its core businesses has also been a major focus under Kahl. New manufacturing capacity added in its international operations in Brazil, England, Germany, and Australia have boosted the company's output of refractory and ceramic products. In addition, new operations in Niagara and Erie counties have continued to upgrade production capacity and strengthen the company's position in domestic markets.

That future will most certainly include continuing involvement in the Niagara Falls community. A recent example of this is

Carborundum Centennial Park, located along the Niagara River rapids and part of the Niagara Frontier State Park, created for public enjoyment, and dedicated in 1991 in honor of the company's 100 years of community service.

Today, as part of British Petroleum and its BP Chemicals group, The Carborundum Company continues to thrive. With worldwide employment figures reaching 4,500 people, and western New York employment figures reaching 1,200, the company remains a dominant force in industry. Its expertise in advanced ceramics technology ensures that it will retain that place, as it helps answer world need for specialty materials and products to meet the demanding design requirements of new products and processes on the drawing boards of tomorrow.

In September 1991, The Carborundum Company celebrated 100 years of achievement—a proud Niagara Falls heritage sure to continue.

ABOVE:
Carborundum® igniters.

FAR LEFT: In the 1940s Carborundum created Fiberfrax® , a fiber that could retain its chemical and physical identity at 3,000 degrees Fahrenheit. By the early 1960s Fiberfrax® ceramic fiber was lining furnaces, kilns, and ovens throughout the world and ensured the company's place in the fast-growing market for new ceramic technology.

LEFT: By producing Globar® silicon carbide heating elements, Carborundum introduced a clean, efficient means of controlling temperatures in a wide variety of furnaces. The company continues to manufacture Globar® heating elements in Niagara Falls.

NIAGARA COUNTY
INDUSTRIAL DEVELOPMENT AGENCY

ABOVE: The company's IRB program continues to stimulate economic development in Niagara County. Holiday Inn used this program to finance a new facility in Niagara Falls.

RIGHT: The newest multi-tenant facility nearing completion, located just outside Niagara Falls. This project was funded through NCIDA's Industrial Revenue Bond program.

Creating new jobs is the Niagara County Industrial Development Agency's goal. Established in 1972 by the Niagara County legislature, the NCIDA "is empowered to actively promote, attract, encourage, and develop economically sound commerce and industry, thereby advancing job opportunities, general prosperity, and economic welfare for the residents of Niagara County." Since its inception, the NCIDA has pursued those worthy goals with admirable results.

A nonprofit corporation, the NCIDA offers financial and incentive programs to support start-up companies, attract new businesses, and encourage the expansion of existing firms within Niagara County. Governed by a nine-member board of directors, the NCIDA is staffed by economic development professionals from diverse backgrounds.

Under its first executive director, Irving Clark, the agency began as a traditional bond-issuing entity. Its Industrial Revenue Bond (IRB) program continues to stimulate economic development in Niagara County, offering long-term, fixed-asset financing for capital expansion of existing businesses. The program helps businesses build additional facilities or warehouses,

acquire another firm, or purchase new equipment by providing them with relief from property taxes, mortgage recording taxes, or sales tax on construction materials. IRBs are secured by a first mortgage on the property, a lease between the NCIDA and the company, and the company's guarantee of bond payment.

The success of the IRB program shows in its numbers. During 1989 a record $111,866,545 in bonds were issued, surpassing the total of bonds issued for the previous five years. More than 50 percent of NCIDA bonds—56 out of 108—have been issued since 1984, and the impetus these bonds have provided to business has resulted in the creation of 2,500 jobs.

Many prominent Niagara County firms have received NCIDA bonds. The largest bond to date

was one for $93 million issued to the United Development Group for construction of a co-generation plant in Niagara Falls. With that bond, the NCIDA was ranked the eighth-largest IDA in New York State for bond issuance during the period 1984 to 1989. Among the many other familiar organizations to which the NCIDA has provided support are American Biorganics, which in 1989 utilized an NCIDA bond for $413,000 to construct a new facility in the Summit Business Park; Benderson Development, which received a bond for a factory outlet mall expansion; Pyron Corporation, for the construction of a production facility; and Wurlitzer Industrial Park, to assist in the renovation of an industrial complex.

In 1985 the NCIDA established another financing method: the direct loan program. This program provides low cost "gap" financing for firms unable to finance job-creating projects through conventional sources. In 1989 the

NCIDA's direct loan program helped create 90 new jobs in Niagara County.

With the entrance in 1984 of a new executive director, Leo Nowak, the NCIDA initiated a marketing program designed to lure new business to the county. NCIDA advertising and video promotions have helped spread the word about the attractive business opportunities and comfortable way of life available in Niagara County. The NCIDA participates in Germany's Hannover Fair, one of the world's largest trade shows, to promote Niagara County to European companies. In 1990 the NCIDA expanded its advertising campaign into Japan.

In response to the opening in 1989 of the Niagara County Foreign Trade Zone, and the signing of the United States-Canada Free Trade Agreement, the NCIDA is increasing its marketing of Niagara County to its nearest neighbor, Canada. Through the establishment of a Foreign Trade Zone, Niagara County can offer many advantages to companies dealing in international trade. The Free Trade Agreement provides Canadian businesses with access to U.S. markets, enabling them to open a branch office on the U.S. side of the border and yet manage it from their Canadian headquarters.

The NCIDA, acting as master leaseholder, demonstrated in 1986 the feasibility of international business by financing the construction of the first industrial development project in the Foreign Trade Zone. The planned Rainbow Industrial Centre was designed to provide office space for foreign firms wishing to expand into the United States. The project's success was quickly assured: It was 100 percent occupied

within six months of opening. Two other buildings targeted to Canadian tenants have since been built, and another is nearing completion. The construction and ultimate occupancy of those buildings have brought hundreds of job opportunities to the area.

Another effect of the Free Trade Agreement, capitalized upon by the NCIDA is the increasing number of Canadian retail shoppers in the United States. To meet the needs of this growing customer base, the NCIDA has issued financing to support the expansion or construction of several Niagara County businesses, including the Factory Outlet Mall, Zayre's (now Ames) Plaza, the Rainbow Square Mall, and most of the hotels built recently in Niagara Falls to accommodate Canadian trade.

To further promote expansion in Niagara County, the NCIDA offers yet another option to would-be residents. It gives special financial, energy, and tax incentives for those interested in building in the Niagara Falls Economic Development Zone. Located in the city's north end, this parcel of land, though economically depressed today, has the potential for successful industrial development.

It is estimated that one out of every 10 people in Niagara County works for a firm that has been assisted by the Niagara County Industrial Development Agency. Credited with assisting in the completion of more than 50 construction or expansion projects, and with the creation of more than 3,000 jobs, the NCIDA has proven its ability to meet its stated goals.

A warehouseman moves stock in the main warehouse at Niagara County Foreign Trade Zone (FTZ) #34, located just outside Niagara Falls at the Niagara Falls International Airport. The FTZ operator has received funds through the NCIDA Revolving Loan Fund program.

Cascades Paper, located in the former Kimberly-Clark plant in Niagara Falls, utilized the IRB program through NCIDA to expand its organization.

NIAGARA WAX MUSEUM

RIGHT: Founded in 1961, the museum has attracted thousands of visitors. Pictured here is the museum's new Prospect Street location.

BELOW: Paul Morden, Niagara Wax Museum founder.

While stationed outside London during World War II, a young Niagara Falls native named Paul Morden happened to pay a visit to Madame Tousards' Wax Museum. Inspired by this unique concept and soaked in the lore of tradition-rich Niagara Falls, he decided that someday, he would bring history to life back in his hometown.

Thus was born the idea for the Niagara Wax Museum, and since 1961, literally thousands of visitors have walked through the pages of history with the help of the museum's 46 exhibits, which feature life-size wax figures and historical artifacts of many kinds.

Paul Morden, who runs the museum with his wife, Louise, comes from a family with a long history in the Niagara Falls tourist industry.

His father, Sanford Morden, entered the tourism business in the early 1900s with a multi-seated horse-drawn rig for sightseers. With the coming of the internal combustion engine, he established the Niagara Scenic Bus Lines for tourists and formed a joint venture with a Canadian firm to offer tours of both the American and Canadian sides of the Falls. Sanford Morden's company also sold tours aboard a fleet of 24 seven-passenger Pierce Arrow cars to arriving railroad passengers. The elder Morden ventured into souvenir and gift shops as well, and operated the Niagara Falls museum for its owners. Following in the foot-

steps of this enterprising man were three sons: Sanford, Ted (both deceased), and Paul.

After a year spent selecting wax figures and locating historical objects for background scenery, Paul and Louise opened their wax museum in the the Old Falls Garage, not far from its present location on Prospect Street.

Among the exhibits the museum brings to life are an Iroquois Indian bark house; Joncaire's Mill, the first commercial use of the area's water power in 1759; the Devil's Hole massacre; Old Fort Niagara; a fire hall dating back to the 1880s; and thrilling scenes depicting some of the daredevils who challenged the Falls. One of the museum's biggest crowd pleasers is an exhibit representing Roger Woodward, who survived a plunge over the Falls wearing only a life preserver.

Seventeen years after the museum first opened, the Old Falls Garage was razed as part of the urban renewal in downtown Niagara Falls. After a brief hiatus, the Niagara Wax Museum was relocated in a new building on Prospect Street, its present location. Today, besides the museum, the building houses souvenir and gift stores, a photo shop where people can have their picture taken while appearing to go over the Falls in a barrel, and a snack shop.

Paul Morden clearly inherited his father's entrepreneurial spirit. Combined with his love of the past, that spirit has enabled visitors far and wide to marvel not only at the Falls themselves, but also at the rich history that lies behind them.

M&T BANK

"Ours is a commitment that goes beyond banking to improve the quality of life in areas that we serve." Since M&T Bank began in 1856 as the Manufacturers and Traders Bank, improving the quality of life through its banking and community services has been its primary goal.

During its first half century, M&T provided those services to small and growing business enterprises in Buffalo, a city then booming. In 1902 Manufacturers and Traders Bank merged with Merchants Bank of Buffalo, and, in 1916, it acquired the Third National Bank. A merger in 1925 with the Fidelity Trust Company, a major financial underwriter for the Peace Bridge con-

An M&T branch in 1964 (far left) and the same building today (left).

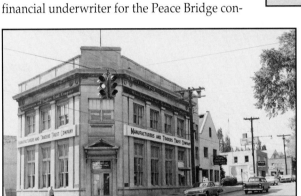

struction project, established the name of Manufacturers and Traders Trust Company.

M&T expanded into Niagara Falls following the Depression, when it acquired the property of Falls National Bank. M&T Bank chartered its Niagara Falls operation at the Portage Road site on June 1, 1939.

Gerry Sdao, an employee at that first Niagara Falls branch, remembers visiting the post office each day to purchase stamps for the bank, and walking checks drawn on Marine Bank to that bank's office on Falls Street. She also recalls the hectic end-of-month activities, as M&T employees carefully prepared customer statements by hand. Over the years M&T has maintained that level of customer service and its number of customers: More than five decades later, two of the first four customers at M&T's Portage Road office still hold accounts there.

The opening of the Portage Road branch was a catalyst for the establishment of other M&T branches in Niagara Falls. The North Main

branch opened in 1953 and served the community for three decades before it closed. In 1956 a third branch was opened on Falls Street. Twenty years later it was relocated to Main Street, where today it is known as the Main-Cedar branch. A Military Road branch followed in 1964, while the most recent of M&T's Niagara Falls branches was established in the Summit Park Mall in 1972.

Today, as the largest subsidiary of First Empire State Corporation, M&T is a financial force in upstate New York, providing its services to more than 250,000 households and businesses. Its 68 offices and more than 2,200 employees make it a leading employer; its $7.6 billion in assets (as of June 30, 1991) supports its position as a leading home mortgage lender.

But M&T's phenomenal growth has not changed its dedication to the communities that it serves. Whether approving the financing of a first home, providing savings options that help realize future dreams, or offering financial support to new businesses, M&T continues to place the highest priority on improving its customers' quality of life.

The North Main branch opened in 1953 and served the community for three decades before it closed.

NIAGARA COUNTY COMMUNITY COLLEGE

RIGHT: NCCC's first home—"Nabisco Tech"—in Niagara Falls.

The phase "from little acorns mighty oaks grow" is applicable to the evolution of Niagara County Community College over the past 29 years.

From its beginnings in 1962 to the present day, NCCC has been a success story in higher education and a tribute to the people of Niagara County. The college is woven into the fabric of life on the Niagara frontier and is regarded statewide and nationally as a premier community college.

The short time frame of 24 months in which NCCC was founded, was called a "miracle of accomplishment."

Those miracles continue.

Interest in a community college for Niagara County was first evidenced in 1959—the result of a study of state community colleges conducted by Edward Pawenski, North Tonawanda supervisor. Although Pawenski was convinced that Niagara County needed a community college of its own, the county's board of supervisors turned down the proposal, citing recent costs for other facilities such as a new jail, hospital, and golf course. But cost notwithstanding, this was an idea whose time had come.

In October 1961 the Youngstown Civic Guild revived the idea and formed a survey committee to poll area schools, parents, and employers to determine their support. The report of its findings—highly positive—was

given to the board of trustees of the State University of New York for approval. The *sine qua non* of starting the school—passing a resolution in the Niagara County board of supervisors—was achieved by the narrowest of margins when a motion made to table the resolution lost by a tie vote. On paper NCCC had become a reality. All that was needed was for SUNY trustees to formally approve the charter for the new community college, and this they did on November 8, 1962.

Within two months, trustees had been appointed. The county government selected five people: Arnold Dutton, Albert Certo, Eugene Swenson, John von Lonkhuyzen, and Edward Pawenski. Governor Nelson Rockefeller appointed the remaining four: Harry Jordan, Samuel Porrath, Bernard Raysor, and Gertrude Tresselt.

Next, a president, Dr. Ernest Notar, then dean of the Erie County Technical Institute, was selected. His credentials were particularly appropriate for the new college. Besides having helped oversee ECTI's move to its new campus, Dr. Notar had also written his doctoral dissertation on community colleges and had an engineering background.

The matter of finances was resolved after some debate. Since the board of supervisors of Niagara County would have to raise $114,000 to open the college, as well as $273,000 for the first year of operation, it struck a compromise with the college's newly appointed trustees. In return

State and local officials cut the ribbons to the new Trott Access Center, a cooperative effort between the college and county, in Niagara Falls in 1989.

for its assistance, the board would have a say in the financial running of the college.

The matter that caused the most debate, however, was the question of where to locate the college. In the early months, Dr. Notar and his secretary had been working from the Parkway Inn (now the Ramada) on Buffalo Avenue in Niagara Falls. The trustees determined that the most economically feasible location was right across the street—in Nabisco's old Shredded Wheat building. This earned the college the nickname, "Nabisco Tech."

Many supplies, furniture, and even a flagpole were donated by local corporate sponsors. Books were obtained from the Fort Niagara library and from book drives, and faculty members were recruited.

Finally, on September 30, 1963, Dr. Notar symbolically opened the college's front door to its first class. In contrast to the 40 curricula of study offered today, the 343 students could select from just five: accounting; secretarial science; electrical technology; liberal arts, humanities, and social sciences; and liberal arts, mathematics, and science.

As enrollment increased, other buildings

were added to the campus, including the former Third Street School, three homes on Buffalo Avenue, the former Olin Laboratory, and the Waldorf-Niagara Motel. The need for a permanent home became evident.

During the ensuing search, no fewer than 18 different locations were nominated, investigated, and debated. In the end, a location to which "all roads led" was chosen. NCCC's permanent home in Sanborn is approximately equidistant from Niagara Falls, North Tonawanda, and Lockport. The cornerstone of its first building was laid in September 1970; classes began in spring 1973.

The campus, designed by Dr. Notar, demonstrates his foresight. It consists of eight interconnected buildings, with ramps for handicapped students. Three distinctive courtyards formed by this layout bring natural light to all parts of the campus and contribute to its striking architecture.

Since 1963 student enrollment has increased to more than 5,500 persons, with a faculty of 210. Reaching out to nontraditional students, including minorities and older students, has been a major factor in NCCC's growth. Noncredit courses attract an additional 15,000. Special community programs, such as CEOSC (Comprehensive Employment Occupational Support Center), which has provided education to more than 200 social service recipients with children, provide positive benefits to the area. And since 1981,

NCCC's corporate training department, Technical Assistant Center, and Small Business Development Center have worked hand in hand with area businesses to offer custom-designed training courses in subjects as diverse as robotics, customer relations, and asbestos removal. All in all, each year, NCCC in some way affects 25 percent of the county's population.

The college's fourth president, Gerald Miller, was inaugurated on November 27, 1989. Miller is the first president to grow up with the college, having first started teaching there in 1966.

Geographically, culturally, and intellectually, all roads do lead to Niagara County Community College.

ABOVE: Dr. Ernest Notar, the college's original president, in front of the administration building at NCCC's permanent home in Sanborn.

LEFT: Gerald Miller, current president, greets a student during his annual student appreciation luncheon, where college administrators serve the students a Thanksgiving dinner.

NIAGARA UNIVERSITY

The Castellani Art Museum opened in September 1990 and houses a collection of more than 3,000 paintings, drawings, sculptures, and prints. The works represent the major aesthetic trends in modern art from the nineteenth century to the present.

Men of God have long been associated with Niagara Falls. The first European to see the cataracts was the seventeenth-century Franciscan named Father Louis Hennepin. And it was another European priest, Father Vincent de Paul, whose teachings in the seventeenth century led to the founding of Niagara University in 1856.

The forerunner of NU was neither in Niagara Falls nor a university, however.

Originally known as Our Lady of Angeles Seminary, located on Best Street in Buffalo, the institution was founded as a seminary by the Vincentian religious order that continues to sponsor the university today.

The seminary moved to a 100-acre farm on Monteagle Ridge—NU's present site—in May 1857. Five years later, its first building, Clet Hall, was erected. A second edifice, Alumni Hall, went up in 1872; but it had to be rebuilt three times, when fires in 1889, 1898, and 1913 caused extensive damage.

Although chartered by the New York legislature in 1863 to confer degrees, it was not until 20 years later that New York State Governor Grover Cleveland signed the documents that changed the seminary to Niagara University. From the very beginning, NU was—and continues to be—a first-rate school, as evidenced by the success of its 20,000 active alumni.

Its Niagara Medical College, opened in 1883, was the first institution in New York State to require four years of study for a medical degree. It merged with the University of Buffalo in 1898, having graduated 137 doctors in its 15-year existence. Buffalo Law School opened in 1887 as part of NU; four years later, it joined the law school of the University of Buffalo.

Mens sana in corpore sano might have been one of NU's early mottos, for it has encouraged participation in sports from its inception. The first intercollegiate basketball game was played at NU in 1905, and a number of its graduates have gone on to careers in the National Basketball Association, including coaches Frank Layden (Utah Jazz), Hubie Brown (New York Knicks), and Larry Costello (Milwaukee Bucks), as well as former Houston Rockets player and all-time NU leading scorer Calvin Murphy.

Over the years, Niagara University has established a number of important educational programs. The College of Business Administration opened in 1930 and the College of Nursing in 1946. The Institute of Transportation, Travel, and Tourism (now the Institute of Travel, Hotel, and Restaurant Administration) was established in 1968. Three other academic areas are part of the four-year liberal arts school: the College of Arts and Sciences, the College of Education, and the Division of General Academic Studies. Graduate studies are also offered in education, business, and biology.

With more than 200 faculty members on its payroll, NU's economic impact on the area is estimated at more than $70 million annually. But even more important is its spiritual and intellectual impact. With 3,000-plus students choosing from more than 700 courses each year, Niagara University is truly an institution of which its "founding fathers" would be proud.

Alumni Hall at Niagara University was originally built in 1872 and has changed considerably over the years due to fires in 1889, 1898, and 1913. In addition to the chapel, the building houses several administrative offices, including that of the president.

CAMEO INN

An interest in decorating and antiques led Greg and Carolyn Fisher of Lewiston to set up one of Niagara County's first bed and breakfasts, the Cameo Inn. This three-story Queen Anne Victorian mansion on the Niagara River has been restored to its former glory, and today the ambience is that of an authentic 1800s home replete with period furnishings.

In July 1990 the Fishers purchased a second home in Youngstown and named it Cameo Manor North. Originally known as the Colbert Estate (named after a Pittsburgh industrialist who owned the home in the early 1900s), Cameo Manor North was used as a retirement home before the Fishers bought it. Built in the style of a grand English manor, it has eight rooms available for guests. The Fishers are developing a full-service "mini resort" and conference center on the site. Legend has it that one of the exquisitely carved mantels inside the home was a gift of local figure Father Baker.

Guests staying at the Cameo Inn or Cameo Manor North find it very easy to love the Niagara County region.

ABOVE: Cameo Manor's decor resembles that of a grand English country estate.

LEFT: Greg and Carolyn Fisher restored this Queen Anne Victorian mansion to its former glory.

RAINBOW HOSPITALITY

Rainbow Hospitality, a bed and breakfast reservation service, offers travelers from both near and far a chance to enjoy the beauty of the Niagara region by arranging stays for them in gracious, often historic "host" homes. Two of Rainbow Hospitality's finest bed and breakfast homes are the Cameo Inn and Cameo Manor.

Georgia Brannan and Cheryl Biggie purchased the business in February 1988. From an original roster of 20 B&B homes, the service now includes over 70 homes throughout the Niagara region.

The service is dual in nature: For travelers, it is a resource listing B&B homes; for B&B owners, it is an administrative manager, which benefits everyone since it leaves hosts more time to enjoy guests.

Rainbow Hospitality is the exclusive B&B reservation service for the Niagara region assisting local and international B&B travelers through its affiliation with the World-Wide Reservation network.

FAR LEFT: (From left) Karen Ruckinger of Rainbow Hospitality assists tourists Elwyn and Paula Richter while company president, Georgia Brannan looks on. Photo by Richard W. Roeller, Buffalo News

LEFT: Cheryl Biggie and Georgia Brannan (seated) purchased Rainbow Hospitality from former owners Gretchen Broderick and Marilyn Schoenherr.

GOODYEAR

The Pathfinder plant became known as Goodyear in 1956.

Say the name "Goodyear" and most people will immediately think of one of two things: blimps or tires.

Even in Niagara Falls, the average person in the street may not associate the Goodyear name with the chemical plant off Baker Avenue that has been a fixture in the town since 1946.

Known as the Pathfinder Chemical Corporation until 1956, the plant owes its presence in the Falls to the shortage of natural rubber resulting from World War II. After the war Pathfinder was formed to produce a PVC plastic product called "Pliovic," which was developed as a selective substitute for natural rubber. Its peacetime uses included clear film for foods and coated fabrics.

Returning GIs originally made up a significant number of Goodyear's employees, and production of the plastic resin was such that by the mid-1950s there was said to be enough of the product manufactured to have furnished every man, woman, and child in the United States with a rain cape. Demand for the resin was even greater after it was approved for use as electrical insulation.

New products were also developed, including rubber chemical products, which proved to

be beneficial to Goodyear and led to the construction of a second Pathfinder manufacturing facility in Niagara Falls in 1954.

The first of these new rubber chemical products was a series of rubber accelerators that sped up the curing process for all types of rubber goods, including tires, belts, foam rubber, and hoses. The second new product line, marketed under the name of Wingstay 100, was a solid-state antioxidant that acts as a stabilizer in synthetic rubber. (The Wingstay name is an amalgam of Mercury's "winged" foot—Goodyear's symbol—and the word "stay," short for "stabilizer.") Subsequently, a liquid form of this product, Wingstay 200, was also introduced. Together, these new product lines manufactured at the Niagara Falls plant enabled Goodyear to make tires that were both longer-lasting and safer.

By 1959 the Goodyear plant's plastic and rubber chemical businesses were operating at peak production levels. Further growth and improvements were in the "wings."

To keep up with the growing demand spawned by American consumer culture, six additional vinyl polymerization reactors were installed at the plant beginning in the 1960s.

Goodyear also increased its vinyl production by building the first of two rotary vinyl dryers to replace the apron dryers it had previously used.

A particularly notable improvement was made in 1967, when Goodyear's own steam plant went on line. This freed the facility from reliance upon outside sources for its steam, which was used to heat up the vinyl reactors, as well as to keep the facility warm through the area's cold winters.

The year 1971 heralded several significant developments. For one, a new rubber accelera-

tor process was developed and put on line at the plant. This created a new generation rubber accelerator for Goodyear under the tradename Morfax. High in quality and exceptionally effective, this product line replaced many of the original rubber accelerators produced here. The same year also saw Goodyear install a recovery unit to convert hydrogen sulfide by-products (formed in the Morfax process) to sulfur, which was then sold to manufacturers for conversion into sulfuric acid. This process, which prevents the release of harmful emissions to the atmosphere, was merely a way point in Goodyear's long history of a continuing commitment to make environmental as well as technological improvements.

During the 1970s Goodyear made many advances in the environmental area. The company improved the working environment at its facility by limiting employee exposure to vinyl chloride monomer, a carcinogen present in the vinyl resin process. In the early days, built-up residue from the manufacturing process had to be manually chopped out of the reactors. Goodyear

instituted a process whereby a solvent could be pumped into the reactor to dissolve the residue, minimizing personal exposure. Another step in this direction was the boiler incineration of left-over vinyl chloride monomer, which was designed to prevent residual monomer from entering the atmosphere.

Since 1980 there have been a number of major developments at the plant. The installation of a direct digital control computer system provides close control of the vinyl reactors, improving safety, efficiency, and the quality of vinyl resin products. On the personnel front Goodyear and its union have demonstrated their desire for improved teamwork and more effective employee participation through a "parnership for the future." This and other innovative approaches bring union and management together to focus on quality in yet another way.

For the future, continued growth is a focal point. The firm has a strong quality position in

vinyl resin, which go into products as diverse as flooring, automobile interiors, wallpaper, and medical examining gloves. Goodyear holds 20 percent of the market for plastisol vinyl resin. And continued demand for the Wingstay 100 product line, which protects and improves tires, will continue to translate into significant sales to tire manufacturers worldwide.

Although it doesn't make tires, the Goodyear plant makes tires better. Rubber chemicals produced in Niagara Falls go into the making of every Goodyear tire in the world. And like the winged foot of Mercury, this vital part of the largest American-owned tire and rubber company has never stood still.

LEFT: After World War II Pathfinder was formed to produce a PVC plastic resin product called "Pliovic," which was developed as a selective substitute for natural rubber. Here an employee weighs 50-pound bags in this 1947 photo.

ABOVE: At the time of this photo, 1955, this chemical plant was known as the Pathfinder Chemical Corporation.

NABISCO BRANDS, INC.

Nabisco Shredded Wheat, known as the "original Niagara Falls cereal."

The history of Nabisco in Niagara Falls is actually the history of the popular breakfast cereal named Shredded Wheat—made there since 1901, and known for many years as the "original Niagara Falls cereal." Yet Shredded Wheat was not invented there, but in Denver. And its inventor was not a baker, as one might expect, but a lawyer named Henry D. Perky.

Legend has it that in 1892 Perky stopped at a hotel in a small Nebraska town, where he noticed a gentleman eating an unfamiliar food—boiled wheat with milk. The man explained that he suffered from indigestion, and boiled wheat was one of the few foods he could enjoy. Perky, who also suffered from indigestion, was impressed by the concoction, and began thinking about a way to manufacture his own whole wheat product.

That same year, he conceived of a machine equipped with a pair of steel rollers that, when water-softened whole wheat berries were put into it, yielded small pillows of moist "shredded wheat." Since the little biscuits had a tendency to spoil if not speedily eaten, Perky baked them. They were not an immediate success, however.

Unfortunately for Perky, who foresaw making his fortune selling the biscuit-making ma-chinery, rather than the biscuits themselves, most people had never tasted boiled shredded wheat before. Perky was quick to realize, however, that a much larger market probably existed for shredded wheat itself than for his wheat-shredding machine.

To test mass production of his product, Perky experimented in a Denver cracker bakery and produced the first commercial Shredded Wheat biscuits later in 1892. After opening a shop in Denver to showcase his new product, Perky headed east to introduce Shredded Wheat to mainstream America.

The first years were difficult, but through dogged persistence and an unfailing belief in the benefits of Shredded Wheat, Perky's product caught on. It was an inspired decision to buy a 10-acre site and put up a $2-million bakery in Niagara Falls in 1901.

The location was ideal. Perky recognized the publicity value of the tourist area, opened the bakery to everyone, and gave away free samples. As part of it still is today, the wheat was obtained from local farmers in the community. The yellow brick, many-windowed plant he proudly called the "palace of light" became a landmark. So magnificent was it by turn-of-the-century standards, that each year it was visited by more than 100,000 tourists.

In 1928 Nabisco—then called the National Biscuit Company—acquired the Shredded

The first Niagara Falls Shredded Wheat Bakery, which opened in 1901, was heralded as the cleanest, finest, most hygienic food factory in the world. Free guided tours led more than 100,000 people through the plant each year.

Wheat Company. The National Biscuit Company had begun in 1898, just three years before the first Shredded Wheat biscuits began streaming out of the new Niagara Falls bakery.

The National Biscuit Company's founder, Chicago attorney Adolphus Green, believed that if bakeries worked together, they could establish standards that would enhance the quality of their merchandise, improve consistency, extend shelf life, and put an end to contamination.

As chairman of National Biscuit Company, Green immediately introduced a new product, shape, name, and method of packaging. It was based upon an improved soda cracker formula, set off with a unique, octagonal shape, and

called a "biscuit" rather than a "cracker," which at the time connoted a stale, soggy product. A package with inter-folded layers of waxed paper and cardboard, named "inner seal," kept the biscuits fresh. The product, Uneeda Biscuit, was immediately popular. Further successes followed, including Oysterettes Crackers, Social Tea Biscuits, Graham Crackers, Fig Newtons, Premium saltines, Nabisco Sugar Wafers, Barnum's Animal Crackers, and Oreo Sandwich Cookies.

During the roaring twenties, American businesses of all kinds were booming. N.B.C. purchased several other baking companies, including the Shredded Wheat Company in Niagara Falls, each with its own specialties. Even during the Depression, N.B.C. flourished, with the most popular cracker in its history, Ritz, introduced during 1934.

Over the years the company continued to grow. It further diversified through the acquisition of international firms in the 1950s and 1960s. Also during this period, as American consumers became increasingly health conscious, the company took steps to make foods that were lower in fats, salt, and artificial ingredients. A name change was also in the wings.

The name "Nabisco" had actually been suggested by Green just after N.B.C. began, but it

was initially rejected by the company's advertising agency as being "a little long and not smooth and pleasant." However, after the National Broadcasting Company came into existence, causing confusion with its identical initials, the name Nabisco was permanently adopted in 1971.

The present company name, Nabisco Brands, Inc., resulted from successful mergers with other giants in the industry. The first of these occurred in 1981 with Standard Brands, whose products included Fleischmann's margarine, and yeast, Royal gelatin, and Planters nuts. In 1985 Nabisco merged with R.J. Reynolds Industries, Inc., an American-based tobacco, food,

and beverage manufacturer that also owned the Del Monte Corporation.

If Henry Perky could stroll through the Nabisco Brands plant in Niagara Falls today, he'd marvel at the modern methods by which his cereal is now produced. However, Perky would surely be delighted to know that Shredded Wheat today is the same 100 percent whole wheat he first shredded in 1892, and that the company that produces his creation, Nabisco, is one of the largest consumer goods companies in the world.

LEFT: At the end of each tour of the "Home of Shredded Wheat," visitors were served a bowl of the cereal with milk and fruit.

BELOW: This photo of the current Niagara Falls Shredded Wheat Bakery was taken in 1932. Today the bakery looks much the same.

CARBORUNDUM ABRASIVES COMPANY

Carborundum Abrasives Company soon found that silicon carbide was useful in many diverse industries.

On July 23, 1983, both a birth and birthday were celebrated. The first marked the completion of the leveraged buy out that created the Carborundum Abrasives Company. The second belonged to the newborn company's current president, Fred Silver, who co-celebrated the day with 38 candles on his cake.

Nearly a century of history was to prelude this event, for it was in 1891 that inventor and Carborundum Company founder William Acheson discovered silicon carbide, the world's first human-made abrasive. It quickly became apparent that the discovery lent itself to the manufacture of abrasive paper for sanding and finishing operations, and in short order Acheson added "coated abrasives" to his company's product line.

Located on Buffalo Avenue in the heart of Niagara Falls' industrial row, the coated abrasive department first introduced its products to the shoe manufacturing trade in 1898 in the form of products for buffing and scouring the soles and heels of shoes. It soon became one of the largest producers of coated abrasives in the world, a position it retains today.

Technical milestones in the company's history include the introduction of paper and cloth coated with the natural abrasive, garnet, in 1908, which opened up the woodworking field to the company; the manufacture of the aluminum oxide abrasive Aloxite in 1909 for metal finishing; the development of waterproof coated abrasives beginning in 1920 for the automobile industry; and a new method for coating abrasive grain on paper, cloth, and combination paper/cloth, invented in 1926.

In 1947 the "department" became the Coated Abrasives Division and moved to a new location on Walmore Road, adjoining Niagara Falls Airport, where it still resides today. A ceremony associated with the move was notable. Instead of the traditional ground breaking with a shovel, company officials cut the airport runway concrete with a

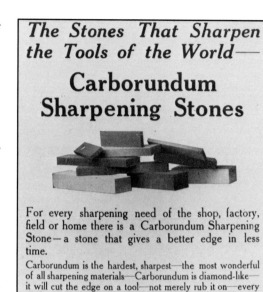

The coated abrasive department of The Carborundum Company first introduced its products to the shoe manufacturing trade in 1898. This advertisement ran in American Shoemaking *magazine.*

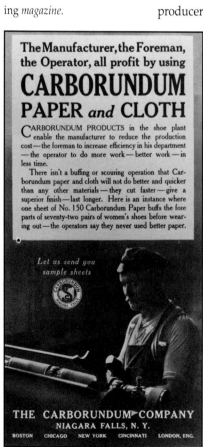

straight-edge concrete cutter equipped with a Carborundum-made diamond wheel.

Following that move, the division was twice bought and sold along with the rest of The Carborundum Company. In 1977 the company was acquired by the Kennecott Corporation. In 1981 the SOHIO Corporation purchased Kennecott. And on a notable day in July 1983, an independent Carborundum Abrasives Company was born in a leveraged buy out by the Peck-Lynn Company, a Chicago-based packaging firm. In 1986 Peck-Lynn sold Carborundum Abrasives to the Norton Company, and in 1990 Norton Company was bought by Saint Gobain, which remains its parent today.

Today, 450-person strong Carborundum Abrasives Company focuses on three markets that are outgrowths of the ones it targeted in the early years of its history: industrial, automobile aftermarket, and the "do-it-yourselfer." Making 50,000 variations of coated abrasive products in operating facilities in Niagara Falls, as well as Los Angeles, California, and High Point, North Carolina, the road looks smooth for this company that has been "rubbing people the right way" for more than a century.

NIAGARA MILK COOPERATIVE

Mention of a land flowing with milk and honey goes back as far as the Bible. Expand the word "milk" to include "whole milk, skim milk, low-fat milk, buttermilk, half and half, and eggnog" and substitute "fruit juices and other drinks" for the word "honey" and the result is a pretty good description of the products made by the Niagara Milk Cooperative.

Formed in 1933 by a group of 25 member farms, including those owned by the Fronczak, Richards, Kroening, Haseley, Milleville, and Stahl families (all still active in the organization today), the cooperative grew rapidly, and by the 1950s could count more than 500 small producer farms as owners. Today the co-op's ownership and distribution base covers Niagara, Erie, Orleans, Wyoming, Monroe, Genesee, and Cattaraugus counties, and its 100-employee plant is the largest of its kind west of Rochester.

At first, the co-op was concerned simply with the distribution of its raw milk to dairies and ice cream and cheese plants, who would themselves bottle, process, and market the final product. But as its membership grew, so did its marketing and operational sophistication.

In 1952, for instance, after two decades of working out of its president's home, the co-op purchased its own headquarters on Pine Avenue, where it remained for almost 15 years.

In terms of marketing, the 1950s also saw the cooperative begin to bottle and distribute its own milk under the name of Diffine's Dairy. Additional purchases of dealer operations and other dairies followed, with the co-op's current home, Wendt's Dairy, acquired in 1966.

As the co-op has grown, so have its member farms and their overall productivity. In the year 1956, for instance, co-op members produced 55 million pounds of milk; over the course of 1989, member farms produced 260 million pounds.

Increased production has also resulted in the elimination of the 10-gallon milk can as the means of transporting milk to city plants. Today 6,000-gallon capacity bulk tank trucks pump milk on from member farms for daily delivery to its Niagara Falls location.

The milk distribution system has evolved from a home delivery system using returnable glass bottles to supermarket deliveries in half-gallon or gallon plastic containers.

Most recently, the co-op has undertaken a multimillion-dollar expansion for an automated high-rise cooler. This is the group's latest effort to meet the needs of an ever-growing market for its products.

Even with its tremendous growth, however, the Niagara Milk Cooperative has managed to remain a close-knit group. It has had the same president, James E. Schotz, a farm owner from Wilson, since 1968. But perhaps the best way to explain this cohesiveness is to recognize that the cooperative's owners are, and always have been, farmers first. As such they are individuals who understand cooperation in its most fundamental sense—between people, animals, and the land.

In 1952, after two decades of working out of its president's home, the co-op purchased its own headquarters on Pine Avenue, where it remained for almost 15 years.

BELOW: A Wendt's bill from 1936.

BOTTOM: Wendt's Dairy, the co-op's current home, was acquired in 1966.

SKW ALLOYS, INC.

Although the name SKW Alloys has been associated with Niagara Falls only since 1979, the company's Highland Avenue manufacturing facility has been a fixture in the local economy for more than seven decades.

SKW Alloys' original predecessor, Pitt-Met (short for Pittsburgh Metallurgical Company), came to the Falls in 1919 due to the availability of low-cost power for its energy intensive business. The first installation consisted of three small furnaces used to produce ferroalloys, which are mixtures of iron and other metallic elements that contribute unique properties to the manufacture of different grades of steel.

Modernization and growth were the rule, notably in the late 1930s under the guidance of Charles Colbert, Jr., then president. The firm's business continued to expand and in 1962 the company was sold to Airco Alloys. Under the Airco ownership, production facilities were further improved and smaller production units were replaced by larger, more economical furnaces.

SKW Alloys, Inc., was formed in 1979 when two plants were purchased from Airco, one located in Calvert City, Kentucky, and the other in Niagara Falls. SKW Alloys is a wholly owned subsidiary of SKW Trostberg AG, a German-based chemical, agricultural, and metallurgical company with facilities worldwide.

Ownership of the company was not the only thing that changed, however. For most of its history, SKW had been a producer of large-volume commodity ferroalloys for steelmakers and foundries. Because the imports were able to undercut domestic prices, however, SKW chose to convert its operations to specialty ferroalloys in the mid-1980s. This market had always been a significant one for its German parent company, so this shift made sense both from a corporate and a market perspective.

However, before it could move into this new market, the company needed to secure a long-term and plentiful source of low-cost power. Following the commitment in 1987 by the New York State Power Authority to SKW of such low-cost power, SKW built an $8.5-million submerged arc furnace for producing silicon metal. Since 1979, SKW has invested approximately $30 million to upgrade and expand its Niagara Falls facilities.

In 1988 SKW Alloys purchased ESM, Inc., a Pennsylvania-based producer of desulfurization agents for the iron and steel industry, representing a significant addition to SKW's North American metals operations. The following year, SKW Alloys also acquired Affival, Inc., a producer of cored wire for the steel industry. These recent complementary acquisitions to SKW's product line further serve to strengthen and broaden SKW's viability as a producer of commodity and specialty ferroalloys.

SKW Alloys, Inc., is here to stay, a fact reinforced by the company's decision effective in 1990 to locate both ESM's and Affival's headquarters in the Cataract City. And although the ferroalloy market for domestic producers is a challenging one, SKW Alloys has managed to position itself for long-term success.

Raw materials are smelted in the SKW Alloys's submerged arc furnace to produce silicon metal.

CITY OF NIAGARA FALLS

On March 17, 1892, an international city that was to become a hub of industry and tourism was created. On that date, the governor of the state of New York, The Honorable Roswell P. Flower, signed into law the bill the state legislature had passed establishing the City of Niagara Falls.

Initially Niagara Falls was governed by a "mayor council," consisting of a mayor and eight aldermen, two from each of the four separate districts or "wards" delineated in the city charter. The first mayor of the City of Niagara Falls elected under this governmental organization was The Honorable George W. Wright.

But on November 3, 1914, Niagara Falls voters elected to replace the mayoral council with a city manager form. Like the mayor council form, the city manager form included a mayor and his or her council. However, the council members were elected by the city as a whole, rather than by their local wards. And, instead of eight council positions, there were now only five, including the mayor. The newly created city manager was to be appointed as the city's chief executive and head of daily operations.

On January 1, 1916, Ossian E. Carr was appointed Niagara Falls' first city manager.

It wasn't until January 1, 1988, that further significant changes were made to the Niagara Falls governmental system. These changes, put into motion with the passage of a 1985 referendum, combined the best of the city manager and city council forms of government. The resulting hybrid system, considered a "strong mayor form of government," consists of an independently elected mayor, who serves as chief executive, seven council members, and a city administrator who retains most of the functions of the city manager. Niagara Falls' first city administrator, Mark R. Palesh, was appointed in 1988 and previously had served two years as the city's last city manager.

Each of Niagara Falls' mayors has left his imprint on the city. Mayor E. Dent Lackey, who held the office from 1964 until 1976, began the

revitalization of Niagara Falls, including the building of the Convention Center. Mayor Michael C. O'Laughlin, who followed Lackey in office, is now in his unprecedented fourth term as mayor of Niagara Falls. His efforts led to the successful revitalization of the city's infrastructure, wastewater and water treatment facilities, and created the public and private partnership for growth that citizens enjoy today.

Facing its second century, the City of Niagara Falls continues to build on its international reputation that marries industry and the preservation of natural resources.

FAR LEFT: Mark R. Palesh, city administrator.

LEFT: Michael C. O'Laughlin, mayor of Niagara Falls.

NATIONAL FUEL

FAR RIGHT: One of National Fuel's predecessors, Niagara Falls Gas Co., provided natural gas to light the nights of Niagara Falls in 1860.

RIGHT: Charles A. Scheiffele, a Niagara Falls Gas & Electric Light Co. engineer, stands by a company serviceman and his truck in this 1927 photo.

An Iroquois Gas employee and his children enjoy a soda in this 1962 photo. Iroquois Gas and numerous other firms were reorganized in 1974 into today's National Fuel System.

In 1935 Niagara Falls Gas and Electric Light Company merged with a competitor, Republic Light, Heat and Power Company, Inc. Some two decades later, Iroquois Gas, one of the "small locals" that had been doing business in Niagara Falls since the mid-nineteenth century, acquired Republic and immediately embarked upon an improvement program.

Iroquois' ambitious program during the 1950s included upgrading the quality of the gas itself (giving one cubic foot almost twice its former energy), laying large transmission lines to extend distribution in the area, and building a new $450,000 service center on Packard Road that is still in use today. Advertisements from this era for the newly built Treadway Inn used the lure of "the modern miracle of gas" to attract guests—not all that different from what the Cataract House had done a century before.

Iroquois Gas and numerous other firms outside Niagara Falls were reorganized in 1974 under National Fuel Gas Distribution Corporation, National Fuel Gas Supply Corporation, and other subsidiaries. The benefits of this were threefold: streamlined administration, enhanced service capabilities, and strengthened gas supplies.

Although its use has changed from the gas lights of the nineteenth century to the hot water heaters and furnaces of the twentieth, natural gas continues, as the *Niagara Falls Gazette* put it back in 1860, "to give great satisfaction."

When Edward VII of England, then Prince of Wales, lodged at the Cataract House in September 1860, he was no doubt delighted with the hotel's newly installed gas lights. A story in the *Niagara Falls Gazette* reported that "the gas was of good quality and gave great satisfaction . . . in the course of a few days gas will be in very general use."

Several monarchs and many years later, gas is indeed in general use, not only in Niagara Falls, but throughout western New York and northwestern Pennsylvania—thanks to the National Fuel System. National Fuel subsidiary companies are engaged in all aspects of the natural gas industry, including exploration and production, pipeline construction and transmission, underground storage and retail distribution.

While natural gas has been provided to Niagara Falls under the National Fuel banner since 1974, many companies and many events preceded the formation of this large, diversified natural gas company.

The first commercial use of natural gas in the world occurred in 1821 in Fredonia, New York, less than 100 miles from Niagara Falls. This sparked an immediate demand, leading to the founding of numerous small local companies to tap the potential of this promising market. These companies were predecessors to the National Fuel known today.

In the Falls, two such pioneers were the Niagara Falls Gas Co., incorporated in 1859, and the Power City Illuminating Company, Inc., incorporated in 1893. The two merged in 1900 to form the Niagara Falls Gas and Electric Light Company, which manufactured gas in a plant along the Niagara River gorge near the present Rainbow Bridge.

NIAGARA MOHAWK POWER CORPORATION

It has all the elements of a good screenplay: a revolutionary theory developed by an unknown scientist, great risk balanced by the potential of great reward, a backdrop of stunning natural beauty, and a dramatic moment in which all the threads of the story are joined in a single hand. Roll the credits on the history of Niagara Mohawk Power Corporation.

Alternating current was the theory, and Dr. Nikola Tesla was the brilliant theorist. The construction of a tunnel that ran more than a mile under the town of Niagara Falls was the risk undertaken by the Niagara Falls Power Company. The reward was nothing short of revolutionizing modern life. And with one of the world's natural wonders in the background, the moment of truth arrived on November 15, 1896, when the hand of Mayor Edgar Jewett threw the switch that transmitted electric power over the then-unheard-of distance of 20 miles. Thus was born the business of long-distance electrical transmission, which Niagara Mohawk Power carries on to this day.

Just as many streams join to form the Niagara River, so too did many power operations merge to form Niagara Mohawk Power.

The Niagara Falls Power Company was formed in 1889 by the merger of four entities, and it was joined in 1918 by the Hydraulic Power Company. In the ensuing years local transmission lines joined together. And finally, on January 1, 1950, the Niagara Mohawk System was formed through the consolidation of Buffalo Niagara Electric, Central New York Power Corporation, and New York Power and

Adams Station.

Light Corporation. Later that year, the Niagara Falls Power Company, the enterprise that started it all, also merged with Niagara Mohawk.

Today this full-service utility enjoys a highly visible presence not only in Niagara Falls (from which approximately 20 percent of its power is still obtained), but also throughout New York State. Its giant transmission towers and switching stations service more than 1.5 million customers over an area of 24,000 square miles.

And while some people might not think of a giant utility as a proponent of energy-use reduction, that is in fact exactly what Niagara Mohawk Power has set as its goal for the 1990s. Building on the company's "demand-side management" philosophy, which emphasizes efficient energy usage, Niagara Mohawk is quick to point out that, compared to building new generating facilities, simple energy conservation not only costs less but also has no negative impact on the environment.

For electricity and many other modern conveniences, the community has Niagara Mohawk Power to thank.

The first alternating current power in the United States, theorized by Dr. Nikola Tesla.

NIAGARA FALLS BRIDGE COMMISSION

RIGHT: It took approximately 5,000 tons of steel to construct the Rainbow Bridge.

BELOW: The story of the Rainbow Bridge begins with a kite. A man named Homan Walsh was the first to span the Niagara River gorge, a feat he accomplished in 1848 by stretching a kite string from shore to shore.

A magnificent steel arch spans the Niagara River approximately 1,000 feet downstream from the American Falls. It is a triumph of engineering, as well as of beauty. It is a vital link between two of the most progressive countries in the world. It has contributed, perhaps more than any other single factor, to the growth of the Niagara Falls tourist industry. It is the Rainbow Bridge, and its story begins with a kite.

An individual named Homan Walsh was the first to span the Niagara River gorge, a feat he accomplished in 1848 by stretching a kite string from shore to shore. Thus began construction of the first bridge to connect the high banks lining the lower Niagara River. Known as the Niagara Falls Suspension Bridge, it consisted of an oak-plank roadway suspended from iron cables.

In 1855 a second span, known as the Whirlpool Rapids Bridge, was built on the same site to carry railroad traffic. It was rebuilt in 1897 without interruption to traffic.

One of the most memorable years in the history of the Niagara Falls bridges was 1938, for it was in January of that year that the Falls View Bridge, predecessor to the present Rainbow Bridge, was torn from its anchorages by ice and collapsed.

Fortunately, the newly formed Niagara Falls Bridge Commission was already well along in its plans for a replacement. On a visit to Canada in 1939, King George VI and Queen Elizabeth II dedicated the site and ground was broken on May 4, 1940.

With the fastest natural flowing water in the world below it, and a river depth of 175 feet, the bridge posed an enormous challenge for its engineers. They were, however, more than up to the task.

The span, which at the time of construction was the longest hingeless arch in the world, consists of approximately 5,000 tons of steel. It also takes advantage of the area's great natural beauty, leaving the Falls and turbulent river below in open view, an accomplishment recognized by an award in 1941 of "first place, class A" by the American Institute of Steel Construction.

Complementing the beauty of the span are the architecture of its terminals and Rainbow Gardens. This may also be the only bridge in the world with its own "musical instrument." The Rainbow Tower Carillon, a 165-foot high tower with 55 tuned bells, is located at the Canadian end of the bridge and received its certificate of inspection on June 11, 1948.

Operated along with the Lewiston-Queenston Bridge by the Niagara Falls Bridge Commission, the Rainbow Bridge is a "link" in the truest sense of the word, bringing together not only two nations, but also two ideals—function and aesthetics—in view of one of the great natural wonders of the world.

KEY BANK

In 1825 two significant events took place in the New York State capital of Albany. One was the dedication by Governor De Witt Clinton of the Erie Canal. The second was the signing into law of a bill to charter the Commercial Bank of Albany. As the canal opened new opportunities, so too did the new bank, which evolved over the decades to become the $23-billion-plus nationally integrated financial services company today known as KeyCorp.

Since it was established KeyCorp has concentrated on offering its financial services to individuals and businesses in the northern United States. Seeing a need for an office in Niagara Falls, it opened its first area branch at Military Road in 1985. The branch became the 39th in its banking network and its third office in Niagara County. Acquisition in 1990 of The Permanent Savings Bank, a local bank specializing in home mortgages, further expanded Key Bank's operation. By the end of that year, the bank had seven offices serving customers in Niagara County. Branch consolidations and the Goldome acquisition in 1991 offer customers nine convenient branch locations in Niagara County.

During the bank's early years explosive growth in commercial industries—including those related to the canal, the railroad, and iron fabrication—nurtured the bank. Six years after it was chartered, the bank became the depository for the funds of the State of New York. On April 29, 1865, the bank was reorganized under the National Banking Act of 1864 and given a

new name, the National Commercial Bank of Albany.

Other mergers and subsequent name changes followed. A consolidation in 1920 with Union Trust Company formed National Bank and Trust Company. In 1971 the holding company First Commercial Banks was established through the affiliation of National Commercial Bank with First Trust and Deposit Company of Syracuse, the largest commercial banking institution between New York City and Buffalo. First Commercial became a major financial force in New York State, with $1.2 billion in assets and 89 offices.

In a move to develop a consistent identity, the name Key Banks Inc. was adopted in 1979 to apply to the bank and its many subsidiaries. To better reflect its position as a diversified financial services company, Key Banks became KeyCorp in 1985.

Since Victor J. Riley, Jr., became president and chief executive officer in 1973, the bank has followed a two-fold management strategy. Focusing its resources in the northern, "snowbelt" states, KeyCorp operates in less-crowded markets. Emphasizing the "basics" of banking, the company avoids risky fads, such as leveraged buy-outs or foreign lending, and concentrates instead on providing banking, loan, trust, insurance, and leasing services to the people and businesses within communities like Niagara Falls.

KeyCorp's strategy, based on sound financial principles and common sense, has garnered great success. In 1990 the organization's credit rating was upgraded to reflect its consistent profitability and successful diversification.

KeyCorp offers financial services to individuals and businesses in the northern United States. The Key Bank branch, located at 2429 Military Road, is one of nine branches serving Niagara Falls customers.

Key Bank branch at 800 Main Street in Niagara Falls.

CWM

Several air monitoring stations, located around the perimeter of the facility, monitor air quality both before and after the air has passed through the site. This enables CWM to assure employees and community members that they are not being exposed to airborne contaminants from facility operations.

The 1990s have been characterized as "the environmental decade" for the United States. Doing its part for the environment by managing hazardous waste in the safest, best possible way is CWM—Chemical Waste Management. The largest company of its kind in America, 200 of CWM's 4,500 nationwide employees work at the company's Model City, New York, facility, just north of Niagara Falls.

The Model City site was originally part of a 7,500-acre land parcel owned and used by the federal government in the 1930s to manufacture TNT and other war-related products. Residues from the processes employed in the manufacture of these products left the land unusable for agricultural or residential purposes. But the abundance of clay present in the site's soil made it especially suitable for waste treatment and storage. Clay's lack of porosity precludes the movement of groundwater, thus limiting the possibility of substance migration, and its structural strength prevents the soil's collapse under a heavy load, such as that of a landfill.

In 1972 Chem-Trol recognized the site's potential and purchased the facility for use as a landfill. SCA Chemical Service, Inc., purchased the site in 1973 and operated it until 1984. In that year CWM purchased SCA, and the company took its place as Niagara Falls corporate citizen.

CWM takes seriously the responsibilities of that citizenship. Aware that successful operation of the Model City landfill is measured by the protection afforded to public health and the environment, CWM has established rigorous monitoring programs to ensure that its facility meets all government regulations. Proud of the community in which it resides, CWM has initiated a series of programs designed to keep its neighbors informed of operations at the landfill.

Government regulation of hazardous waste management was formalized in 1976, when the first regulations applicable to hazardous waste treatment and disposal were instituted. Present-day disposal of hazardous materials is tightly controlled. Operations at Model City are closely monitored by federal, state, and local authorities as well as by CWM's environmental compliance personnel.

Control over the treatment process actually starts before waste is generated. The company's consultants work with generators to identify ways to minimize waste volume and plan safe transporting of the materials. Its Environmental Remedial Action Division (ENRAC) offers remediation services at sites from which the waste is taken.

An average of 50 to 60 trucks a day bring material to the Model City facility for treatment or storage. Sixty percent of the waste

comes from generators in New York State; the
remainder from industries in the Northeast.
Before CWM will accept a waste, generators
are required to submit a sample of it for chemical analysis. A waste profile sheet must accom-
pany the sample to describe the contents of the
waste and the process that produced it. At
CWM's on-site laboratory, trained scientists
analyze the sample to verify its contents and
determine the most environmentally sound
and cost-effective treatment or disposal
method. Once a method is selected, the waste
is scheduled for shipment to the facility. Each
incoming waste is analyzed to verify that it
conforms to the original sample and waste
profile.

CWM's Model City facility offers waste generators a number of treatment and disposal options. These include aqueous treatment, which
renders water-based wastes harmless and suitable for discharge to the Niagara River; a stabi-
lization process that mixes cement and other
additives to waste, rendering them nontoxic
and suitable for deposit in the secure landfill;
and a blending program for organic liquids

such as dry cleaning and paint solvents so that
they can be used as a fuel in cement kilns.
Residues from treatment processes, contaminated soils, and wastes for which there is no
other treatment are deposited in the secure
landfill. The landfill is designed and
constructed with a special composite liner and
capping system to prevent it from leaking, thus
protecting the environment.

CWM's long-range plans for Model City include constructing a rotary kiln incinerator for
the destruction of organic solids and liquids.

CWM considers community outreach very
important. The company was among the first
in the country to establish a community liaison committee to promote dialogue between
interested citizens and the facility operation's
people. An open-door policy encourages people in the community, students, and other interested individuals and groups to tour the
facility.

Working with local schools and universities,
CWM supports educational programs such as
the Chemical Education for Public Understanding (CEPUP), which promotes a knowledge and
understanding of science and technology.

The next decade promises tremendous
growth for CWM and the waste treatment industry. By federal law, all 50 states must make
provision for the disposal of all hazardous
wastes generated within their borders over the
next 20 years. CWM, with its expertise in hazardous waste management and its network of
storage and treatment facilities, will assuredly
thrive. The demand for incineration is expected
to increase, and the projected need for site remediation services will provide opportunities
for the company's ENRAC division. CWM's
labs will continue to develop and implement
improved waste management technologies.
And, as America works to reduce its volume of
waste, the company will increasingly be called
upon to provide waste minimization consulting
services.

Protection of tomorrow's environment requires effective waste management today.
CWM, with its eye on the future, will continue
to lead the way.

*Safety at the Model City
facility is of primary
importance. The safety
manager works with
employees and contrac-
tors working on the site
to make sure all jobs and
procedures are done in a
safe manner.*

UNITED DEVELOPMENT GROUP

United Development Group has given new meaning to the old saying "carry coals to Newcastle." In fact, coal is being carried—but to Niagara Falls, not Northumberland. And it's being used to generate—or more accurately, co-generate—power in a city already famous for its abundant hydroelectric resources.

The history of United Development Group and its Niagara Falls co-generation power plant begins with John Fair, a lawyer from Columbia, South Carolina. In the early 1980s Fair perceived a growing need for inexpensive power among industrial manufacturers in a variety of markets. The lawyer knew that co-generation, which is the production of two kinds of energy at one time (in the case of Niagara Falls, electricity and steam produced by the burning of coal) can provide energy more efficiently than can a utility company. Acting on this insight, Fair formed United Development Group in 1983.

Initially, the company simply investigated the co-generation market. In 1985, however, UDG actually built a small co-generation plant in Georgia. During the same year, it also became involved with two 120-megawatt projects in Virginia representing $360 million in capital investment. Coincidentally, Goodyear Tire & Rubber Co. became interested in the possibility of developing a co-generation facility in the Niagara Falls area at about the same time.

In short order, United Development Group set up a limited partnership and purchased a four-acre site from Goodyear, adjacent to its plant on 56th Street. That was the simple part, as the next hurdle UDG had to get over was the permitting process.

Working closely with the Department of Environmental Conservation and other environmental groups, UDG designed a facility capable of producing up to 486,000 pounds of steam per hour, as well as electricity. The plant utilizes "fluidized bed" technology, which mixes limestone with coal to trap pollutants in the resulting ash.

In July 1989, the Niagara County Industrial Development Agency approved $93 million in bonds to finance the plant, the largest offering ever handled by the county IDA up to that time. Ground breaking took place in September 1989, and in 1991, the plant went on line, culminating an eight-year development process.

The 52-megawatt plant now supplies inexpensive steam power to the Goodyear Plant and sells electricity back to Niagara Mohawk Power Corp. With a final cost of $103 million, the project has had a highly positive economic impact not only on local industry, but on local employment, as well. Nearly 250 area workers were employed during construction and approximately 40 permanent jobs have been created.

Niagara Falls and the generation of power have been linked for nearly 250 years. United Development Group is simply the latest name in a tradition that includes Joncaire, Tesla, and Moses.

United Development Group's 52-megawatt plant, which went on line in 1991, supplies inexpensive steam power to the Goodyear Plant and sells electricity back to Niagara Mohawk Power Corp.

ELKEM METALS COMPANY

"The best of both worlds" is an apt phrase for the history of Elkem Metals Company. The company was founded on July 1, 1981, when the Norwegian ferroalloy firm Elkem a/s acquired Union Carbide's metals business. The merger brought together the production facilities and technical know-how of the leading ferroalloy producers on each side of the Atlantic Ocean.

Union Carbide had been the leader in the United States. Starting with modest facilities in Niagara Falls at the turn of the century, Union Carbide's ferroalloy business spread throughout the United States and Canada to provide the

muscle for the industrialization that is taken for granted today.

The Niagara facilities provided the impetus for this growth. Besides a production facility, Union Carbide built research and development facilities at Niagara Falls that sparked major advancements in stainless steels, wear-resistant alloys, tool materials, metal ceramics, and numerous alloys so vital to the automotive, aircraft, aluminum, and chemical industries. When Union Carbide decided to consolidate its core businesses in chemicals and plastics, the sale of the ferroalloy sector to Elkem was a natural choice.

Elkem had been a ferroalloy leader in Europe since 1917. Taking advantage of Norway's hydroelectric power, the company had become a highly respected producer of ferroalloys for steel and iron. Elkem was also known for its innovations in furnace design, engineering over

350 ferroalloy furnaces that were built in some 40 countries.

The new global thrust of Elkem's consolidated business has meant changes at Niagara Falls. Instead of focusing on commodity materials, the Niagara plant is using its unique facilities to serve specialty markets. Using such diverse technologies as powder metallurgy, vacuum processing, and conventional smelting, Niagara's dedicated staff produces specialty products for steel, superalloys, ceramics, and refractories.

Elkem's worldwide facilities have become known for their customer-driven motivation. In the United States major customers have recognized this focus on quality and meeting customers' needs through awards such as General Motors' "Marks of Excellence," Ford's "Q1," and General Electric's "Partners in Quality." This attitude of value-added quality and enhancement carries into the products made at Elkem's Niagara Falls plant today.

LEFT: The first person to discover how to make calcium carbide and ferroalloys in an electric furnace was James Turner Moorhead (third from left). Based on his discovery, a ferroalloy plant was built in Niagara Falls, New York, near the turn of the century. Part of this plant produces specialty alloys for Elkem Metals Company today.

BELOW: These New York financiers bought Moorhead's operations and formed the companies that developed the calcium-carbide and ferroalloy businesses in the United States. They are posing in front of the Whirlpool Bridge in Niagara Falls, New York—not far from one of their earliest plants that is operated by Elkem Metals Company.

NIAGARA COUNTY TOURISM

Niagara County is more than just the home of Niagara Falls, shown here. Niagara County Tourism department invites visitors to "Come see the Falls, then stay and look around."

Fred Bonner, outdoor writer from Garner, North Carolina, hoists a trophy spring chinook salmon from the productive waters of Lake Ontario off the mouth of the Niagara River. Niagara County shorelines offer key fishing locations for a variety of fish species throughout the year—some of the best sportfishing and access facilities in the state for shore fishermen and boaters alike. Photo by Bill Hilts, Jr.

For many years, Niagara County appeared to many only as a context for the glory of Niagara Falls. Since the seventeenth century, when Father Hennepin became the first white person to see the Falls, visitors have hurried to the Cataract, leaving unnoticed the beauty of the land that surrounds it.

But in 1976 the Niagara County legislature, following the leadership of Richard Shanley, took a dramatic step to change all that. Recognizing tourism dollars as a potentially tremendous source of revenue, and certain that the county's attractions, once known, would easily draw those dollars, the legislature created the Niagara County Tourism department. What then seemed a step has proven to be a leap.

Two years after it was established, Niagara County Tourism became part of the "I Love New York" campaign. The campaign, designed to bring visitors to the state as a whole, brought visitors to Niagara County, too. In the first year of the "I Love New York" campaign, the number of visitors to the state increased dramatically and tourism—both for the state and for Niagara County—continues to grow. In 1988 the state spent $15.2 million on advertising and received $2.3 billion in tax revenues from tourists. In 1990 Niagara County Tourism spent $1.2 million on its advertising, and received $13 in revenue for every dollar spent.

Part of these advertising dollars go to pro-

duce the Niagara County Guide, the major promotional brochure of Niagara County Tourism. The agency also prepares materials detailing single areas of interest such as Niagara County restaurants, hotels, power projects, and fishing spots. Prospective tourists within a 500-mile radius are targeted to receive this material, and a regional marketing program is directed at bringing in tour groups from surrounding counties. Niagara County Tourism also sends representatives to England, Germany, and Japan; foreign visitors bring significant revenues to the county, spending almost six times as much as a domestic traveler.

Promotion of the county has paid off. In 1986 Niagara County Tourism received 13,500 inquiries from prospective visitors. Four years later, there were more than 350,000—a remarkable increase. Sport fishing, now Niagara County's second most popular attraction, has grown astronomically. The county issued only 71 nonresident fishing licenses in 1982, but by 1987, there were more than 16,000 visiting anglers trying their luck in Niagara County's waterways.

The word is out—Niagara County is more than just the home of Niagara Falls. Tourists from all over the world are taking up Niagara County Tourism's invitation: "Come see the Falls, then stay and look around."

Niagara University was founded by Vincentian Fathers and Brothers as a seminary. In 1883 it was chartered as a liberal arts university and today has approximately 2,400 undergraduates and 660 graduate students. The Alumni Chapel is pictured here. Courtesy, Niagara University

PATRONS

The following individuals, companies, and organizations have made a valuable commitment to the quality of this publication. Windsor Publications and the Niagara Falls Area Chamber of Commerce gratefully acknowledge their participation in *Echoes in the Mist: An Illustrated History of the Niagara Falls Area.*

Broda Machine Company*
Cameo Inn*
Carborundum Abrasives Company*
The Carborundum Company*
Certo Brothers Distributing
    Company*
City of Niagara Falls*
CWM*
John W. Danforth Company*
DCB Elevator Co., Inc.*

Du Pont*
Elkem Metals Company*
Empire Builders Supply Co.*
Goodyear*
Helmel Engineering Products*
Key Bank*
Maid of the Mist Corporation*
M&T Bank*
Moore Business Forms*
Nabisco Brands, Inc.*
National Fuel*
Niagara County Community
    College*
Niagara County Industrial Development Agency*
Niagara County Tourism*
Niagara Falls Bridge Commission*
Niagara Milk Cooperative*
Niagara Mohawk Power Corporation*

Niagara University*
Niagara Wax Museum*
Nuttall Gear Corporation*
Occidental Chemical Corporation*
Ohmtek*
Rainbow Hospitality*
SKW Alloys, Inc.*
Smith Brothers Construction Company*
TAM Ceramics, Inc.*
United Development Group*
Washington Mills Electro Minerals
    Corporation*
Waste Technology Services, Inc.*

*Partners in Progress of *Echoes in the Mist: An Illustrated History of the Niagara Falls Area.* The histories of these companies and organizations appear in Chapter 7, beginning on page 123.

BIBLIOGRAPHY

(various authors), American Revolution Bicentennial bi-weekly local history series, The Buffalo Courier-Express (Buffalo, N.Y.), 1976.

———*Lewiston Sesquicentennial 1822-1972*; Sesquicentennial Committee (Lewiston, N.Y.), 1972.

(various authors, including Niagara County Department of Economic Development and Planning staff and county historian Richard Reed), "Welcome To The Niagara Trail," also known as the Niagara Trail Tabloid, Official Bicentennial Publication of the Niagara County Legislature (Lockport, N.Y.), 1976.

ADAMS, Edward Dean, *Niagara Power: History of the Niagara Falls Power Company 1886-1918,* Vols. 1 and 2; privately printed for the Niagara Falls Power Co. (Niagara Falls, N.Y.), 1928.

BABCOCK, Louis L. *The War of 1812 on the Niagara Frontier*; Buffalo and Erie County Historical Society publication series, Vol. 29 (Buffalo, N.Y.), 1927.

CRUIKSHANK, Capt. Ernest, *The Battle of Lundy's Lane*; Welland, Ontario, Canada, 1893. Reprinted Lundy's Lane Historical Society (Niagara Falls, Ontario, Canada), 1984.

DeVEAUX, S., *The Traveller's Own Book to Saratoga, Niagara Falls and Canada*; Faxon and Read (Buffalo, N.Y.), 1841.

DOW, Charles Mason, *Anthology and Bibliography of Niagara Falls, Vols. 1 and 2*; State of New York (Albany, N.Y.), 1921.

DUNNIGAN, Brian Leigh, *Glorious Old Relic: The French Castle at Old Fort Niagara*; Old Fort Niagara Association (Youngstown, N.Y.), 1987.

DUNNIGAN, Brian Leigh, *History and Development of Old Fort Niagara*; Old Fort Niagara Association (Youngstown, N.Y.), 1985.

DUNNIGAN, Brian Leigh, *Siege -1759: The Campaign Against Niagara*; Old Fort Niagara Association (Youngstown, N.Y.), 1986.

DUNNIGAN, Brian Leigh, *Forts Within A Fort: Niagara's Redoubts*; Old Fort Niagara Association (Youngstown, N.Y.), 1989.

FAIRBANKS, Phil, "An Unnatural Disaster, The Trashing of Niagara Falls," Buffalo Magazine, The Buffalo News (Buffalo, N.Y.), March 18, 1990.

FOX, Austin M., *Designated Landmarks of the Niagara Frontier*; Meyer Enterprises (Buffalo, N.Y.), 1986.

GROMOSIAK, Paul, *Niagara Falls Q & A*; Meyer Enterprises (Buffalo, N.Y.), 1989.

GROMOSIAK, Paul, *Soaring Gulls and Bowing Trees*; Meyer Enterprises (Buffalo, N.Y.), 1989.

KIRBY, William, *Annals of Niagara*; Lundy's Lane Historical Society (Niagara Falls, Ontario, Canada), 1896. Reprinted 1972.

MIZER, Hamilton B., *Niagara Falls 1892-1932: A City is Born, A City Matures*; Niagara County Historical Society series No. 24 (Niagara Falls, N.Y.), 1981.

MIZER, Hamilton B., series of history articles in Business Insider; Niagara Falls Chamber of Commerce (Niagara Falls, N.Y.), 1980-1985.

O'BRIEN, Andy, *Daredevils of Niagara*; Reyerson Press (Toronto, Ontario, Canada), 1964.

PARKMAN, Francis, *Frontenac and New France Under Louis XIV*; Little, Brown & Co. (Boston), 1899.

POWER, Michael, *A History of the Roman Catholic Church in the Niagara Peninsula, 1615-1815*; Roman Catholic Diocese of St. Catharines (Ontario, Canada), 1983.

SEVERANCE, Frank H., *An Old Frontier of France, Vols. 1 and 2*; Buffalo and Erie County Historical Society publications series, Vols. 20 and 21 (Buffalo, N.Y.), 1917-1918.

SEVERANCE, Frank H., "The Story of Joncaire," article in Buffalo and Erie County Historical Society publications series, Vol. 9 (Buffalo, N.Y.), 1906.

SEVERANCE, Frank H., *Studies of the Niagara Frontier*; Buffalo and Erie County Historical Society publications series, Vol. 15 (Buffalo, N.Y.), 1911.

STEVENS, Paul L., *A King's Colonel at Niagara*; Old Fort Niagara Association (Youngstown, N.Y.), 1987.

VOGEL, Mike, "The Power Behind the Niagara Frontier," 25th anniversary articles on the Niagara Power Project, The Buffalo News (Buffalo, N.Y.), Feb. 9, 1986.

VOGEL, Mike, "War!" ; folio reprint, with introduction, of 175th anniversary front page reportage of the Campaign of 1814, The Buffalo News (Buffalo, N.Y.), 1989.

VOGEL, Mike, and MacCLENNAN, Paul, Love Canal series of articles describing the history and progress of pollution problems at the Love Canal; The Buffalo News (Buffalo, N.Y.), Aug. 2, 1988.

WELCH, Thomas V., "How Niagara Was Made Free: the Passage of the Niagara Reservation Act in 1885," article in Buffalo and Erie County Historical Society publications series, Vol. 5 (Buffalo, N.Y.), 1902.

WHALEN, Dwight, "The Rival Daredevils of Niagara Falls," Buffalo Magazine, The Buffalo News (Buffalo, N.Y.), Dec. 2, 1984.

WILLIAMS, Marjorie F. (City Historian), *A Brief History of Niagara Falls, N.Y.*; Niagara Falls Public Library (Niagara Falls, N.Y.), 1972.

Index